I0813615

The Who

The Who

Album by Album – Listening To You

Dante DiCarlo

WHITE OWL
AN IMPRINT OF PEN & SWORD BOOKS LTD.
YORKSHIRE – PHILADELPHIA

First published in Great Britain in 2025 by
White Owl
An imprint of Pen & Sword Books Limited
Yorkshire – Philadelphia

ISBN 978 1 39905 868 1

A CIP catalogue record for this book is
available from the British Library.

Typeset by Mac Style
Printed in the UK by CPI Group (UK) Ltd, Croydon, CR0 4YY.

The Publisher's authorised representative in the EU for product safety is Authorised Rep Compliance Ltd., Ground Floor, 71 Lower Baggot Street, Dublin D02 P593, Ireland.
www.arccompliance.com

For a complete list of Pen & Sword titles please contact

PEN & SWORD BOOKS LIMITED
47 Church Street, Barnsley, South Yorkshire, S70 2AS, England
E-mail: enquiries@pen-and-sword.co.uk
Website: www.pen-and-sword.co.uk
or
PEN AND SWORD BOOKS
1950 Lawrence Road, Havertown, PA 19083, USA
E-mail: uspen-and-sword@casematepublishers.com
Website: www.penandswordbooks.com

Contents

Acknowledgements

I would like to thank the following people, who helped in some way with the writing of this book:Mike Vishnick, Benn Kempster, John Foote, White Fang, Chris Charlesworth, Helen Fiona Bryant, Craig Addecott, Horace Austin and Justin Harris.

I would also like to thank Marc Burrows for putting me in contact with my publishers, and my publishers for taking on a first-time writer.

Additional thanks to the following people for the encouragement – Emma Dawson, Sue Ralton, Heather Weldon, Charlotte Casimir, Mae Horak, Dean K, Dennis Dine, Sarah Sheldon, Max Edwards, Karl Moulden, Andy Hughes, Naomi Corney-Punch, Alex Gilblom, Vince Pross, Gav Shirley and my family.

This book is dedicated to the memories of Keith Moon, John Entwistle, my dear friends Charlene Tinsley and Paul Wills, and my uncle Gerard.

Foreword

It is one of life's small ironies, that just as I was entering existence, my future favourite band was exiting it. I was born in October 1983, just ten months after The Who had played the last gig on their 'farewell' tour, even though at the time, it was seen as more a goodbye to full-scale touring rather than the complete end of the band. In December 1983 though, Pete Townshend announced he had left the band, effectively breaking up the group after nearly twenty years. Of course, that was not quite the end. The band reunited in 1985 for Live Aid, before gathering for a massive tour in 1989, a *Quadrophenia* revival in 1996 and 1997, and coming back as something of a permanent touring outfit in 1999.

In the meantime, I had started my path as a Who fan. Growing up with a brother ten years my senior, I had been raised on The Beatles from day one, and over the years I heard bits and pieces from most of the prominent bands of the 1960s and 1970s, as well as some contemporary rock artists. I was familiar early on with 'Substitute', 'Pinball Wizard' and perhaps 'My Generation'. A particularly crucial moment was hearing 'The Kids Are Alright' on the radio, on the way to school with my dad, aged about 7. I instantly fell in love with a song I guessed might have been by The Beatles, as it seemed to speak to my feelings of isolation and social unease – quite profound for a kid of my age. It wasn't long after this that I saw a clip of the band on a show called *Sounds Of The 70s*. This BBC programme was a compilation of various musical performances from a variety of bands, largely gathered from the archives of *Top Of The Pops* and *The Old Grey Whistle Test*. The Who were miming to a sacrilegiously pruned-down version of 'Won't Get Fooled Again' on *Top Of The Pops* – it would be a few years before I heard the glorious full-length version, but a mental note was made: there was definitely something about this band.

In my early teens, I began to buy vinyl records. I cast my mind back to *Sounds Of The 70s* and which bands and artists had impressed me enough to be worth my hard-earned pocket money. There was Alice Cooper, David Bowie, Deep Purple and, ah yes, The Who! I think the first record I bought was *Live At Leeds*, a live album which blew me away but contained only six tracks, just three of those being original songs. At some point I accidentally picked up Lou Reizner's

1972 orchestral *Tommy*, believing it to be The Who's version. After being more familiar with the *Tommy* film soundtrack, this caused further confusion: just how many bloody versions of *Tommy* were there, and where could I find The Who's original version?

A bootleg of their BBC radio sessions introduced me to their early singles, but my first proper Who studio album was a copy of *Who's Next* that I still own. Bought in a record market in Penge, South-East London, it was a watershed moment. Knowing next to nothing about the band's discography, I picked out the record, noted that the year of 1971 was probably a good indication of quality (even at this time, I was highly suspicious of anything from the 1980s), and as an extra seal of approval it contained 'Won't Get Fooled Again'. That album spent much time on my turntable. This was around 1999, and Pete Townshend had recently started reviving *Lifehouse*, the story that had given birth to the *Who's Next* album, producing a radio play based on the story and assembling a massive boxset containing many of his demos and unused ideas. Around this time, there was also an episode of the *Classic Albums* series of TV documentaries, centred on the making of this very record. It all seemed to come together perfectly, and looking back through some *Record Collector* magazines from the past year or so, I found more information about a series of CD reissues that had got underway in the mid-1990s. Of course, I set about buying all these albums, on both CD and vinyl, trying to absorb as much Who music as I could.

As a shy, young, budding solo songwriter and guitarist, I was especially taken with how it was that the slightly awkward guitarist of the band did most of the songwriting – you mean, I didn't need a McCartney to my Lennon, or a Jagger to my Richards? I was impressed too by his skills at recording his own demos, something which also greatly interested me.

Between those days as a teenager, when I was just really discovering a band, and the present day, The Who have never left me. I'd end up seeing them live over forty times and counting (not an impressive number compared to many hardened fans, but not an amount to be sniffed at either), and I even joined a Who tribute band called Who's Next. Despite this huge amount of Who activity, I've never got bored with the albums, but in writing this book, I've come to listen to them in a new light and from interestingly different angles. I've been forced to listen to records and songs that I simply wasn't that engaged with at first, and discovered new things, sometimes in the songs themselves, but perhaps also in me. I've always thought certain music is forever tied to its place in your history – the album that sums up the summer when you were fresh out of school, or when you met your first girlfriend. Sometimes those records can only ever be appreciated through assuming the memories and feelings of who you were at that specific time in life, for the songs simply no longer speak to who you are now. But the best bands are those that can write music that will still strike a chord in you decades later. Maybe the song will still be relevant in the same way, or perhaps in a completely different one; maybe it will be the tunes you previously skipped that you now find yourself playing on repeat. For me, The Who manage to both speak to my teenage self who fell in love with the band in the first place, and the adult I've become, as songs that once passed me by seem to have hit the spot at last. That's not to say there aren't still some tracks that get a pass from me; but then again, give me another twenty years and who knows? Still, this has been an interesting and fun period writing this book. I hope you enjoy it just a little, because as Pete said in one of his solo songs (and thus not covered in this book), 'Just a little is enough'.

Introduction

The Who were one of the first and most important classic rock bands. Belonging to the 'British Invasion', like The Rolling Stones, they managed to make the transition to something altogether different in the 1970s. For although The Who had started off as pop contemporaries of The Beatles, they would end up in the same bracket of such rock behemoths as Led Zeppelin, Deep Purple, AC/DC, Queen and others who typified the louder, bigger and heavier approach of the Seventies. During their first half-decade or so, the West London four-piece went from being a singles band to embracing the LP format, in the process helping to revolutionize it.

The Who produced two of the most famous concept albums of the Sixties and Seventies – 1969's *Tommy* and 1973's *Quadrophenia*. Both double LPs were landmark moments in rock album history and spawned movies based on them. Even before this, the band had pioneered the 'mini opera' on their second album, 1966's *A Quick One*, and developed a concept album of sorts in the ode to pirate radio, *The Who Sell Out*, in 1967.

Whereas The Beatles were hugely prolific in their relatively short life, releasing eleven full albums as well as a double EP in just eight years, and The Rolling Stones stayed together as a band on an unbroken run that still continues, releasing albums in seven consecutive decades, The Who were a different story.

Their heavy touring schedule often got in the way of recording, and several plans for albums were abandoned or downsized. Many songs that were recorded were released as stand-alone singles, never to emerge as part of an album, the prolific Townshend moving on to new compositions as the band's album output struggled to keep up with the growing collection of songs dripping from his pen.

The band reached the end of the line in 1982, having released ten studio albums in seventeen years. The Who would reunite to play concerts many times over the years, but through the majority of the 1980s and the entire 1990s, no new albums materialized. The Who had become a greatest hits touring band, apparently uninterested in recording new material, until eventually in 2006, after twenty-six years, an eleventh album, *Endless Wire*, finally appeared. The album received a somewhat mixed reception, and after such a long wait to produce anything new, it seemed the band had recorded their studio swansong. The

Who once more carried on as a touring band until the somewhat surprising release of a twelfth album, *Who*, in 2019. The album was an unexpected turn of events from a group that was perceived by most to be grinding their way into retirement via protracted 'farewell' tours, with only two remaining members. The record was generally met with positive reviews, showing that there was life in the old dog yet.

Looking back through the band's history, although twelve albums in a 60-year career is by no means prolific, one is struck by the number of ideas that never made it, as well as the different ground the band managed to cover. We have the early days, when The Who were a pop art band, writing about youth culture and quirky stories with the likes of 'My Generation', 'Substitute', "A Quick One While He's Away' and 'Tattoo". Then we have the spiritual concept album years, where Townshend's writing was about finding a deeper meaning in life, this being the driving force behind *Tommy*, *Who's Next* and *Quadrophenia*. After this we have the dark confessional and artistic self-questioning period, summed up by the next few albums such as *The Who By Numbers*, *Who Are You* and even *Face Dances* and *It's Hard*.

This book takes a careful look at the entirety of the band's studio album discography, delving into the stories behind the recording and the songs themselves, as well as taking occasional note of the music theory and production inherent in the material.

Note on This Book

In this book, I've decided to include only studio albums. Although I was tempted to feature *Live At Leeds*, such is its importance as an album, I felt doing so would open the door to including other live releases. I also wanted to focus more on The Who in the studio, for while *Live At Leeds* is arguably the greatest live album of all time, it is a snapshot of just one of many outstanding live performances by band.

I have also decided to include the compilation album *Odds And Sods*, but not other compilations such as *Meaty, Beaty, Big And Bouncy*. *Odds And Sods* was comprised almost entirely from previously unreleased material and was very much considered a new release, with overdubs performed at the time to several songs, making it much more than just a compilation. Other compilations tended to focus on singles and B-sides, and thus were not as much albums in their own right.

I've also made the hard call to include albums in their original form, in other words with no CD bonus tracks. The main reason for this is the sheer number of different reissues with different bonus tracks. Further to this, many of these songs exist in different versions across the multiple rereleases, some in rough early takes, and even in the form of Pete's demos. As I've attempted to not only discuss the song, but also the arrangement and mix, describing multiple different versions of several songs would be a bit tiresome. No doubt some would love to read all this, but my decision is not born out of laziness but the desire to keep things somewhat concise.

From Dancehalls to the Studio

On paper, The Who shouldn't have worked. Whereas The Beatles were a tight-knit group of friends who shared a sense of humour, The Who were, by their own admission, four 'orrible geezers who didn't seem to share anything, except a love for making a noise.

Roger Daltrey (born on March 1, 1944), John Entwistle (born on October 9 of the same year) and Pete Townshend (born May 19, 1945) all grew up around Acton, West London. Although Pete and Roger attended the same school, they didn't become friends, the older Daltrey being a somewhat intimidating figure for Pete, thanks to his tough image and reputation for being handy with his fists.

Entwistle and Townshend, however, would develop a friendship, and in the late 1950s formed a trad jazz band together called The Confederates, with Pete on banjo and John on trumpet. However, this group would not last very long, and by 1962 Entwistle had moved on to playing bass, a fact which caught the eye of Daltrey, who was now lead guitarist in his own act called The Detours. After Entwistle joined The Detours, it wasn't long before Townshend was recruited as well, first on rhythm guitar and then as lead guitarist, as Daltrey switched to lead vocals, having fired their singer.

The band decided to change their name, and brainstormed ideas with Townshend's friend, Richard Barnes. Townshend came up with The Hair, while Barnes suggested The Who. Townshend considered combining the two – The Hair And The Who – but it was felt it sounded too much like a pub name, so they stuck to The Who after Daltrey made the decisive call.

The group would eventually acquire a manager named Helmut Gordon, a middle-aged man who owned a doorknob-making factory. By all accounts, Gordon fancied himself as the next Brian Epstein, but although he did buy the band equipment and stage clothes, he was not cut out to take them to mainstream success. Into the picture stepped Pete Meadon, a young mod with a desire to emulate Andrew Loog-Oldham, the young manager of The Rolling Stones. Meadon and Gordon shared a barber called Jack, and after hearing about Gordon and his band from Jack the barber, Meadon got involved, trying to prise The Who away from Gordon. Meadon would also restyle the band as mods and change their name to The High Numbers, this name being a cheeky drugs joke, 'number' being a term for a low-level mod in the social hierarchy.

Someone else who wasn't cut out for the next stage in the band's career was drummer Doug Sandom, who was a decade older than the rest of them and a slightly fatherly presence. However, at an audition for Fontana Records, the band were firmly told that Sandom wasn't up to scratch, and after an argument with Townshend, he left the band.

The group were using a stand-in drummer at a gig when the final piece of the puzzle fell into place. Keith Moon (born August 23, 1946), at the time in a surf band called The Beachcombers, walked into the pub the band were playing at, and either he or his friend (depending to which story you go by) announced to them that he was better than their drummer, asking to sit in with them on a song. The band took him up on his request and realized they had stumbled upon something extraordinary when Moon proceeded to smash the life out of the poor drummer's kit. From that moment on, Moon was in the band.

As well as effectively becoming the band's manager, Pete Meadon would also write their first two songs: 'Zoot Suit', which was a shameless rewrite of a track called 'Misery', and 'I'm The Face', which was just as shamelessly a copy of 'Got Love If You Want It' by Slim Harpo. The resulting single did poorly though, and the band would release nothing further with Meadon.

However, all was not lost, and soon the band had managed to attract the attention of Kit Lambert and Chris Stamp. These two unlikely friends and business partners couldn't have been more different. Lambert was an upper-class Oxford graduate, whose father was the classical composer Constance Lambert. On the other hand, Chris Stamp was a working-class lad, brother of actor Terrence Stamp. Lambert and Stamp shared an interest in filmmaking, having been assistant directors together, and in 1964 were intent on finding a group they could manage and make their own film of. One day, walking into a venue, they found their band.

Under Lambert and Stamp, the group would change their name back to The Who, and would wind up cutting their first single, 'I Can't Explain', with Kinks producer Shel Talmy in late 1964. Talmy would bring in Jimmy Page for the session, but he would only end up playing on the B-side. The A-side, 'I Can't Explain', would also feature a vocal group, The Ivy League, on backing vocals, as Talmy believed The Who were not up to scratch. The single was a hit, reaching number eight in the charts, priming the band for further success and possibly an album, though this would prove more difficult than expected.

Chapter 1

My Generation (1965)

Produced by Shel Talmy
Released in the UK on 3 December 1965 as Brunswick LAT 8616 (Mono)
Released as *The Who Sings My Generation* in the USA on 25 April 1966 as Decca DL 4664 (Mono) DL 74664 (Stereo)
Chart position – UK = 5, USA = did not chart
Recorded at IBC Studios in London, April and October–November 1965
Pete Townshend – Guitars and Vocals
Roger Daltrey – Vocals
John Entwistle – Bass, Vocals and Horns on 'Instant Party'
Keith Moon – Drums
Nicky Hopkins – Piano

My Generation is really the only album by The Who for which their Marquee residency poster tagline, 'Maximum R&B', could be accurately used as a description of the music within. Never again would the band fully embrace the Motown and soul influences that they had built their short live career around. It would also be another six years before The Who released an album on which Roger Daltrey was as vocally confident.

But in the mid-1960s, the goalposts were moving fast. The die had been cast by The Beatles, whose first album, *Please, Please Me,* had contained eight original songs and six covers. The Rolling Stones had entirely ignored the coming trend for self-penned material by offering nothing but covers on their self-titled debut, but had since branched into original compositions, while their Liverpudlian rivals had upped the ante by putting out two albums of entirely self-composed tracks. These were 1964's *A Hard Day's Night* and 1965's *Rubber Soul,* released on 3 December, the very same day as *My Generation.*

Of the twelve tracks on the UK edition of *My Generation*, nine are originals, and of these, eight are composed by Townshend, the remaining song being a group-credited instrumental. Two of Townshend's songs (the title track and 'The Kids Are Alright') are still Who classics, at home on any best-of compilation and regularly performed in concert over fifty years later.

The fact that the vast majority of the album is made up of originals is a testament to Townshend's burgeoning skills as a composer, and the whole lot could have been if they had elected to include the top ten singles 'I Can't Explain' and 'Anyway, Anyhow, Anywhere'.

In their time as a group, The Who had rather cleverly built a live set, not around blues and rock and roll covers, like The Rolling Stones and many other bands of the early to mid-1960s, but instead the soul and R&B of Motown and Stax. There was more than enough material in their repertoire to comfortably squeeze out an album showcasing a typical Who concert, but Townshend, who had already published his first song, 'It Was You', in 1963 (later recorded by The Naturals) was on a creative roll. Spurred on by the enthusiastic reaction of the regular crowd to 'I Can't Explain', he had embraced his role as spokesman for a generation of frustrated, inarticulate kids. Given a new brief to write songs that reflected The Who's audience, the tracks began to pile up, many of the band's staple set of covers falling by the wayside.

The band had inevitably started to change direction and purpose. Pete, however, smoothed this transition with a selection of songs that covered varied ground, including attempts to write original R&B tracks that more or less blended in with their regular covers set. Despite Townshend's growing talents, the truth is that the band did almost release a standard covers album instead.

My Generation was recorded over a period of several months, primarily in two different sessions, seven months apart. The first of these was in April 1965, from the 12th to the 14th, at IBC Studios, where they produced the band's second single, 'Anyway, Anyhow, Anywhere'. This was a concerted attempt to replicate the live power and chaotic energy of The Who's live shows. The freak-out instrumental middle section, with its pounding drums and bass, topped off with guitar string pick-scrapes as well as howling feeding back and Morse code-like noises (performed by flicking the pickup selector between pickups, one of which has the volume completely off), is in stark contrast to the somewhat sedate recording of 'I Can't Explain'. So groundbreaking and unorthodox was the overall effect that the band's US record company, Decca, sent the tapes back, assuming there had been a technical error.

As well as 'Anyway, Anyhow, Anywhere', The Who also recorded the Townshend original 'Out In The Street' as well as the covers 'I Don't Mind', 'Please, Please, Please' and 'I'm A Man', all of which would end up featuring on *My Generation*. In addition to these tracks, the band committed to tape several songs which didn't make the final cut, including 'Daddy Rolling Stone', 'Leaving Here', 'Lubie (Come Back Home)', 'Shout And Shimmy', '(Love Is Like A) Heatwave', 'Motoring' and 'Anytime You Want Me'.

In this session alone, The Who had recorded enough songs for a debut album, and indeed the original intention was to comprise an LP from these tracks. Mere days after this session, *Record Mirror* reported it would be a USA and

French release only, as manager, Kit Lambert was quoted as saying that those markets were screaming out for an LP, but he didn't think it was the right time for one in the UK. Yet the USA and French release never happened, and in July, after allowing journalist John Emery to listen to a nine-track acetate preview, the group and their managers had a major rethink. While the resulting review offered some praise, it did bemoan the lack of originality offered up (ironically, one of the covers that was met with favour was 'Leaving Here', which ended up on the cutting room floor), so the intended release date was postponed so that more of Townshend's originals could be recorded. Kit Lambert, coming clean, released a press statement in *Melody Maker*, informing the public that the group were largely dropping R&B in favour of 'hard pop'. In the meantime, though, it was not so easy to reconvene to record a new selection of songs, as The Who were still a busy touring band. Not only this, but the group were in crisis. They may have been one of Britain's hottest new acts, with two top-five singles to their name and an eagerly awaited debut LP in the pipeline, but they were also in serious danger of splitting up before that album could even be finished.

September 1965 proved to be a particularly turbulent time for the group. On 2 September, the band's van was stolen, with £5,000-worth of equipment inside. In a bitter slice of irony, the van had been parked outside Battersea Dogs' Home while roadies enquired about buying a guard dog. Although some of the equipment was eventually recovered, the band was left with the task of fulfilling European tour dates with no gear. Venturing across Holland and Denmark to make TV appearances and play gigs with hired equipment, things were about to come to a head. A gig in Aarhus, Denmark, was abandoned after only minutes when the crowd overran the stage. Things got much worse, however. Of the four members of The Who, Daltrey was the only one to rarely partake in drugs. While this other three were popping pills left, right and centre, Roger avoided anything which dried out his throat or gave him a sense of not being in control. As the months elapsed, Daltrey had become increasing frustrated with his bandmates' narcotic intake and what he perceived as its impact upon their live performances. Moon was especially out of control. Townshend's long-time friend and group associate, Richard Barnes, would recall an incident at the Richmond Jazz and Blues Festival that year, where Moon had swallowed Barnes' entire stash of around twenty purple heart pills in one gulp, after he held out a handful of them when the drummer had asked for 'something in the upwards direction'. In Denmark, the proverbial shit hit the fan, Daltrey snapping and flushing Keith's supply of pills down the toilet. Moon, never a fighter, foolishly attacked Daltrey with a tambourine. Roger, though short in stature, had always been known as someone who was more than handy in a fight, and his resulting retaliation got him kicked out of the band. Well, sort of.

The Who still had touring commitments to honour, but a plan began to form in which Roger was out of the band, to be replaced by future King Crimson and Bad Company bassist Boz Burrell. Boz was at the time vocalist in the band Boz People, and there were rumours of him also playing second bass. Bizarrely, a second drummer was also mooted for the new version of The Who, whilst Daltrey had ideas of forming his own breakaway band. This, however, became a forgotten idea when The Who scored a number two single with their third release, 'My Generation'.

'My Generation' was recorded at IBC in October in the same session as the other classic from the album, 'The Kids Are Alright', amid all the uncertainty surrounding the band's future. Although Daltrey had been reinstated in the band days after his dismissal, his status in the group was rather shaky until the chart success of the song which would become the title track of their debut album. With this kind of commercial result, any ideas of breakaway bands and disrupting the obvious winning formula – built out of the four very different individuals in the band – seemed foolish.

Thus, the delicate ecosystem of The Who, which seemed liable to collapse at any moment, was cemented (though by no means being safe from destabilization over the years) for well over a decade, until the untimely death of Moon in 1978. Daltrey was back in the band, with the proviso that he would leave his fighting days behind him. However, despite the hit single and The Who's effort to put in-band disputes behind them, the press had got wind of the inner turmoil. On 20 November 1965, *Melody Maker* ran with a front page entitled 'The Who Split Mystery', detailing the possible replacement of Daltrey with Boz Burrell, which was denied despite having been discussed at one point.

By this point, The Who had already returned to IBC Studios on 10 and 12 November, to finally tape a selection of Townshend originals designed to complete a more original debut album. During these two days, the band recorded 'The Good's Gone', 'La-La-La Lies', 'Much Too Much', 'It's Not True', 'A Legal Matter' and 'The Ox'.

My Generation was released in the UK on 3 December 1965 and reached number five in the charts. The album is a snapshot of The Who in their raw youth, and even today is a startling collage of energy and palpable excitement. Shel Talmy proves himself as the perfect producer for this stage of the band's career, and the record is arguably the best-sounding Who LP until 1971's *Who's Next*. It may be no co-incidence that the producer of that album, the legendary Glyn Johns, served as engineer for the sessions that produced *My Generation*. Talmy achieved the sound of the album by placing a series of microphones at different distances and blending them, which produced a raw but tight live sound that gloriously bursts from the speakers. The vocals are crisp and direct on this album, and Roger Daltrey is in his element, seizing every chance to delve into his dark, growling, bluesy vocals. It's easy to forget he was a mere 21 years old. Pete Townshend does an excellent job of wringing the standard blues licks out of his Rickenbacker, as well as creating jangling and choppy chord rhythms. Even at this time, Keith Moon is a revelation on drums; it's largely down to him that even the poppiest tracks on *My Generation* carry a heaviness and energy that sets The Who apart from most other bands of the time. John Entwistle, of course, manages to change rock music forever, and with it the lives of bassists all over the world, with the legendary solo on the title track. This idea had actually sprung from a Townshend home demo but is realized on 'My Generation' in groundbreaking fashion by the man who would come to be known as 'Thunderfingers'. And let's not forget the unofficial fifth member of The Who on this album, the wonderful Nicky Hopkins, whose piano work fills in gaps and adds energy and colour to the heavy four-piece.

My Generation was a bold musical statement. This was a band unlike any of their peers, not only musically but in attitude. If The Rolling Stones were considered the 'bad boy' answer to The Beatles, then The Who were something even more dangerous, a group that wasn't here to steal your daughters, but instead seemingly wanted to dismantle the establishment and everything it stood for, or at least stick two fingers up at it. The cover reflects this attitude, with the four of them looking up towards the camera, surrounded by oil drums, with Entwistle draped in a Union Jack flag jacket. Though a popular symbol, available on thousands of products today, to do anything with the Union flag in 1965 apart from run it up a pole was seen as practically treasonous. Indeed, when seeking to have the jacket made, the band were flat out refused by several tailors. This was pure defiance, a redefinition of what the flag stood for; this was a new Britain, the Britain of a younger generation who rejected the old ideals and institutions.

In America, the album was retitled *The Who Sings My Generation* and released by Decca on 25 April 1966. The US release also featured a different cover, opting instead for a shot of the band in front of London's Big Ben. The record also substituted 'I'm A Man' with 'Instant Party', a song that had been intended as the band's next single and one that would soon play a part in a complicated legal battle.

In the press, the band themselves appeared less than enthusiastic about the record. In *Record Mirror* on the eve of the album's release, Townshend went through the album track by track, slating most of the songs, though this may have had more to do with the souring of the band's relationship with Shel Talmy than any faults in the record itself. Over the months, The Who and their managers had become increasingly unhappy with the deal that had been signed with Talmy and the percentage of royalties they were on. Lambert and Talmy had a particularly bad relationship; in fact, Talmy has maintained the only one he ever had a problem with was Kit. These frustrations led to The Who splitting from the producer and their record label Decca/Brunswick, signing instead with Robert Stigwood's newly formed Reaction, which, as a breach of contract, prompted legal action from Talmy. This had both a short- and long-term effect. In the short term, it put The Who into the unusual position of releasing new songs while at the same time Decca were salvaging all they could from their short time together by releasing several extra singles from the *My Generation* album, without the involvement or blessing of the band members themselves. Three singles were released in 1966: 'A Legal Matter' (a somewhat apt title given the litigation going on at the time),'The Kids Are Alright' and 'La-La-La Lies', none of which managed to crack the top thirty. All the while, The Who were having a run of top-five singles with their latest songs which were a world away from their first album compositions. It was an unusual point in time for the band, but even when matters were eventually resolved later in 1966, the long-term effect of this falling out remained for many decades. *My Generation* would soon fall out of print, and although it was reissued by Virgin Records in 1980, this too was short-lived and soon out of print again. Over the years, various attempts were made to reissue the record and produce a stereo version, but Shel Talmy owned the recordings and it wasn't until 2002 that a deal was finally struck with him. Incredibly, Talmy had placed the master tapes for sale on eBay with an asking price of $500,000, a fee that The Who's current record company were not willing to pay. At this point, avid Who record collector David Swartz stepped in and convinced the producer to lower his price. Talmy agreed and ended up remixing the album for release. However, although the resultant remix sounded wonderful, it was discovered that some overdubs had been recorded directly onto the master tapes, meaning that they were impossible to separate to mix in stereo. Sadly, this affected the biggest track of all, the title song, with Pete's lead overdub during the bass solo having been one of these parts. Consequently, the 2002 stereo mix on this version is simply missing these lead fills, with the same being the case for 'A Legal Matter'. Despite these drawbacks, the remix was well received, with even Townshend stating that he loved the new mixes. This 2002 edition was also expanded to a two-disc set, containing many bonus tracks.

In 2014, the album was once again remixed by long-time Who sound man Bob Pridden and Richard Whittaker, and remastered by Jon Astley, this time Pete Townshend recording new parts through vintage equipment in an attempt to recreate the missing fills. Daltrey was also brought in to add a few lost backing vocals and the resultant mix was released online before getting a physical release as part of the Super Deluxe boxset in 2016.

TRACK BY TRACK

1. 'OUT IN THE STREET'

Written by Pete Townshend
Produced by Shel Talmy
Recorded at IBC Studios, London, 12–14 April 1965

Originally titled 'You're Going To Know Me', 'Out In The Street' opens with an intro stolen straight from The Who's second single, 'Anyway, Anyhow, Anywhere', but transposed three semitones higher as Pete tremolo strums the F, E flat and C chords instead of D, C and A. This appears to be on a guitar tuned a whole step down.

The rest of the song is an authentic R&B original, with Daltrey delivering bluesy vocals and Pete and John providing the high backing. Pete's feedback and noise solo separates it from most standard R&B fare, even at this point marking himself out as a guitarist cut from a different cloth. The middle section, with Pete sliding up to a C chord repeatedly, is a nice change in dynamics and also recalls the sliding A chord of 'Anyway, Anyhow, Anywhere'.

Apparently, Kit Lambert was unhappy with the original lyrics and wrote new ones, although received no credit. Upon release, Townshend would state to *Record Mirror* that he wasn't going to take the blame for any of them.

2. 'I DON'T MIND'

Written by James Brown
Produced by Shel Talmy
Recorded at IBC Studios, London, 12 April 1965

The Who's cover of James Brown's 'I Don't Mind' is one of the few inclusions of songs from their regular live set and shows that the band were certainly a very tight and capable R&B band. Though barely 21 years old at this point, Daltrey was able to dig deep into the sort of bluesy vocals that already showed his great promise as a singer, and you can tell he is in his element tackling this sort of material. Townshend also shows a deft touch at playing the generic but fairly slick blues licks and solos. Indeed, much is made of Townshend being mainly a rhythm guitarist, but even at this early stage he more than holds his own with contemporaries like George Harrison (The Beatles), Keith Richards, Brian Jones (both The Rolling Stones) and Dave Davies (The Kinks), even when playing in a style he largely avoided.

Pete and John also provide the excellent backing vocals, which like much of the backing vocals on this album, leave you wondering why The Ivy League were hired to sing on their first single, 'I Can't Explain'.

3. 'THE GOOD'S GONE'

Written by Pete Townshend
Produced by Shel Talmy
Recorded at IBC Studios, London, 10 November 1965

Even in the early days, The Who seldom wrote conventional love songs, and 'The Good's Gone' presents a strikingly dark and haunting take on the genre. Opening with a chiming droning riff in the key of B that lives in the same territory as The Kinks' 'See My Friends', the song soon launches into its relentless mid-paced groove, with Daltrey delivering a remarkably low-register vocal in a sneering performance that exudes menace. Townshend commented at the time that the slight-of-stature singer sounded 6 feet tall on this. Pete and John's harmony vocals on the chorus immediately sweeten things, especially Pete, who takes the major third. The song also has a chordal, rhythmic guitar solo, with Keith helping to build the tension, until the middle eight, a somewhat simple change that really only serves as a short break before returning to the guitar riff. As the song winds towards the end, Pete adds a single 'It's gone forever' as the haunting riff re-enters once again, possibly one of Townshend's most catchy guitar hooks, albeit in a somewhat obscure early track.

4. 'LA-LA-LA LIES'

Written by Pete Townshend
Produced by Shel Talmy
Recorded at IBC Studios, London, 10 November 1965

One of the most throwaway tracks on the album, 'La-La-La Lies' is still a catchy and enjoyable track, largely due to the harmony vocals, Nicky Hopkins' piano work and Keith's enthusiastic drumming. The structure is a simple I–IV–V chord sequence in the key of G, which moves up a whole step for an instrumental section and remains there for the rest of the song. As with much early Who material, even when not the best-written song, the group had an ability to turn virtually anything into a worthwhile listen thanks to their energy and dynamic nature. As lightweight and poppy as the track may be, it's hard to not be swept up in the tom fills of Moon and be charmed by the rich harmony vocals for the relatively short duration of the track, which was said by Townshend to have been influenced by several singles by Sandie Shaw.

After the band's messy split with Talmy, the song was issued as a single in 1966, which failed to chart.

5. 'MUCH TOO MUCH'

Written by Pete Townshend
Produced by Shel Talmy
Recorded at IBC Studios, London, 10 November 1965

Perhaps the great early Who hit single that never happened, 'Much Too Much' is a hidden highlight of *My Generation*, a song pitched somewhere between 'The Kids Are Alright' and the sort of R&B that The Who had built their career on playing.

The song starts with an a cappella chorus refrain, the band singing in glorious harmony. As the track kicks in properly, Daltrey serves up another low and rather mono-tonal vocal, and Keith slashes away behind the kit. The song quickly builds the tension as it switches to a minor chord with the melody brilliantly opening up, in contrast to the verse's stark use of notes, leading to the uplifting and rousing chorus, this time with the full instrumentation backing up the vocals.

Again, Nicky Hopkins is an important element in the sonic mix, but one cannot overlook Townshend's chiming guitar as the guiding light of the song.

Pete has said that the song might have been inspired by his involvement with 22-year-old Anya Butler, who at the time was managers Chris Stamp and Kit Lambert's personal assistant, and whose sexual appetite was an eye-opener for the 19-year-old Townshend.

6. 'MY GENERATION'

Written by Pete Townshend
Produced by Shel Talmy
Recorded at IBC Studios, London, 13 October 1965

The impact of 'My Generation' cannot be overstated, a prime example of a song which emerged extremely early in a band's career, yet remained as popular and adaptable to the various changes they would go through. This is despite its most famous line, 'I hope I die before I get old', which has oft been thrown back in their faces as the band has entered each new decade.

Much of the inspiration for the song came in the wake of Pete Townshend having his vehicle towed away on the orders of the Queen Mother. At the time, Townshend was living in the upmarket Belgravia area of London and his unusual choice of car was a Packard hearse. However, one day it was spotted by the Queen Mother, who, reminded of her husband's death, ordered it to be removed. Townshend was, understandably, livid, and channelled his frustrations into a new song which was at first a slow blues shuffle in the style of Jimmy Reed, with a whiny vocal intended to emulate Bob Dylan. Townshend made home demos of the new song, and it's at this early stage that two key trademarks came into existence. Firstly, Townshend came up with the idea of a bass solo and played a rudimentary one on his demo. The other idea was the stuttering vocal which sets 'My Generation' apart from any other song at the time. According to Townshend, this was inspired by blues artists, but other accounts lay the inspiration with Daltrey's real-life stutter, with Kit Lambert and Chris Stamp then encouraging it, as it also sounded like he was wired on amphetamines. However, Townshend's demos clearly show a less pronounced version of the stutter and thus back up his insistence that it was his idea.

When it came to recording the bass, things didn't go quite as planned. For a while, John Entwistle had been using a Danelectro Longhorn bass; or to be more specific, he had gone through three of them. These short-scale basses were a joy to play, with great upper fret access and a slim neck, and also came with very thin strings that allowed for super dexterous playing which wasn't possible with the thicker strings usually available. However, with a busy touring schedule, John kept breaking strings and replacement sets weren't available – hence why John had ended up acquiring three of the basses, needing them just for their strings. When it was time to record 'My Generation', complete with its solo, John had broken strings on all three Longhorns and so had to play it on a Fender Jazz bass, strung with La Bella tape-wounds. Up until this point, his solos had apparently been more complex, which is an eye-watering thought, considering the seismic shock John's 'simplified' solo nevertheless sent through the music world.

'My Generation' is a young band at the peak of their powers. Daltrey delivers his vocal with passion and the authentic, impudent scowl of an entire generation of pissed-off youths. His stuttered vocals build tension, especially the 'f-f-fade away' line, teasing the unspeakable swear word as people held their breaths in anticipation of something that never comes. Despite this, the effect is made; in essence, this is the first punk song.

Moon's drums lurch in and out of action, pausing for the vocals, only to batter the listener over the head in the fills at the end of each verse. When the bass solo enters, it's a revelation, one that still not many others are able to do justice to, even to this day. We may never know what more complex versions John had up his sleeve, but they were not needed as his final version is note-perfect, inspiring many musicians to choose a bass over the guitar.

Structurally, the song starts off with a simple two-chord riff from G to F before introducing key changes, starting with the verse directly after the bass solo, a neat trick which gives life and interest to a simplistic song, likely inspired by The Kinks' 'You Really Got Me'.

The ending of the song is a glorious cacophony, with Keith unleashing all manner of hell on the drum kit, the tumbling rolls resembling a wonderfully musical explosion in a drum factory.

The 2002 stereo remix of the song for the Deluxe reissue is missing Townshend's guitar fills during the bass solo, these having been recorded directly onto the master tapes and thus not existing as an isolated track. In 2014, the album was once again remixed and remastered, for which Townshend rerecorded these parts using vintage equipment in an attempt to produce a stereo version as close to the original recording as possible. Although distinguishable from the original, this rerecorded version is close and a good compromise. For my money, however, the original mono version still wins out.

'My Generation' was released in the UK as a single preceding the album on 29 October 1965, reaching number two in the charts. Amazingly, The Who would never better this chart position with any single release.

7. 'THE KIDS ARE ALRIGHT'

Written by Pete Townshend
Produced by Shel Talmy
Recorded at IBC Studios, London, 13 October 1965

The second most well-known and highly acclaimed track from The Who's debut album, 'The Kids Are Alright' is the closest a Townshend song ever came to sounding like The Beatles. A beautifully melodic composition in the key of D, it was partially influenced by 'The Gordian Knot Untied' by classical composer Henry Purcell. Written with just a handful of chords, it marks The Who out once more as a band entirely different from their pop peers. The narrator of the song is an ordinary lad who doesn't mind leaving his girl to dance with other guys, as he feels the need to get away from the crowd and find solace in his solitude. Sharing a theme of fitting in, or rather *not* fitting in, with The Who's later *Quadrophenia* LP, this could very well even be the character of Jimmy from the 1973 concept album featured in this song. This is not a happy love song, a song about breakups, unrequited love or even betrayal; in fact it's not even a love song at all. This is a song about the feeling of claustrophobia, born from social unease. Even in 1965, Townshend was tackling subjects that most other artists had never dreamed to articulate. The fact that the 20-year-old Townshend does articulate it is impressive enough, but that he does so by way of such a perfectly crafted piece of melodic pop was a huge feather in the cap for the young writer.

The song starts with a shimmering D chord, strummed on Pete's twelve-string Rickenbacker (an instrumentation choice which adds to its Beatles flavour), then the harmonized vocals enter before the whole band kicks in, led by Keith's insistent drumbeat and Pete's chiming arpeggiated guitar chords. One thing to note is an early appearance of Keith's regular unplanned vocal contributions, namely his screaming. Whilst recording drums, Keith would often scream during fills, something that the drum mics would pick up, leaving them indelibly baked into the track. 'The Kids Are Alright' is an example of this; listen for his screams at the end of the middle eight at around the 1.23 mark.

An instrumental break (often edited down for compilations) showcases the power of the band, with Pete laying down chiming chords on top of a brutal rhythm section. It's their sheer power and heaviness as a band that really sets this apart from anything The Beatles might have done, despite the melodic sensibilities and guitar sounds shared with the 'Fab Four'.

'The Kids Are Alright' was perhaps strangely never intended as a single, despite its catchy pop melodies, but released by Shel Talmy in 1966 without the band's involvement or support after they had parted ways with him, it reached a lowly forty-one in the UK charts and only eighty-five in America. By this point the band had moved on, having already released 'Substitute' as their first release on Reaction Records.

The song was dropped from live play after 1966 but would return to the set in the 2000s, where it was often performed in a prolonged version, featuring new autobiographical lyrics sung by Daltrey towards the end. One such version can be found on the Teenage Cancer Trust concert from 2000, available as an audio and video recording.

8. 'PLEASE, PLEASE, PLEASE'

Written by James Brown and John Terry
Produced by Shel Talmy
Recorded at IBC Studios, London, 12 April 1965

Another of The Who's R&B repertoire and another James Brown track, 'Please, Please, Please' again finds Townshend mining more traditional blues playing, but listen out for his trademark pickup toggle switch flicks at the end of the solo. Daltrey provides an earnest soul vocal with solid support on backing vocals as usual, but the sedate nature of the track fails to utilize the natural energy of the band in the same way that more up-tempo tracks do and it is one of the weaker moments on the album.

9. 'IT'S NOT TRUE'

Written by Pete Townshend
Produced by Shel Talmy
Recorded at IBC Studios, London, 10 November 1965

Though by no means one of the best songs Townshend would write for The Who, 'It's Not True' is nonetheless an energetic and fun track from their early catalogue. Driven along by the bubbling piano work of Nicky Hopkins and the effervescent drumming of Keith Moon, with its fantastic clattering drum fills, the song offers a neat mix of R&B pastiche (reminiscent of Solomon Burke's 'Everybody Needs Someone To Love') and quirky lyrical humour.

The track tells the tale of a man faced with a raft of false rumours, including being born in Baghdad, having eleven kids, having killed his father, and even being half-Chinese. Daltrey also sings of not having a wife, which though true for Townshend, who had written the song, was not for Daltrey, who had wed in 1964. At a time in which John Lennon had tried to hide his own marriage amid media speculation, this line is particularly wry. Indeed, in the notes for the Super Deluxe reissue of the album in 2016, Pete explained that, like The Beatles, The Who attempted to hide any relationships from the public, alas to no avail, as they would receive letters from girls stating that they knew the truth.

The humour contained in the lyrics is not typical of Townshend, and if one didn't know better, one might think this was a John Entwistle track, at least lyrically, as the musical structure is a little upbeat and conventional to be typical of his style

The track is a fairly straightforward rhythm and blues shuffle, but halfway through, it shifts tone to something more sinister, as the opening verse lyrics are repeated but with a new melody, sneered with menace by Daltrey. This melody plays out over Townshend's doom-laden fuzz chord strikes, while in the gap between verses, Townshend introduces a simple savage string bend. The fuzz guitar might be the heaviest a Rickenbacker had ever sounded on record at the time.

The song was later covered by The Untamed, and was also produced by Talmy, while Pete had talked about giving the song to a country group called The New Faces, stating that he himself hated the song.

10. 'I'M A MAN'

Written by Elia McDaniel
Produced by Shel Talmy
Recorded at IBC Studios, London, 12 April 1965

The album's final cover song starts off as one of the weaker moments, but slowly builds momentum and springs into life. Daltrey's vocal is a little unconvincing as the 21-year-old tries his best to affect the dirty growl of a hardened blues artist, and it's not until he opens up his higher register, just past the minute mark, that he really sounds like the engaging singer he was proving to be. Likewise, Moon sits back and plays a minimal beat until the song slowly starts to build in intensity. Townshend lets out a blast of feedback followed by pick-scrapes whilst John holds down a deep bass groove and Nicky Hopkins tinkles away authentically at the piano. This build-up goes on until we suddenly break through to a slick blues groove, Townshend's signature style of guitar work giving way to standard blues licks, before the song wraps up with a flurry of drums.

In America, the song's lyrics were considered too racy and the track was dropped from the US edition, being replaced by the Townshend-penned track 'Instant Party', a substitution which improves the album.

11. 'A LEGAL MATTER'

Written by Pete Townshend
Produced by Shel Talmy
Recorded at IBC Studios, London, 12 November 1965

Pete Townshend's sole lead vocal, 'A Legal Matter' is an up-tempo R&B number, rudimentary in structure but carried off with aplomb. A standard I–IV–V blues progression, the song takes an amusing but slightly chauvinistic swipe at marriage, as Pete sings of backing out of a wedding so that he can carry on doing 'dirty little things' instead of working in an office just to bring his money home to the poor girl he is singing to. The track was partly inspired by an ill-fated dalliance with a mod girl Townshend had met at a show in the West Country and who spent time with him at his London flat. Townshend explained that one night whilst he was on too many purple hearts (amphetamine pills favoured by mods), he had a rather nasty comedown and sent the girl off in a huff after becoming rude. Although no intentions of marriage or children had ever emerged, Townshend was nonetheless inspired to write the song.

The track opens with a three-note riff and then launches into its brisk pace, Nicky Hopkins' piano and Keith Moon's drums driving full tilt, with the latter providing wonderfully upbeat work on the ride cymbal and more quick-fire drum fills leading into the chorus, where one can again hear shouts from him. For the chorus, the chord sequence of the song merely switches from I–IV–V to IV–V–I and speeds up the changes. Pete's vocal is nicely assured and a good contrast to Daltrey's surly, bluesy voice, a dynamic that would be used to full effect over the course of The Who's career.

The mono version features guitar-fill overdubs that are not present on the stereo remix of 2002, these parts – like the guitar overdubs on the title track – having been recorded directly onto the master. For the 2014 remix version, Pete Townshend rerecorded these parts, as he did with the overdubs on the title track.

'A Legal Matter' was released as a single by Talmy in 1966, going up against The Who's first single for the Reaction label, 'Substitute', reaching number thirty-two.

The song was revived in concert by Pete Townshend on his solo tour in 1996, and was played by The Who briefly in 1999.

12. 'THE OX'

Written by Pete Townshend, Keith Moon, John Entwistle and Nicky Hopkins
Produced by Shel Talmy
Recorded at IBC Studios, London, 12 November 1965

Credited to Townshend, Entwistle, Moon and Nicky Hopkins, but much associated with Entwistle thanks to the title, which was also a nickname of his, 'The Ox' is a protracted jam owing much to the surf music that Keith Moon adored. The track is a basic I–IV–V in the key of D, with Moon delivering a drum beat not unlike The Safaris' 'Wipeout', moving between his rack and floor tom, whilst Entwistle slides up and down his bass. Pete offers up some simple blues riffs and lead fills throughout, and there is nothing much to the track to create any contrast or interest, apart from a stop in the middle of the song which leaves Nicky Hopkins' piano on its own (save for a few drum stabs) for a few moments. The track nearly reaches the four-minute mark, and while it does illustrate The Who's energy and power as a band, it is a rather throwaway ending to the album.

13. 'INSTANT PARTY' ('CIRCLES')

Written by Pete Townshend
Produced by Shel Talmy
Recorded at IBC Studios, London, 12 January 1966

Not featured on the original UK version of *My Generation* but included on the US Decca release in place of 'I'm A Man', 'Instant Party' which in fact was really called 'Circles', had been intended for release as The Who's follow-up single to 'My Generation'. However, after deciding to part ways with Talmy, the band would end up rerecording the song and releasing it on the B-side of 'Substitute', their first single for their new record label, Reaction, prompting legal action from Talmy. This led to the band withdrawing the single and issuing it again, with the song now credited as 'Instant Party', which was in fact nearly the title of a completely different song, 'Instant Party Mixture', which the group had recorded with Talmy at the same session as his version of 'Circles'. Complicating matters even further, the B-side of 'A Legal Matter', the single Talmy had released within days of The Who issuing 'Substitute', was his version of 'Circles', which was also erroneously entitled 'Instant Party'.

Nevertheless, the original version of 'Instant Party'/'Circles' was superior to the remake, and indeed makes the American version of the album a better record.

One of Townshend's early pop gems, the song opens with Pete's strummed riff, before the band kicks in, complete with wonderful brass by Entwistle, which seems to enter slightly late, behind the backing vocals which take the same melody. The first appearance of Entwistle's brass on record, his understated line is rousing and majestic, like a clarion call to the youth, rising above the streets of Swinging Sixties London. The song finds The Who moving towards the slightly psychedelic vibe that The Beatles would soon enter with songs like 'Rain' and 'And Your Bird Can Sing', with ringing guitars and rich harmonies pulling the listener in. Its chorus (ushered in by Moon's fantastic tumbling rolls) is simple but effective, played over a single B minor chord. The middle eight, with its climbing chord sequence, sung by Townshend with vocal answers from Roger, is effective at lifting the track, and an instrumental section builds tension, utilizing Townshend's dissonant chord stabs and Moon's frenetic drumming. During this, Entwistle's single-note brass in the background sums up a faint air of doom, before an unexpected and slightly jarring key change, moving up a semi-tone to A sharp.

One of the best early Who songs, it is a shame that it was fated to end up mis-titled and virtually abandoned, apart from its inclusion on the American edition of the album, although the song was recorded and released as a single by the band Fleur-De-Lys in 1966.

The 2002 remix of this song omitted the brass part, which was later restored for the 2014 remix. Both the 2002 and 2014 versions appear to feature a single lead vocal track instead of the double-tracked vocals of the original mono mix.

Chapter 2

A Quick One (1966)

Produced by Kit Lambert
Released in the UK on 3 December 1966 as Reaction 593 002 (Mono)
Released as *Happy Jack* in the USA in May 1967 as Decca DL 4892 (Mono), Decca DL 74892 (Stereo)
Chart position – UK = 4, USA = 51
Recorded at IBC Studios in London and Pye Studios in London, August–November 1966
Pete Townshend – Guitars, Vocals and Penny Whistle on 'Cobwebs And Strange'
Roger Daltrey – Vocals, Trombone on 'Cobwebs And Strange'
John Entwistle – Bass, Vocals, Harpsichord on 'I Need You' and Trumpet on 'Cobwebs And Strange'
Keith Moon – Drums, Percussion and Vocals
Al Kooper – additional Organ

Filled with uncertainty but also creative progression, 1966 would be a strange year for The Who. In January, the band reconvened at IBC Studios to record 'Circles', one of Townshend's pop gems that was intended to be their next single. However, the relationship with producer Shel Talmy was breaking down, with Talmy and Kit Lambert on rocky ground, the group now unsatisfied with their deal with the producer with its royalty rate and five-year duration. Breaching their contract, they signed to Robert Stigwood's new Reaction label and released 'Substitute' as a single, a track which was issued three times as the band withdrew the release over legal action owing to the fact the B-side was a rerecorded 'Circles', for which Talmy still had rights. A second release of the single kept the song, simply changing its name to 'Instant Party', but this didn't fool Talmy, so the single was released a third time, featuring not The Who on the flip side but The Graham Bond Organisation, credited as The Who Orchestra (featuring Ginger Baker, who later that year formed Cream with Eric Clapton and Jack Bruce, Baker also writing the track under the alias of Harry Butcher), with an instrumental track entitled 'Waltz For A Pig', the title thought to be a dig at Talmy. This single was followed within days by the non-band-sanctioned release of 'A Legal Matter' by Talmy, backed with the version of 'Circles' he'd produced, also credited as 'Instant Party'. The Who were in the awkward situation of having to compete with themselves in the singles charts, although they did come out better than Talmy's release, scoring another top-five hit.

With a court case hanging over their heads, The Who were forced to concentrate on touring and TV appearances rather than recording. In the midst of this, they were once again facing a split at any moment as Roger almost left the band, and Keith might have been hedging his bets when he recorded 'Beck's Bolero' with Jeff Beck and Jimmy Page in May. Shortly afterwards, Keith temporarily quit after a bust-up onstage which carried on post-gig, when he and John turned up to the show over two hours late and found that Pete and Roger had recruited the rhythm section from the support group and started the performance without them.

Legal proceedings with Talmy eventually resulted in an out-of-court settlement and The Who were free of Talmy and Decca (except in America, where Decca would continue to release the band's output until 1971), but at a cost: Talmy would make 5 per cent on all recordings made in the next five years, a bitter price to pay. However, the band were now free to release music and another single. 'I'm A Boy', followed in August, thankfully another hit for them.

The Who commenced work on the second studio album (originally with a working title of *Jigsaw Puzzle*) in August 1966, most of it being taped at CBS Studios in October, with some work done earlier at Pye. In September of that year, Roger, talking to *Record Mirror*, spoke of several new songs slated for inclusion on the new album, which he stated would be ready in about a month. These songs included a cover of 'Barbara Anne' and Pete's 'Disguises', which Roger said was his favourite of the new songs. These two tracks were instead released on the *Ready Steady Who* EP in November, a month ahead of the release of *A Quick One*.

The Who's second album is a record which has often been referred to by the group themselves as the most fun LP to make. However, although the fun is clearly evident, *A Quick One* is the weakest effort during the Keith Moon years. There are several reasons for this. Firstly, the band were in a period of transition. Their first album had already seen them shift away from R&B covers towards Townshend's original compositions, but Pete had still kept one foot in their R&B roots, even though he was moving into melodic pop and even tinges of psychedelia. For *A Quick One*, Townshend had almost completely abandoned R&B, but the band's new direction wasn't entirely clear. 'Substitute' and 'I'm A Boy' had both been great pop singles, but while one dealt with gritty realism, with barbed lyrics about fashion and social standing, the other got its lyrics from a science fiction musical idea of Pete's called *Quads*, about a future in which the gender of babies could be chosen.

It also must be said that despite any dissatisfaction the band had with Shel Talmy as far as their contract went, the American certainly knew how to produce a good record, and although Kit Lambert was a great ideas man, he was not experienced in a technical sense. An example of this can be found in a story related by Brian Carroll, who was employed at IBC Studios in the 1960s in the disc cutting room. He recalled that on an early single produced by Lambert, The Who's manager pointed to the sound meter and asked what the red bit was for. This red portion of the meter indicated that the volume was too high. When told this, however, Lambert was immediately convinced that this was exactly the volume at which they should be cutting the single, and insisted that Carroll turn up the volume until the needle was all the way into the red.

Kit encouraged the band to experiment and have fun in the studio, which produced some wonderful moments of odd and unique enjoyment for both the band and the listener, but the quality of recordings doesn't match their debut album, and the sense of raw live power captured on *My Generation* is mostly lacking on their follow-up LP.

Perhaps the biggest reason for the lesser quality of the album, though, is Pete Townshend's diminished role as a songwriter. As part of a new publishing deal with Essex Music, secured for Entwistle, Moon and Daltrey, they would receive a bonus if the three of them contributed two songs each to the album. While this had a positive result in discovering the genuine songwriting talent of John Entwistle, who would come to contribute several great tracks to The Who's discography over the years, especially later in the band's career, it did relegate Townshend's own output in favour of a few sub-par tracks. John contributes the novelty fan favourite 'Boris The Spider' and 'Whiskey Man', which is quite frankly the better of the two tracks, albeit much more obscure. Keith contributes 'I Need You' and the throwaway instrumental goof around 'Cobwebs And Strange', whilst Daltrey only manages one song, the Buddy Holly-influenced 'See My Way'. This leaves just four Townshend compositions on the album, and oddly, only one song on the entire first side, the opening 'Run Run Run'.

In truth, Pete was somewhat low on songs, which is perhaps why the band elected to include a cover of Martha And The Vandellas' 'Heatwave'. However, this shortage of songs and the need to fill another ten minutes of runtime did lead to the birth of the composition from which the album gets its title, 'A Quick One While He's Away', with the groundbreaking mini opera being written simply to plug the gap. Of course, there perhaps would have been just enough songs, had the band chosen to include the previous singles for Reaction, and one can't help feeling that if the weaker tracks had been replaced with 'Substitute' and 'I'm A Boy', the LP could have been a marked improvement on their debut, even allowing for the inferior production. No matter, the album is still a landmark record, not just in The Who's own catalogue but in the pantheon of 1960s albums. It attains this status due to the title track alone, a shockingly bold move in 1966 that showed The Who were charting their own course and trying to achieve something different to all their peers.

Overall, the album is an interesting and slightly disjointed listen, with the four different members all bringing something to the table that doesn't really make for a cohesive record, but the creativity and bold risk-taking cannot be doubted. Strangely, it is the only Who album that features lead vocals from all members apart from Townshend, who only sings a small section in 'Heatwave' and the last section of 'A Quick One While He's Away'.

In America, the recently released single 'Happy Jack' was added to the record in place of 'Heatwave', with the album being retitled after it. Decca were not keen on the risqué title of the album alluding to sex, and also wished to cash in upon the relative success of the single. The US version was released in 1967, though unlike *My Generation*, it featured the same artwork as the UK release, a cartoon by Alan Aldridge featuring each member of the band (John and Pete apparently playing ten-stringed instruments), with the title of one of their individual songs flowing out from their instruments. Interestingly, John's song is 'Whiskey Man', perhaps indicating that at the time this was seen as the better of his two offerings.

In 1995, the album was reissued on CD, containing several bonus tracks, including those from their *Ready Steady Who* EP.

TRACK BY TRACK

1. 'RUN RUN RUN'

Written by Pete Townshend
Produced by Kit Lambert
Recorded at IBC Studios, London, October 1966

'Run Run Run' sees the last remnants of the 'Maximum R&B' version of The Who that featured on their first album, and nicely opens an album that then veers into very different territory. A classic blues tale about bad luck, the song has a great groove and backing vocals from Pete and John, with Pete's nimble and wiry guitar and John's bass amalgamating into a fierce attack, while Keith plays relatively restrained for once. After the second chorus, the song comes to a stop with the drums dropping out, leaving an air of tension before Pete's climbing guitar run leads into a solo. Again, the song grinds to a halt and then rumbles back into life straight into a key change. Daltrey's double-tracked vocals as always sound cool and surly, while an answer vocal on the later choruses is a little buried in the mono mix, but a bit more prominent in the stereo version. The song was first released by a band called The Cat, which was produced by Townshend.

2. 'BORIS THE SPIDER'

Written by John Entwistle
Produced by Kit Lambert
Recorded at Pye Studios, London, October 1966

The status of 'Boris The Spider' as John Entwistle's most famous and popular song is both inexplicable and totally reasonable. A long way from the best song he would ever write, it is, however, so unusual – both musically and lyrically – that it was always destined to be popular, with even Townshend admitting it should have been a single.

The song's birth was fairly spontaneous. One night, Entwistle had been at popular London nightclub The Scotch Of St James with various musicians, who were trying to come up with silly names for animals. John came up with Boris the spider, but scarcely thought any more of it until Townshend asked him if he had completed a song to go on the album. Put on the spot, John lied and claimed to have written one called 'Boris The Spider'. When asked how it went, Entwistle had to come up with something very quickly, but the end result was well received.

The song opens with a straight chromatic rundown from D to B flat before a rise from F to G, which forms the simple chorus line, with Entwistle delivering a low growl in stunning contrast to his usual high backing vocals. The verse then plays around several differing phrases in G minor pentatonic, with the bassline providing the melody in an unorthodox fashion. John's bass dominates the song, as seems fitting, with the guitar sparse and offering mainly single-chord sweeps and Pete's usual Morse Code pickup flicks.

The odd and slightly gothic nature of the music is interesting enough, but the real highlight is the hilariously offbeat lyrics, which are so far removed from anything on their first record that it's remarkable this is the same band just a year down the line. 'Boris The Spider' would often be played in concert in every decade of the band's career, up until Entwistle's death.

3. 'I NEED YOU'

Written by Keith Moon
Produced by Kit Lambert
Recorded at Pye Studios, London, October 1966

Written by Keith Moon, 'I Need You' was originally titled 'I Need You (Like A Hole In The Head)'. The high vocals from Keith and baroque harpsichord (played by an uncredited Entwistle) make for an unusual track, complete with a middle section containing barely audible chatter that includes a Beatles impersonation provided by the band's northern roadie, Gordon Molland. This was inspired by the Fab Four's Scouse in-joke humour, which Keith found hard to decipher and speculated might be aimed at him when he had met them previously. This might have been at the Ad Lib Club in London, which is said to have provided the inspiration for the song. According to Townshend, it was extremely difficult to work out what melody Keith was singing when he attempted to demonstrate the song, as his singing was awful.

4. 'WHISKEY MAN'

Written by John Entwistle
Produced by Kit Lambert
Recorded at IBC Studios, London, November 1966

John's Entwistle's second track, and the superior of his two contributions, 'Whiskey Man' is the hilarious tale of a man and his imaginary friend who appears as the result of alcohol consumption. The structure is slightly unconventional, featuring two sections that function as alternating verses, plus a chorus. Entwistle double-tracked his vocals, explaining that he had trouble singing the 'R' in the word 'friend', and so sang 'flend' on one track and 'fwend' on another, hoping they would blend together as 'friend'.

Entwistle's tight but simple bass helps drive the song, but his trump card is the fantastic brass, including a lovely solo towards the end of the track, adding a sense of movie drama.

5. 'HEATWAVE'

Written by Holland/Dozier/Holland
Produced by Kit Lambert
Recorded at IBC Studios and Pye Studios, London, 30–31 August 1966

The initial sessions for The Who's debut album, *My Generation*, had seen the group taping several covers, one of which was 'Heatwave', made famous by Martha And The Vandellas. However, a major rethink had led to them abandoning many of these covers in favour of Townshend-penned compositions. For their second album, though, The Who decided to rerecord 'Heatwave', perhaps owing to a lack of original songs. The track had been a staple of The Who's live set, and it shows, the band tackling the song with a tight energy that makes it a worthy addition to *A Quick One*. Keith is especially dynamic on the track, with his customary quick-fire drum rolls and swishing cymbals, while Pete and John provide solid backing vocals underneath Daltrey's cool lead. In America, the track was replaced by the single 'Happy Jack'.

6. 'COBWEBS AND STRANGE'

Written by Keith Moon
Produced by Kit Lambert
Recorded at Pye Studios, London, October 1966

Keith Moon's second song for the album is as throwaway as it gets, being an off-the-wall instrumental of pure mayhem that not only perfectly sums up the drummer, but also the fun and carefree experimentation that typified the recording process. Sounding like the most chaotic big band in the world, the song begins with Pete Townshend playing penny whistle and recorder, before the song (whose working title was 'Showbiz Sonata') launches into full marching band madness. Keith smashes cymbals, Roger blows into a trombone and Entwistle plays trumpet, cornet and tuba. What then follows is a crazy duel between Moon smashing the hell out of his kit and Pete delivering strummed chords like a deranged ukulele player on speed. In amongst the chaos there are screams, and at the end, for added drama, Pete plays climbing diminished chords, evoking silent movie suspense music. As part of the experimentation, Kit Lambert had the band marching past a microphone, hoping to create a stereo effect, an interesting but flawed idea, not least because as they came to overdub more parts, they would find themselves unable to hear what had been previously recorded and drift out of time.

Although the song is frivolous, one can't help but warm to its sense of fun, humour and sheer weirdness. Townshend would even open shows on his 1993 solo tour with the song, and you can hear shades of it on The Who's next album in the form of 'Heinz Baked Beans'.

7. 'DON'T LOOK AWAY'

Written by Pete Townshend
Produced by Kit Lambert
Recorded at IBC Studios, London, November 1966

This acoustic-based, country-tinged track is one of the more unusual Townshend songs from his early catalogue, and you can't help but feel it would have been sold off to another artist if Pete had been more flush with quality original compositions at the time. Indeed, it's a fun track but it doesn't quite suit The Who. The enthusiastic rhythmic gallop of the song is engaging and the harmonies are extremely pleasing, but it is nonetheless one of Pete's most lightweight and forgettable tracks, though it is somewhat lifted by its simple but fun solo. An interesting moment is the Beach Boys-type section at the end of the chorus, perhaps written for Keith Moon, who was an avid fan of the Californian pop group and surf music in general. In 2023, a live version of the song from San Francisco in February 1968 surfaced on Youtube. This audio recording, made by Marc D'Ercole and passed onto Edoardo Genzolini, author of the book *The Who: Concert Memories From The Classic Years, 1964–1976*, shows the band raising it to greater heights thanks to their customary heavy approach to even the most meek and inoffensive songs.

8. 'SEE MY WAY'

Written by Roger Daltrey
Produced by Kit Lambert
Recorded at IBC Studios, London, November 1966

Opening with a slightly corny vocalization, 'See My Way' is unfortunately one of the weak points on the album, being Daltrey's only writing contribution to a Who LP. It must have been difficult to even attempt to pen material for The Who when Pete was clearly so suited to it. Perhaps for this reason, Roger chose to write something rather old fashioned and owing to 1950s music, particularity Buddy Holly, whose rhythms for songs like 'Peggy Sue' one can hear in this track. Keith ended up playing drums on cardboard boxes to get the deadened sound that Daltrey desired, another example to the experimental nature of the album's production that Kit Lambert brought to the table.

9. 'SO SAD ABOUT US'

Written by Pete Townshend
Produced by Kit Lambert
Recorded at IBC Studios, London, November 1966

An undoubted highlight of the album, 'So Sad About Us' is one of the most enduring songs in The Who's early catalogue, a spiritual and sonic sister to 'The Kids Are Alright' and perhaps one of their most conventional, theme wise. Basically a simple break-up song, the track does, however, contain a touch more realism in its bitter melancholy than many others of similar ilk. Opening on a jangly chord riff based around Townshend's by now trademark suspended chords, the song inhabits a similar feel to The Beatles' 'Ticket To Ride' from a year previously. It then takes flight as the whole band kicks in, the harmony vocals following the melody in the chord riff, over a standard I–VI–IV–V progression. Entwistle's harmony vocals shine on this, and Keith Moon, as usual, adds so much heavy energy to an otherwise melodic pop track that you can positively hear the angst and frustration that the song is trying to convey.

The middle eight injects even more emotion as Daltrey reminds us that 'apologies mean nothing, when the damage is done'. After a reprise of the opening section, the band launch into a key change (a technique that Townshend would often use over the years), taking us up to B, the song soaring even higher now, before simmering down for its mellow end.

'So Sad About Us' was never issued as a single but became a favourite with many fans, and was especially associated with the mod movement, particularly when it was covered by The Jam in 1978. It has also been covered by Primal Scream and notably featured as a duet between Pete Townshend and Paul Weller live at the Royal Albert Hall in November 2000 in a concert for the Teenage Cancer Trust, which is available as an audio and video release. It was first released by The Merseys in July 1966.

The song was played live around the time of its release (an especially blistering version from The Marquee having been filmed and released on the *Thirty Years Of Maximum R&B* video), but was not played for the majority of The Who's career (save for the 2000 duet with Weller) until their 2014 *The Who Hits 50* tour, where it was reintroduced for several shows.

10. 'A QUICK ONE WHILE HE'S AWAY'

Written by Pete Townshend
Produced by Kit Lambert
Recorded at IBC Studios, Pye Studios and Regent Sound Studios, London, Autumn 1966

As the adage goes, necessity is the mother of invention, and this proved the case in the creation of the album's closer and standout track, 'A Quick One While He's Away'.

Despite the fact that Entwistle, Moon and Daltrey were all contributing songs to the record, it was found that they still had around ten minutes of run time to fill. Perhaps the Essex Music publishing deal these three had signed had relieved the pressure on de-facto chief songwriter Townshend a bit too much, and had the effect of leaving him short of songs. Perhaps he had simply used much of his best material in the singles 'Substitute' and 'I'm A Boy'. Whatever the truth, the band simply needed more songs. Kit Lambert then proposed an interesting idea to Townshend and suggested he write a ten-minute song. Pete insisted that songs had to be two to three minutes, prompting Lambert to float the idea of one composition made up out of several two-minute songs. Thus, the mini opera was born, with Pete composing a track comprising six different sections: 'Her Man's Been Gone', 'Crying Town', 'We Have A Remedy', 'Ivor The Engine Driver', 'Soon Be Home' and 'You Are Forgiven'.

The story centres on a Girl Guide who, after being separated from her lover while he travels afar, is seduced by an engine driver. The young man eventually returns to find his love with the engine driver, but ends up forgiving her in the rousing finale. This mini opera features Entwistle playing the part of Ivor the engine driver and Townshend as the Girl Guide.

The song was quite clearly recorded section by section, opening with an a cappella harmony, setting up the scene of the girl and her man who has been gone for nearly a year. The song then bursts into life on the back of an arpeggiated riff in the key of D from Townshend, as it enters the second section, Daltrey's low vocal contrasting with the very high backing from John. The third section enters in a somewhat jarring cut, this one is in the key of A and based around another typical Townshend riff of suspended variations of the home chord. The section ends with Pete's mock American-accented declaration, before John Entwistle assumes lead vocals as Ivor. 'We'll Soon Be Home' takes the form of a traditional country and western movie ballad, even containing the throwaway line 'come on old horse', but it's on the final section that the song really picks up pace. A series of crashing chords lead into the band playing at full tilt, with backing vocals singing 'cello, cello', simply because they didn't have the money to hire real cello players. In this section, Pete sings as the Girl Guide as she explains her indiscretions to the returning lover. As the lover forgives her, we are treated to Daltrey, Townshend and Entwistle all singing 'you are forgiven' in contrasting parts, Entwistle reaching an insanely high falsetto towards the end.

'A Quick One While He's Away' was a groundbreaking moment in pop and rock music, and the song would go on to feature in live shows up until 1970, before being revived in concert in 2014 for the band's *The Who Hits 50* tour. A notable performance of it is from *The Rolling Stones' Rock And Roll Circus* concert, and it is theorized by some that The Who's blistering rendition at this one-off filmed event caused the shelving of its release when The Rolling Stones judged themselves to have been upstaged. Whatever the case, the entire *Rock And Roll Circus* wasn't released until 1996, but part of The Who's performance of 'A Quick One While He's Away' was featured in the 1979 film *The Kids Are Alright*, with the full version later being restored.

11. 'HAPPY JACK'

Written by Pete Townshend
Produced by Kit Lambert
Recorded at CBS Studios, London, November 1966

Released as a single on 3 December 1966 in the UK and 18 March 1967 in the USA, 'Happy Jack' was another departure for The Who, one that Daltrey would call a 'German Oompah song'. The tale of an odd man who lives on the Isle Of Man and remains happy, despite the taunting and cruel treatment by local kids, became a minor hit in America – the band's first Stateside success, prompting its inclusion on the American album release in Spring 1967, which was also retitled *Happy Jack*.

During the recording of vocal overdubs, Keith Moon was so distracting that he was ordered to lie down flat and keep out of sight. At the very end, when the drummer popped up, Pete cried out 'I saw ya!', which can be clearly heard on the record.

Musically, the song is indeed a strange one, opening with a cheery lick from Pete and John before moving straight to the verse with its interesting timing, which inserts an extra beat at the end of each line. The rest of the song is awash with nice harmonies and has an extremely catchy chorus, as well as two slightly different instrumental sections where all hell breaks loose in contrast to the mellow verses.

The song reached number three in the UK charts and was featured live for many years, being played at their *Live At Leeds* 1970 gig, eventually being released on the expanded edition of the album in the mid-1990s.

Chapter 3

The Who Sell Out (1967)

Produced by Kit Lambert
Released in the UK on 15 December 1967 as Track 612 002 (Mono) and 613 002 (Stereo)
Released in the USA on 6 January 1968 as Decca DL 4950 (Mono) and Decca DL 74950 (Stereo)
Chart position – UK = 13, USA = 48
Recorded at Pye, CBS, IBC and De Lane Lea Studios in London, Talentmasters and Mirasound in New York City, Bradley's Barn and Columbia in Nashville, and Gold Star Studios in Los Angeles between March and October 1967
Pete Townshend – Guitars, Vocals and Keyboards
Roger Daltrey – Vocals
John Entwistle – Bass, Vocals, Horns and Keyboards
Keith Moon – Drums, Percussion and Vocals
Al Kooper – additional Organ

The Who Sell Out is a very loose concept album. The songs have no real connection to each other and there is no overall narrative, but the record plays like a pirate radio station, complete with jingles. Some of these were real radio jingles produced by PAMS (Production Advertising Merchandising Service), which would end up causing trouble since the band had not obtained the rights to use them, while others were written by the band themselves. Of the band-composed adverts, we get full-length songs like 'Odorono' as well as short unlisted jingles such as 'Charles Atlas', 'Premier Drums' and 'Rotosound Strings', that merely connect the tracks. The shorter jingles such as the one for Premier Drums were made up by John and Keith in the pub, and the final 'Track Records' snippet that features on the album's run-off groove was sung down the phone from the pub and recorded at the other end with a microphone.

The birth of the album and its concept was down to a combination of factors that seemed to come together in a somewhat fortuitous way, though by no means from an ideal situation. In 1967, The Who's managers Chris Stamp and Kit Lambert, decided to start their own record label, Track Records. The Who would of course be the first act on the roster, soon to be followed by Jimi Hendrix. In April, The Who released their first single on Track, 'Pictures Of

Lily', another perfectly crafted pop single that hid its cheeky masturbation theme within the prettiness of its melody. The song was another hit, reaching number four in the UK. After this success, The Who somewhat set themselves back by releasing a cover of 'The Last Time' by The Rolling Stones, backed with another cover of theirs, 'Under My Thumb'. This was done in support of The Rolling Stones, who were facing trial over drug offences. More Stones covers were intended if the band were not released, but the matter resolved itself and so no more appeared. However, the single barely scraped the top fifty and perhaps obstructed the chart momentum The Who had built up.

Their next single, 'I Can See For Miles', was a song which Townshend had envisioned as a secret weapon that would finally land the group a place at the top of the singles charts, but when it was released, it too struggled relative to the band's recent run of singles, and only just cracked the top ten.

By the time 'I Can See For Miles' was released, work had already begun on *The Who Sell Out*, albeit not in any organized fashion. Throughout 1967, the band had recorded various songs amid their busy touring schedule, but when told by Chris Stamp that they needed a new album, with him proposing the selection of songs they had in the can, Townshend was unsure. Feeling that the tracks were a ragbag of tunes that didn't make for a focused album, he sought something to connect them. Looking through the songs they had, one highlight was 'Odorono', which was not meant as an advert but would perfectly serve that purpose. By this time, The Who had recorded real radio adverts, such as one for Great Shakes which was a powdered milkshake drink, and had also written a couple for Coca-Cola which featured in cinemas. Another track they had was 'Jaguar', an ode to the car company and reportedly a somewhat optimistic attempt to obtain one of their vehicles in sponsorship. Thus, an idea began to form for an album that sounded like half an hour of a pirate radio station.

The timing of it couldn't have been more serendipitous, as 1967 was the year that new legislation outlawed pirate radio stations. These stations – such as Radio London and Radio Caroline – had made use of a legal loophole which meant that they could avoid any UK broadcasting laws, so long as they operated offshore in international waters. Pirate radio quenched the thirst the public had for pop music, which was being ignored by the BBC. However, 1967 saw the loophole closed and the BBC finally elected to give pop music the place it deserved with the overhaul of its broadcasting network and the creation of Radio One, even hiring DJs from the pirate stations to helm its new shows. *The Who Sell Out* thus forms both a homage and a fond farewell to pirate radio, the perfect idea at the perfect time, a way of giving the band's third album a different and unique angle as well as a superficial thread of connection. The original plan had been to sell advertising space in-between the songs, a Townshend suggestion, though according to Richard Barnes, Barnes himself had originally suggested it to Daltrey, who passed the idea on to an initially unimpressed Townshend. Sadly, the approached companies found the projected sales too low to be interested.

Though a great and entertaining album, it's easy to see why Townshend felt they needed a theme to tie it all together. The record splits itself into many fragments, though definitely displays more coherence than *A Quick One*. There are notable Beach Boys influences on 'Our Love Was' and 'Rael', possibly due to Moon being a fan of them. A Townshend demo from around this time, 'Inside Outside', which is featured on the Super Deluxe rerelease of the album, also has a Beach Boys vibe and borrows a lyric hook from their song 'Surfin' USA'. We also get dark psychedelia on 'I Can See For Miles', as well as touches of the raw sound that the band were developing onstage in the instrumental fracas at the end of 'Relax'. Of the advert songs, there is also a surprising moment of true brilliance in 'Odorono' as well as more light-hearted material in tracks like 'Medac' and 'Heinz Baked Beans' that are fun, though little more than jingles dressed up as songs.

The still partly disjointed nature of the record not only lends itself perfectly to the theme of pirate radio, but was mirrored by the nature of its recording. Not only were the songs written and recorded sporadically, but with The Who constantly on the road, they were also forced to use many different studios, both in the UK and USA, taking tapes with them and recording in an almost ad hoc fashion. Indeed, many songs were started at one studio only to be finished in another on the opposite side of the Atlantic, and a few were recorded more than once, at different studios, in an attempt to produce a satisfactory result. It was a highly unusual process.

The album is also unusual in featuring a whopping four lead vocals from Pete Townshend, in contrast to their previous album in which he did not feature as main lead vocalist on any track. This was partly due to much of the material being unsuitable for Daltrey's voice, or at least this being the feeling within the band.

The Who Sell Out was released in the UK on 15 December 1967, having missed its intended release date of 17 November while legal agreements with Heinz, Odorono and Charles Atlas were made. It peaked at a disappointing thirteen, whilst charting even lower at number forty-eighty in America when it was released in January of the following year. The first 1,000 copies of the album (500 mono and 500 stereo) came with a psychedelic poster designed by the artist Adrian George.

The artwork of the album itself is a good indication of the crazy nature of some of the zany music contained within. Designed by David King and Roger Law, who also came up with the double-meaning album title (a working title had been *Who's Lily?*), and photographed by David Montgomery, the front cover features Townshend with a giant stick of Odorono deodorant and Roger Daltrey in a bath of baked beans. The back of the album has Entwistle (looking positively ecstatic that he had landed the best role) with a fake tattoo, in an animal skin, clutching a teddy bear, and a blonde girl who is wearing a leopard print bikini. In the right-hand panel, Moon is applying a giant Medac tube to his face (though the Australian release changed the tube branding to Clearasil). Daltrey really did get the short end of the stick, as the beans were freezing and the attempted solution of shoving a heater under the bath only made matters worse when it heated up part of Daltrey whilst leaving the rest of him still cold, causing him to become ill afterwards. To add insult to injury, original copies would misspell his name as 'Daltry' on the front cover, an error which was corrected on later issues.

Though the album was not a commercial success upon release, it has come to be much more widely appreciated in recent times. Journalist Nik Cohn felt it had the potential to be great but didn't deliver on its promise, since it largely drops the pirate radio idea after 'Medac'. *Rolling Stone* liked the album, calling it fantastic and praising the musicianship and humour contained within. In America, however, the number one pop radio station, WMCA, went so far as to ban the record after the music director called it disgusting (for unknown reasons) and asserted that he wouldn't even let his children look at the cover.

The Who Sell Out is a quirky and extremely creative snapshot of a small time period in the 1960s when pop music was breaking out of the shadows and into the mainstream, with the BBC finally realizing the worth of the bands that were capturing the imaginations of the youth. For Who fans, it's also an interesting point, with the band still trying to find their direction but showing signs of what would come on the album *Tommy*. There was a whole batch of unreleased tracks from around this period, not only from Townshend but Entwistle, Moon and even Roger Daltrey with the great song 'Early Morning Cold Taxi', co-written by Roger and Who roadie Cy Langston. Many of these songs are excellent and can be found on the album's expanded 1995 release, 2009 two-disc Deluxe edition and 2021 Super Deluxe boxset. In 2021, *The Who Sell Out* was also featured in a Sky Arts-produced *Classic Albums* documentary, to go alongside the release of the Super Deluxe boxset.

TRACK BY TRACK

1. 'ARMENIA CITY IN THE SKY'

Written by John 'Speedy' Keen
Produced by Kit Lambert
Recorded at CBS Studios, London, 28–29 May, and IBC Studios, London, October 1967

Unusually for a Who record, *The Who Sell Out* starts with a song not penned by Townshend or any of the band, but one composed by Pete's friend, and at the time chauffeur, John 'Speedy' Keen, who would go on to form the band Thunderclap Newman and score a chart-topper with the Townshend-produced 'Something In The Air' in 1969.

A weird psychedelic freak-out (Keene himself speaking the words 'freak out' towards the end), which enters on faded-in backwards brass, after the initial PAMS Radio London jingle, the song title, according to Keen, is actually meant to say 'I'm an ear, sitting in the sky'.

The vocals sound speeded up (commonly known as 'varispeed'), producing high-pitched singing that is somewhat unidentifiable but is in fact Roger Daltrey, who is then joined on the chorus by an uncredited Keene. Once again, Keith's screams can be heard in the background amidst the brass, guitars, pick-scrapes and toggle switch effects, all of which make for a mesmerizing soundscape. Although not as strong as Townshend's own material, it is nonetheless an arresting start to the record.

An original 'Wonderful Radio London' jingle features at the end.

2. 'HEINZ BAKED BEANS'

Written by John Entwistle
Produced by Kit Lambert
Recorded at IBC Studios, London, 11 October 1967

Employing the same brass band vibe as 'Cobwebs And Strange', albeit in a less chaotic manner, 'Heinz Baked Beans' gives writer John Entwistle the chance to display his brass skills once more, forming the first song on the album that serves as an advert for an actual product. Though little more than a jingle, a lot of humour is derived from the vocal performances which take the part of a family, all asking the question, 'What's for tea?' These sound like Keith as the child, Pete as the husband and John as the grandparent. If the first track wasn't bizarre enough, 'Heinz Baked Beans' lets the listener know they are in for a wild ride.

A 'More Music' jingle features at the end.

3. 'MARY ANNE WITH THE SHAKY HAND'

Written by Pete Townshend
Produced by Kit Lambert
Recorded at De Lane Lea Studios, London, 24 October 1967

'Mary Anne With The Shaky Hand' was recorded several times, including an electric version released as the American B-side of 'I Can See For Miles', but the version that ended up on the album opted for a stripped-back acoustic arrangement with a Latin feel to it. A song that appears to contain the same sort of sexual innuendo as 'Pictures Of Lily', delivered via a sweet melody and soft harmony vocals, it is a fairly simplistic three-chord track. According to Townshend, however, it was really inspired by a girl at an Arthur Brown concert, whose unique dancing style involved her waving her hands around as if swatting flies, rather than by any sort of sexual acts. You, the listener, can decide! As if two versions weren't enough, a third found its way onto the 1995 expanded reissue of the album, while the B-side version with Al Kooper playing organ can be found on the expanded *Odds And Sods* CD, and both are also on *The Who Sell Out* Super Deluxe release. Records indicate at least one live performance of the song in 1967, and it did briefly find its way back into The Who's set in 1999 and 2000.

The song is followed by the 'Premier Drums' jingle.

4. 'ODORONO'

Written by Pete Townshend
Produced by Kit Lambert
Recorded at IBC Studios, London, 11 October 1967.

An obscure and overlooked gem in the band's catalogue, 'Odorono' is Townshend''s first lead vocal of the album, and although on the face of it a slightly humorous song advertising deodorant, it is a remarkably well written track with a beautiful sense of melody. Charting the tale of a girl hoping to get a showbiz part only to be turned down, the sting only emerges at the very end when the reason for being spurned becomes apparent – her deodorant has let her down! The song is a masterstroke, which leads the listener down a path of emotional investment, only to play the joke card at the end, letting us know that this is all an advertisement, thereby exposing the cynicism of the advertising industry.

Pete's voice is a standout performance, capturing the emotion perfectly and soaring in the chorus sections, while his trademark suspended chord stabs sit bold in the mix. The character of Mr Davidson might have been inspired by the real-life impresario Harold Davidson, who was a prominent booking agent and promoter at the time.

A final chorus was removed from the song but ended up appearing on the 1995 expanded CD release, while a full unedited version made its way onto the Super Deluxe boxset.

An original 'Wonderful Radio London' jingle is included at the end.

5. 'TATTOO'

Written by Pete Townshend
Produced by Kit Lambert
Recorded at IBC Studios, London, 12 October 1967

'Tattoo' is a particularly unusual song, both musically and thematically, which relates the story of a boy who, along with his brother, goes to get a tattoo to prove that he is a man. Today, tattoos are more popular than ever, but at the time were not so much, and indeed no member of The Who appears to have had any tattoos. The tricky and somewhat unsettling arpeggios that start the song and form its verses demonstrate Townshend's use of unconventional spins on chords. Here we basically move from B flat to F, to C and back to B flat or alternatively D, but Townshend utilizes an open E string throughout to inject dissonance and transform each chord into something more unusual. The short interlude section features Townshend singing about his father not liking long hair (very topical for the times) and telling him to get inked, while the chorus contains one of the funniest lines as the protagonist promises his tattoo that 'I expect I'll regret you, but the skin graft man won't get you'. The tattoos backfire when the father beats the brother for getting 'mother' tattooed, while the song's protagonist is beaten by his mother for getting a nude lady etched on his flesh.

Daltrey sings in a high, pure voice, atypical for him, while Keith keeps a restrained presence on drums, focusing on deft cymbal work and minimal bass drum hits, playing even less in the chorus.

'Tattoo' would become a live favourite and can be found on the expanded edition of *Live At Leeds*. It has also been featured by the band in several acoustic gigs in the 2000s.

An original 'Radio London' jingle is included at the end.

6. 'OUR LOVE WAS'

Written by Pete Townshend
Produced by Kit Lambert
Recording details unknown

Strangely credited as 'Our Love Was, Is' in America, this track finds Pete again taking the lead vocal and finding some influence in The Beach Boys and is one of the highlights of the album. The song is fairly simple, but the arrangement keeps things interesting by adding parts and building intensity during its course.

The 'love, long' section is glorious with its host of harmonies and allows Keith to finally unleash as the song launches into a more intense verse, while John's brass also injects added emotion and colour. The mono and stereo mixes of the song contain completely different guitar solos, the former containing a melodic and clean slide solo, while the latter has a searing Hendrix-type guitar line.

An original radio jingle is included at the end, followed by the 'Speakeasy, Drink Easy, Pull Easy' and 'Rotosound Strings' jingles composed by Entwistle and Moon.

7. 'I CAN SEE FOR MILES'

Written by Pete Townshend
Produced by Kit Lambert
Recorded at CBS Studios, London, 28–29 May 1967, Talentmasters Studio, New York City, July 1967, and Gold Star Recording Studio, Los Angeles, September 1967

Released as a single preceding the album, in September 1967 in America and October of the same year in Britain, 'I Can See For Miles' would be both Pete Townshend's proudest moment and most bitter disappointment to date. Pete had originally demoed the song in 1966, the group feeling that the demo would be hard to improve upon, but held it back for when the band were in real need of a hit. However, having finally played their intended trump card, it fell inexplicably flat. Considered by him to be the finest thing the group had recorded and the best bet for a number one single, the song ended up only charting at number ten in the UK, not only a long way off the top spot but a drop in their usual UK chart performance. Though it did better in America, where it became their highest-charting single on the US hot 100 so far, reaching number nine, Pete Townshend metaphorically 'spat on' the record-buying public. Listening to the song, it's not hard to understand Townshend's feelings.

The track evokes a dark, brooding psychedelic atmosphere, every part of its arrangement creating tension. Built around a drone in E, over which other chords are played (a familiar Townshend songwriting trick), the track deals with betrayal and exudes drama. Keith's drums have an orchestral air to them, and he eschews a standard 4/4 beat in favour of a pounding rhythm for the verse, only picking up the pace into a more standard rock groove for the chorus. Daltrey delivers his vocal in the way only he could, filled with cool menace and wired paranoia, especially on his 'oh yeah' that ends certain sections. Townshend keeps things simple, delivering a single-note guitar solo that may well have influenced Mick Ronson's solo on David Bowie's 'Jean Genie' half a decade later, as well as fuzz-infused chord stabs and the siren-like guitar bends during the chorus and other sections. Towards the end, the song, in true Who style, shifts to the key of A, jolting us into an even higher level of energy for the rousing finale. The song was recorded across three separate studios, with it being started at CBS, before vocal overdubs were added at either Bradley's Barn in Nashville or Talentmasters in New York and finishing touches at Los Angeles' Gold Star Recording Studio.

One of the best crafted and most well-arranged songs of the mid–late 1960s, 'I Can See For Miles' was possibly too dark and complex to ever become the chart hit that Townshend felt it should have been. Pete spoke of wanting to create the nastiest song thus far, an intention which Paul McCartney apparently took up as a challenge, writing 'Helter Skelter' in response. Due to its complex nature and layered backing vocals, 'I Can See For Miles' was barely played live until The Who's 1989 tour, before being virtually ignored again until its more regular inclusion from 2014 onwards. In 2015, the track became the fourth Who song to be used in the American *CSI* TV franchise, appearing as the theme for the series *CSI: Cyber*.

8. 'CAN'T REACH YOU'

Written by Pete Townshend
Produced by Kit Lambert
Recorded at unknown studio and date, and De Lane Lea Studios, London, 5 July 1967

The opening track on side two, and Townshend's third lead vocal, is another gem, demonstrating the beginning of his golden period as a composer. Driven by piano played by Townshend, and opening with a pretty, almost classical motif, the track does still give Keith a chance to mildly unleash on the kit, providing the perfect hard edge to an otherwise soft and gentle song, which lyrically uses several metaphors for not being able to emotionally and perhaps physically connect with someone.

The song is based in C major, but the middle eight shifts to A minor, taking us into darker waters. Here Townshend sings of briefly connecting before being torn apart by his mind, a beautiful piece of psychological lyric writing. A trademark Who key change lifts the song for the final chorus, with Townshend's voice sailing high over the bright backing arrangement.

The song, which was credited as 'Can't Reach You' originally but on later reissues is titled 'I Can't Reach You', is said to have been partly inspired by a bad flight, something which influenced several songs, most obviously 'Glow Girl', which was recorded in January 1968 and released on *Odds And Sods* in 1974.

This song is preceded by the 'Charles Atlas' jingle by John Entwistle, featuring him and Townshend speaking as part of the advert.

9. 'MEDAC'

Written by John Entwistle
Produced by Kit Lambert
Recorded at unknown studio, October 1967

Another jingle dressed up as a song, the second of John Entwistle's compositions is an ode to spot cream and is featured on the back of the album, with Keith Moon applying a giant tube of it to his face. Throwaway in nature, the song also signals the end of the advert tracks, with no more jingles appearing until the final 'Track Records' refrain on the run-out groove of the vinyl. On the American release of the album, this track was retitled 'Spotted Henry', possibly due to legal rights associated with the name Medac.

10. 'RELAX'

Written by Pete Townshend
Produced by Kit Lambert
Recorded at Mirasound Studios, New York City, 7 August 1967, and Columbia Recording Studios, Nashville, 17 August 1967

Fitting in perfectly with the burgeoning hippie movement, 'Relax' adopts a more 'peace and love' approach for a band that had often dealt with frustration and pent-up energy. Here they sing of forgetting problems and letting the music of the band in, as opposed to angry defiance or social ostracism. The track opens with a jazzy figure played in unison on guitar and organ (which is played by Al Kooper), and is simple in structure and chords, but again veers towards basic jazz in its middle eight as Townshend hits a B ninth chord, leading to a short section sung by him. Midway through, the song proceeds to rev up the energy as it enters an instrumental section in D, Townshend again shifting into more heavily distorted lead playing that would become a part of the band's live sound very soon.

A live version of 'Relax' is featured on the *Live At The Fillmore East* album, a concert from April 1968, in which the song is dragged out to over ten minutes of experimental jamming, pointing the way to the band's post-*Tommy* live sound, although the song itself would be dropped from their sets by the end of 1968.

11. 'SILAS STINGY'

Written by John Entwistle
Produced by Kit Lambert
Recorded at unknown studio, October 1967

Out of Entwistle's three contributions to the album, 'Silas Stingy' is easily the best, the only one that is a fully formed song rather than being little more than a jingle. As usual for Entwistle, it is a humorous character-based song, this time dealing with a somewhat Dickensian-type skinflint, obsessed with money and nicknamed 'Mingy Stingy' by the kids. Entwistle's medieval-style music is arranged with gothic organ and even some mariachi-type trumpet towards the end. John takes lead vocals, joined by Roger, and Pete sings the middle eight. Keith also provides excellent tom work for a great group effort that delivers dark comic relief.

12. 'SUNRISE'

Written by Pete Townshend
Produced by Kit Lambert
Recorded at unknown studio, October 1967

Pete's fourth and final lead vocal is really a Townshend solo track, in the same way as 'Yesterday' had been for Paul McCartney in The Beatles. One of his earliest compositions, Townshend had first written a version of the song all the way back in 1964 – although at first with very different music – before being inspired to rewrite it by a book of jazz chords. Conceived as a song to impress his mother by showing her he could write 'proper' music, Pete fits in a host of jazz chords, many of which are similar shapes moved up and down the neck, their striking and unusual nature in pop music highlighted further by being played on a twelve-string guitar tuned down a full step. The first real example of Townshend as an excellent acoustic player, a middle section includes a fast fingerpicked part with descending suspended chords that foreshadow the 'Pinball Wizard' riff from their following album, *Tommy*. Pete's tender, reverb-drenched vocal is a standout moment for him as a singer, while as a songwriter, the track reveals him again to be far deeper than simply the angry master of the power-chord he is sometimes portrayed as.

It appears that the song wasn't intended for inclusion until late on, being missing from prospective track listings, and according to Townshend, Moon didn't want it on the album at all.

The very early demo of 'Sunrise' is available on the *My Generation* Super Deluxe boxset, while another very different, more pop-oriented demo features on *The Who Sell Out* Super Deluxe boxset.

13. 'RAEL'

Written by Pete Townshend
Produced by Kit Lambert
Recorded at Talentmasters Studio, New York, July 1967

Pete Townshend's second mini opera started life as a proposed full-length opera, not even intended to be recorded by The Who, but with fellow Track Records artist Arthur Brown as a possible vocalist. The story ran into over twenty scenes, but ultimately was condensed into a single song of different sections, forming a mini opera not unlike 'A Quick One While He's Away'. The lyrics for an unused song from Pete's original opera, 'Party Theme From Rael', were published in *Eye* magazine in September 1968.

The story of a war between The Red Chins and the country of Rael, the song is notable for containing musical motifs that would be reused as 'Sparks' and 'Underture' on The Who's next album, *Tommy*.

The recording itself was salvaged after tapes were thrown in the bin by a careless cleaner at Talentmasters Studio in New York and had to be rescued from a nearby dumpster. After piecing together the missing tape, it was discovered that the intro of the song was either missing or too damaged to use. Luckily, recording engineer Chris Huston had made the precaution of taking home a mono mix-down, and this was used to fix the track, although it does mean the intro is in mono, even on the stereo version. There is a story that Pete Townshend was so enraged by the mishap that he threw a chair through the glass window of the studio control room, but this has been debunked by Huston himself in his notes for the album's Super Deluxe release.

On the original release of the song there are some rather savage cuts. For instance, the first chorus of the first section cuts in slightly abruptly around the twenty-four second mark, and this is also where the stereo version switches into true stereo from the salvaged mono mix. As we enter the section that is essentially 'Sparks' from *Tommy* there is another bad edit, as a guitar enters late in the right-hand side of the mix, in mid strum at around the 3.37 mark. The 1995 reissue tries to fix this, adding back a half-verse and fixing the bad cut to the chorus of the first section as well as the cut in the 'Sparks'-type part, but the Super Deluxe issue restores the original version, bad cuts and all. The band attempted to remake the track entirely at IBC Studios, but, unsatisfied, chose to use the patched-up Talentmasters version.

The run-out groove of the original copies contains a badly recorded 'Track Records' jingle, sung by John and Keith down the phone at a pub and recorded from the other end of the call. The last part of this plays on an endless loop until one switches the record off, in a similar vein to the gibberish contained on the run-out groove on The Beatles' *Sgt. Pepper's Lonely Hearts Club Band* album, released earlier that year.

Chapter 4

Tommy (1969)

Produced by Kit Lambert
Released in the UK on 23 May 1969 as Track 613 013/4
Released in the USA on 17 May 1969 as Decca DL 4950 (Mono), Decca DXSW 7205
Chart position – UK = 2, USA = 4
Recorded at IBC Studios in London and Morgan Studios in London between 19 September 1968 and 7 March 1969
Pete Townshend – Guitars, Vocals and Keyboards
Roger Daltrey – Vocals and Harmonica
John Entwistle – Bass, Vocals, French Horn, Flugelhorn and Trumpet
Keith Moon – Drums, Timpani, Gong, Tambourine and Vocals

Pete Townshend had always envisioned The Who as a band with a limited shelf life, and in their few years as recording artists they had certainly walked a fine line, with no end of disasters and inner band tensions that threatened their very existence. In 1968, the group experienced a crisis like never before, for although they had come close to splitting up many times, their chart success had always held them together. However, this run of success had finally slightly gone off track with 'I Can See For Miles', which only just hit the top ten, and things got much worse for them in 1968 as their next few singles continued a downward spiral.

Townshend was growing as a songwriter every day, but his abilities were if anything too eclectic, and given the added complication of writing for such an idiosyncratic band of four musically unique individuals, his task as main songwriter was becoming increasingly difficult.

In March 1968, the band released 'Call Me Lightning' in America. It was a curious backwards step, more reminiscent of the R&B that they had practically dispensed with after the release of the debut album, and it just about limped into the top forty. Townshend had several tracks that had been recorded following *The Who Sell Out*, including some absolute gems in songs like 'Glow Girl', 'Melancholia' and 'Little Billy', but these never saw the light of day, although

'Glow Girl' would play a significant part in the creation of *Tommy.* As these tracks were recorded throughout the year, there was some talk around this time of a fourth Who album, which was to be titled *Who's For Tennis?* and released in time for Wimbledon that year, an idea possibly more insane than *The Who Sell Out* and one that ultimately never came to fruition.

In the UK, their next single was 'Dogs', a song unlike anything the band had previously recorded. This unconventional love story revolving around a dog racing track was a good enough song, but its cheeky charm, complete with Daltrey affecting a cockney accent, was an odd fit for The Who. Indeed, it was later suggested by Daltrey that it simply should have been given to the Small Faces, whose single 'Lazy Sunday' adopted a similar cockney charm, to much more successful results. 'Dogs' charted at a lowly twenty-five, The Who's lowest ever position, not including the unsanctioned Brunswick singles after their split from Shel Talmy and their cover of The Rolling Stones' 'The Last Time'.

Picking themselves up and dusting themselves down, the band released another single, this time an old track of Pete's called 'Magic Bus', built around acoustic guitars, claves and a Bo Diddley-style rhythm. However, this fared even worse and stalled at number twenty-six. The Who were now once more in turmoil, this time not from within but from outside the band, as for the first time the public were rejecting them. It was make or break time and their next album would either catapult them to a new level or bury them once and for all. With his back firmly against the wall, Pete Townshend took his biggest risk so far and wrote *Tommy.*

In a way, the desperate situation the band found themselves in was the perfect opportunity for Townshend to throw caution to the wind and write what had been on the cards since he penned the mini opera 'A Quick One While He's Away'. He had flirted with the idea of writing a proper opera with 'Rael', but this never materialized and instead had been condensed into another mini opera, recorded and released on their third album, *The Who Sell Out.* Another joke opera he came up with. 'Gratis Amatis', didn't get far either. Now, however, Townshend would embark on writing a full-length rock opera. In this venture, Kit Lambert was the perfect right-hand man. An avid classical music and opera buff, and son of the composer Constance Lambert, Kit had the knowledge as well as the belief in Townshend to nurture the project from conception to birth.

Although a solid concept for the opera initially eluded Pete, he felt inspired to write something spiritual. The real beginnings of his spirituality began shortly after the Monterey Festival in 1967, when he experienced a bad acid trip aboard the flight back to the UK, which manifested itself as an out-of-body experience. Shortly after, he was introduced to the teachings of Indian spiritual leader Meher Baba by his friend, Mike McInnerney, who gave him a book called *The God Man*.

For his opera, Townshend toyed with the idea of a protagonist who experienced vibrations in an unconventional way, perhaps even as an animal or a being from outer space, before eventually the idea of someone without senses came to him. He then drew up a chart, depicting two aspects of reality experienced by the story's protagonist. This chart and other material including a short essay dealt with the idea of repeated reincarnation leading to enlightenment. The initial idea, which Pete developed on tour buses during the band's spring run of American gigs in 1968, had the hero experiencing seven lives, each with its own afterlife. In a way, Townshend was trying to create a story based on several ideas of spiritualism he had picked up and married together to create something new.

At first the project had various titles, such as *The Amazing Journey*, which came from an epic poem Townshend had written and was described by him as being so long it stretched from Twickenham to the far reaches of the universe, as well as *Brain Opera*, *Journey Into Space* and *Deaf Dumb And Blind Boy*.

In an interview with *Rolling Stone* writer Jann Wenner, printed in September 1968 just as sessions for *Tommy* were beginning, Pete spelled out the idea, which was still in its infancy, pressuring himself into delivering. This strategy of announcing projects to the press and thus forcing himself to pursue them was something he would admit to in the book *The Who: In Their Own Words*. For Townshend, talking to Wenner and other journalists was crucial, as the process of brainstorming his ideas out loud to the press actually helped to focus them.

As the idea gained shape, Pete decided the story would feature a character who would go through great suffering, thereby attaining enlightenment. Our hero would then become a powerful figure for many, but would ultimately end up misusing this power and paying the price. Townshend decided that the catalyst for the character's sensory deprivation would be emotional trauma rather than anything physical. In Townshend's mind, this would be a type of autism, which was something still not fully understood at the time, so he began researching it to give him a clearer understanding, even finding one case of a boy who stared at his own reflection in a mirror, which became a key part of his story. At the time, Pete gathered that childhood trauma could cause autism and that music often had an immense ability for reaching even the most withdrawn children. Thus, his idea that music and vibration should play a part in this seemed entirely fitting. As well as the character's sensory deprivation being a link to autism, Pete saw it as a way of mirroring the general population's spiritual deprivation, essentially showing us that we were deaf, dumb and blind to our higher potential. As the story progressed, the lead character gained the name Tommy, a name Pete plucked out of the air, but he did note that it was a term for a British soldier and that it contained the sound 'Om' within it, the Hindu symbol representing a sacred sound.

The basic story of *Tommy* is as follows. Tommy Walker is born during the First World War while his father is away fighting, soon to go missing, presumed dead. His mother meets another man, and they live happily together until one night the father, who is very much alive, returns home and, finding his wife with someone new (in contrast to the betrayed lover of 'A Quick One While He's Away'), kills the other man. The young Tommy witnesses this but is told by his parents that he didn't see or hear anything, and is instructed that he shouldn't tell a soul what happened. This creates trauma and causes Tommy to become deaf, dumb and blind. As the years go on, Tommy remains locked in his own world, and is abused by his uncle and bullied by his cousin who is left to mind him. Tommy only seems interested in staring at his reflection in a mirror and, later, playing pinball machines, which he inexplicably becomes a champion at. Meanwhile, his parents seek a cure for his condition from various people, but nothing works until one day, in frustration, his mother smashes the mirror Tommy stares into, which breaks the spell and returns Tommy's senses. At this point, news breaks out of the deaf, dumb and blind pinball champion's miracle cure and Tommy gains a cult following, becoming a messiah-like figure. As his followers seeks to be like him, Tommy opens up his home, which takes the form of a British holiday camp, and informs them all that in order to become like him, they have to become deaf, dumb and blind through the use of blindfolds, headphones and a mouth gag. Eventually, the followers revolt and turn against Tommy, with his fate left unknown at the end.

Though the story is rather crazy, with Entwistle claiming he only understood it when he saw the film version in 1975, it has enough meat to provide a structure to write the songs around. 'Amazing Journey' formed the central point of the album, and once this song, which had lyrics taken from Pete's epic poem, was utilized, many others fell into place around it. Townshend had previously written songs that he managed to fit into the story, including 'We're Not Gonna Take It', 'Welcome' and 'Sensation'. For the dark songs depicting Tommy's sexual and physical abuse at the hands of Uncle Ernie and cousin Kevin, Townshend felt unable to write them, as his own childhood abuse made the subject too traumatic. He handed the task to Entwistle, who responded brilliantly. Originally, there was another song called 'Cousin Kevin, Model Child', which was more upbeat and depicted Kevin pleading with his parents to be allowed to look after Tommy rather than accompany them to the theatre. This could have served as a prelude to 'Cousin Kevin' but was dropped from the track listing, later appearing on the CD reissue of *Odds And Sods* as well as the *Tommy* Deluxe release, but strangely not the Super Deluxe. As a side note, this track is credited to Entwistle on *Odds And Sods*, but to Townshend on the Deluxe edition of *Tommy*.

The band arrived back in England back from the US in September 1968 and immediately began preparations for the album. Things were not simple, though, as they found themselves in the position of having to play shows in order to fund the recording, an odd situation as record companies are usually there to pay for sessions.

On 19 September 1968, sessions began with a recording of 'Young Man Blues', a Mose Allison cover that The Who had made a part of their set for several years. This was intended to be worked into the album along with another Allison song, 'One Room Country Shack', but both were dropped from the final track listing, 'Young Man Blues' later appearing on the Deluxe and Super Deluxe editions. However, sessions were soon on hold as the band set off on a UK tour of over twenty shows as well as promotion for the doomed 'Magic Bus' single.

In October, in an interview with *Record Mirror*, Entwistle talked about the rock opera, calling it *Deaf, Dumb And Blind Boy*, speculating that it would probably cover one side of the new album and mentioning that they were all writing for the record, indicating that the band were still far from cementing things. They also had to squeeze in a New Year's Eve special for French TV, taped in late November, where they performed 'I'm A Boy', 'I Can See For Miles' and 'Magic Bus', three tracks that felt a lifetime away from The Who's current musical direction. They also managed to fit in a show-stealing performance at The Rolling Stones' *Rock And Roll Circus* in December. Whilst all this was going on, Townshend was still wrestling with *Tommy*, refining the story and songs.

Sessions resumed in January 1969, but being in financial difficulties whilst trying to record the most ambitious album of their career put The Who in an awkward situation. IBC cutting room technician Brian Carroll recalled that sometimes the band were waiting for cheques to clear before they could start a session. At this point, Keith had also run out of drum kits, with Premier Drums unwilling to send any more, so a kit had to be borrowed from roadie Tony Haslam to record with in the studio.

The sound of *Tommy* is quite unlike any Who album before, lacking the raw, in-your-face punch of their debut and being much cleaner and crisper than their subsequent two Kit Lambert-produced records. Lambert, who had no formal experience producing records, had often encouraged discs to be cut as loud as possible, making some of The Who's recordings with him sound rough, dirty and lacking in clarity. Townshend had begun to pick up on this around the time of 'I Can See For Miles', and as someone who was becoming proficient at the art of recording due to the hours he put in at his home studio, he began to question his manager's methods. For *Tommy*, it was clear even to Lambert that a different approach was needed. This was not quite the same loud, brash rock group whose main goal was to make sonic mayhem. This, to paraphrase Keith Moon's often-used live introductions for *Tommy*, was 'a bleedin' opera!', and although the power of the band would not be completely stifled, it was important to capture something much more refined than previously committed to tape.

The track listing changed as time went on. As well as dropping 'Cousin Kevin, Model Child' and the two Mose Allison songs, other discarded pieces were 'Trying To Get Through', 'Success' and an odd intro called 'I Was'. These can be found on subsequent Deluxe and Super Deluxe reissues. In contrast to dropping songs, Pete managed to recycle ideas from previously recorded material, most blatantly 'Glow Girl' and 'Rael', but parts of *Tommy* bear passing resemblance to other recent tracks too, including 'Sunrise' and the unreleased 'Melancholia' and 'Glittering Girl'. Originally, Townshend also planned more impressionistic instrumentals to follow the more narrative songs, but the final album would see only two such compositions.

During the making of the album, the band would generally gather around to listen to Pete's demos before working on the songs without prior rehearsals. Studio engineer Damon Lyon-Shaw was impressed by how spontaneous the process was, with the group managing to arrange and adapt Pete's demos quickly and efficiently. Keith often played in isolation with headphones to be able to hear the rest of the band, while Pete and John recorded together, with screens set up to separate the sounds as much as possible. A special box, nicknamed 'Colin' after Colin Peterson, the drummer of The Bee Gees for whom it was created, was used to help Moon control the headphones.

Once basic backing tracks were recorded, Pete and John would overdub acoustic and electric guitars, as well as brass parts. Roger tended to be brought in later on, when the songs were ironed out and nearly completed, for him to add his vocal. Overall, though, the sessions were lengthy and sometimes featured the band rerecording songs as changes were made to the narrative structure, but the group were in good spirits and had much fun during the recordings. The sense of camaraderie was high, with John, Roger and Keith remaining fully behind Pete's creative vision, embracing it and rising to the challenge of bringing this bold project to life.

Lambert, however, was unreliable during sessions, with the band and engineers often waiting at length for him to arrive. When he did turn up, sometimes he would appear with takeaway food, or on one occasion a portable roulette table, which he proceeded to try to teach everyone to play on. Another time he took everyone to the nearby pub, while time in the expensive studio ticked by. Kit also seemed keen on adorning the record with a full orchestra, an idea Townshend flatly refused, being adamant that the band should play everything themselves, the only orchestral instruments being John Entwistle's brass parts.

Initially, casting the vocal roles provided some interesting dilemmas. Roger's voice was thought to be too rough and bluesy to portray the younger Tommy or his inner voice, so Townshend claimed these songs for himself, as well as 'Amazing Journey', the idea being that Roger would play the adult Tommy. However, this meant his first song was 'I'm Free' and that the first half of the album would feature Townshend as main vocalist instead of their lead singer. Daltrey thus worked to find a different voice, his own inner Tommy, and after singing 'See Me, Feel Me' in falsetto, Townshend realized that Roger had nailed it. Thus, Roger became Tommy, although Pete still ended up assuming the character's voice at points during the album.

Tommy is a huge step forward for the band on all fronts. Production-wise, as already stated, it's cleaner and clearer, with much more room for the instruments to breathe. Townshend's songwriting has also developed, and although there are some throwaway moments in such tracks such as 'Miracle Cure', 'Do You Think It's Alright' and 'There's A Doctor', these are basically not even songs but simply link pieces to provide greater narrative structure. Some of the full-length songs might be a little weak compared to Townshend's best writing, but there are moments of clear genius. 'Pinball Wizard' is without doubt not only one of The Who's best singles, but one of the best singles by anyone in the 1960s, managing to combine weird subject matter, unconventional structure and some nice nods to classical composition into a catchy-as-hell hit. The 'See Me, Feel Me' and 'Listening To You' sections are sublime, like a modern-day hymn, and would captivate audiences all over the world.

Individually as well, the band are on fire. Townshend is understated on electric guitar, but his acoustic playing is skilled and textural. This album begins a trend where Townshend would use acoustic guitar as the bedrock for a large part of the band's recorded sound. His weapon of choice from here on in was a Gibson J-200 bought from Manny's guitar shop in New York. Electric guitar-wise, he also made use of a Fender Electric XII twelve-string and possibly a Jazzmaster.

Keith's drumming is brilliant and orchestral at times, expressive and wild as ever, but with a touch more maturity and even more musicality than before. Entwistle really begins to grow as a bassist on the album, his lines becoming more melodic and starting to enter the picture as a lead instrument even more, not to mention his brass which at times is key in elevating the record from a mere rock LP to something worthy of the rock opera tag. It is also on this album where Daltrey begins to discover his truest voice. Having shown incredible promise on their debut album, Daltrey had spent the time since trying to find a way to deliver Townshend's material, which had moved away from the R&B of their beginnings. Although having done a great job, the more pop direction the band had gone in and the several turns they had taken had left him slightly out of his comfort zone. Though it wouldn't be until *Tommy* went on tour that Daltrey really discovered his rock voice, there are signs of it on tracks like 'The Hawker' and 'Smash The Mirror'.

When recording was finished, Kit Lambert unexpectedly took a holiday to Cairo, leaving engineer Lyon-Shaw to mix the album. Lyon-Shaw was stunned by this decision but undertook the task using notes that Lambert had made, many of which were apparently on the back of cigarette packets. Pete was unaware that Lambert had not mixed it, but overall was pleased with the result, although he thought the vocals were too loud compared to the music, which resulted in the album lacking a little of the punch that the band was well known for. Though this is true, the idea may have been to make the vocals louder than usual so that every word could be clearly heard. On the other hand, Daltrey felt his vocal was too prominent, while Pete's was mixed better with more echo and placed further behind.

Listening to the record, although beautifully crisp, it is a world away from the band's live sound. Indeed, there is more of a similarity between the band's live shows and tracks like 'Relax' from *The Who Sell Out* than anything on *Tommy*. Some have speculated that Lambert may have been leaving room in the mix for the full orchestra he had wanted, but no such idea was ever pressed by Lambert to Lyon-Shaw and his decision to leave for Cairo meant that any possibility of a last-minute orchestral addition was out of the window for good.

According to Lyon-Shaw, Paul McCartney once remarked to him that *Tommy* was very under-produced. Whether meant as a compliment or a criticism, there is no doubt that its production is quite stark compared to The Beatles' *Sgt. Pepper's Lonely Hearts Club Band*, but this basic arrangement made it easy for the band to reproduce it onstage, and in most people's opinion to better it. The LP would be taken on the road extensively in the UK, Europe and across America, and it's these live performances that would grow the popularity of the album, centring around a landmark performance at Woodstock in 1969, immortalized on film.

In March, The Who released 'Pinball Wizard' as a single. Though labelled as 'sick' by DJ Tony Blackburn (who, according to Townshend in an interview with *Zig Zag* magazine in 1974, got a drumstick in the eye on *Top Of The Pops* as a result of his comments), the song was a success, even removed from the album and its story, and reached number four in the UK charts.

For the artwork, originally Pete had wanted to get Alan Aldridge, who had provided the cover for *A Quick One*, but having spent much time discussing the album and the themes and philosophies behind it with his artist friend and fellow Meher Baba devotee Mike McInnerney, he turned to him instead. Townshend was familiar with McInnerney's work, having been to his Soho design studio, and together they worked on concepts and ideas without input from the rest of the band. McInnerney's approach was somewhat abstract and was more concerned with depicting Tommy's own perception of the world around him rather than showing the titular hero himself. Aside from just the cover, which was produced in a triple-gatefold sleeve rather than the conventional double for a two-LP set, McInnerney also designed a booklet to illustrate the story. This booklet would contain images as well as lyrics, and a full libretto, with the initial run also being individually numbered.

As McInnerney would work on the artwork, so too would Pete on the songs, the process becoming a two-way creative street with each demo by Pete inspiring McInnerney, but also Townshend being influenced by the concepts coming back from him. McInnerney would often hear Pete's demos before the rest of the band and became an important part of Townshend's creative process. *Sgt. Pepper's Lonely Hearts Club Band* had been a landmark, but this was pushing the boat out even further, and McInnerney received an astonishing £1,000 for his completed package, a huge step up from the £200 given to Peter Blake for his iconic Beatles cover.

The cover of *Tommy* is still striking today, a blue and cloudy, dream-like sky, in which holes are punched, rendering it like a latticework. Inside the black holes we get each member of the band reaching out with ripples, as if attempting to break through from one reality into another. This was in fact a last-minute addition to the record after Decca in America objected to a cover that did not feature the band, so The Who were quickly assembled for a photo shoot in order that they could be added.

McInnerney was given full artistic freedom by Townshend to guide the album concept and overall cover design, and Pete's occasional visits to the studio to converse and play demos were helpful but non-intrusive in the creative process. Upon delivering the finished work, it was met by universal praise, the entire band and management being stunned by the final result, while Polydor – who distributed Track records – were excited at the thought of producing a groundbreaking triple-gatefold album and fully supported McInnerney.

As the album neared release, Pete Townshend looked back on the process with great appreciation for his bandmates and how they had supported his creative process, drawn-out and haphazard as it may have been. His vision for the record might have taken time and great energy to pull into focus, but the result was remarkable, mature and powerful. The band knew they had something special on their hands, but that was only half the job done. Winning over his bandmates might have been an unexpected doddle, but winning over the press could never be relied upon so easily. It was decided the best way to launch the album was with a live performance especially for the press. The band rehearsed the album in church halls, refining and reworking it for live performance, with all of them feeling that what they had would be a success.

Although *Tommy* wouldn't be the first rock opera, Townshend felt he had started it all with 'A Quick One While He's Away'. By the time *Tommy* would be released, though, The Pretty Things had released *SF Sorrow*, while the Small Faces had produced the concept album *Ogden's Nut Gone Flake*. *Arthur* by The Kinks was also on the horizon and had been announced at a press conference in March as an album to tie in with a television play, even though the album itself wouldn't be released until the autumn of that year. Thus, there may have been a feeling that The Who were jumping on a trend even though this was more due to their inability to move at a fast-enough pace to fully realize all of Pete's ideas.

On 1 May 1969, The Who launched *Tommy* at Ronnie Scott's jazz club in Soho. The atmosphere from the attending press was hostile, and after being heckled, the band turned up the volume and proceeded to blow them away. Against the odds, The Who won them over and finished their set to a standing ovation. Despite this, reviews were a little mixed. The *NME* carried a review that called the album sick as well as over-ambitious, and expressed disappointment with its style, stating that the record wasn't representative of the band, and that if this was their new sound, the old one was much preferred. Chris Welch of *Melody Maker* was more positive though, declaring it as an important facelift to the battered image of pop, while legendary conductor and composer Leonard Bernstein was reportedly enthusiastic about it, expressing this in person to Townshend.

The band took the show out to opera houses in Europe and across America, The Who breaking into the mainstream but also finding themselves potentially being swallowed up by the pretentiousness of upper-class society. Entwistle felt they should have smashed up the opera houses, while Townshend bemoaned the fact that the front rows would be filled with Polydor executives. The Who were a band for the youth, but the success of *Tommy* made them a hot ticket and a status symbol for the wealthy and cultural elite, latching on to the novelty of rock as a highbrow means of entertainment.

At Woodstock in August 1969, The Who played a pivotal part, but Townshend hated the event, not least because he found himself on an unplanned acid trip. As a stark indication that The Who were at odds with the drop-out hippie, peace and love movement, Townshend ended up assaulting stage invader Abbie Hoffman, who had run on to protest about the jailing of writer and activist John Sinclair for possession of marijuana. In a moment that cameras missed, Townshend hit Hoffman over the head with his guitar and sent him offstage. Despite this brutality, it's undeniable that the rousing finale of 'See Me, Feel Me' as the sun came up in the early hours of the morning was a moment of unity between band and audience, the sort which might have inspired Townshend's next idea – *Lifehouse*.

Tommy transformed The Who from a pop art singles outfit into a serious albums band, and helped define the LP as an art form in its own right. This may have started with such records as *Pet Sounds* by The Beach Boys, but a double album carrying a narrative and marketed as a rock opera certainly broke new ground.

Tommy was reissued as two-disc Deluxe version in 2003, followed by a four-disc Super Deluxe edition in 2013.

TRACK BY TRACK

1. 'OVERTURE'

Written by Pete Townshend
Produced by Kit Lambert
Recorded at IBC Studios, London

It was Kit Lambert who suggested the album should begin with a formal overture to gather the main themes of the record, so even though the track opens *Tommy* it was in fact one of the last to be written. Beginning with the descending chord sequence from '1921', the rest of it is mainly made up of 'Go To The Mirror', complete with its 'See Me, Feel Me' and 'Listening To You' sections, which are more often thought of as parts of 'We're Not Gonna Take It' but do actually originate from 'Go To The Mirror'.

The track opens brightly, the piano helping to carry the chords, before we enter the 'See Me, Feel Me' section and Townshend's strummed guitar begins to take us into melancholy territory.

The signature riff from 'We're Not Gonna Take It', backed up with brass, is the next section of the song, which then leads via a fantastic drum fill to the 'Go To The Mirror' riff in the key of G, before modulating down a tone to F, the vocal melody played majestically by Entwistle on horns.

The song pulls the listener around with its different sections, repeating in different keys, before it ends with the first appearance of the 'Pinball Wizard' riff, the brass playing the two-note strike that is played on guitar on the full track. The riff here is played in G and moves down to F before we land on a D chord played on acoustic guitar by Townshend. Having revealed himself as an adept acoustic player on the previous album's 'Sunrise', Pete ups the ante here with a skilled and impressive display of strumming and picked chords, mixing blues, country and shades of folk. Pete as the narrator then tells us Captain Walker is missing in action during the war and presumed dead. His wife, meanwhile, is about to give birth to his son, the child Tommy, who he will never know.

2. 'IT'S A BOY'

Written by Pete Townshend
Produced by Kit Lambert
Recorded at IBC Studios, London

Short in length, 'It's A Boy' finds its origins in the then-unreleased song 'Glow Girl'. One of the best tracks from early 1968, 'Glow Girl' was a song written about a girl going through the contents of her bag on a plane as the engines fail, dooming the passengers to certain death (see the chapter on *Odds And Sods* for further details). The end refrain of that song, 'It's a girl Mrs Walker', is reused, via a gender change, as a song that announces the birth of our protagonist. The key is changed from 'Glow Girl's' B to the key of D, up a tone and a half, requiring Townshend to display his high vocal range, hitting a C5 note towards the end.

Segueing in seamlessly to '1921', the song is also founded on Townshend's acoustic guitar, but gloriously lifted by Entwistle's brass which is warm and heralding. The song deviates from its 'Glow Girl' template with a simple ending that leads to the next track.

3. '1921'

Written by Pete Townshend
Produced by Kit Lambert
Recorded at IBC Studios, London

In '1921', the story turns to Mrs Walker and her new lover, blissfully looking forward to what lies before them in life. But Captain Walker returns home alive, and upon finding his wife and her lover, engages in battle with the latter, who ends up dying. This murder is witnessed by the infant Tommy, who, traumatized enough by the sight, is further damaged by his parents' insistence that he didn't see or hear anything, and that he will not tell a soul the truth. The pressure of this sends Tommy deaf, dumb and blind.

The song begins with the same descending pattern that opens the 'Overture', this time with the piano playing a repeating three-note figure over the top until we reach the verse of the song, a G suspended fourth to G major chord change, with Pete taking the lead vocal role once more.

On original US releases of *Tommy*, this track is titled 'You Didn't Hear It'.

4. 'AMAZING JOURNEY'

Written by Pete Townshend
Produced by Kit Lambert
Recorded at IBC Studios, London

The song which in a way forms the central point of the opera sprang to life from an epic poem Pete had written, which contained over 200 lines. A stream of consciousness that Townshend described as containing both great and terrible lines, he discarded 90 per cent and pared it down to the lyrics we know. The original poem dealt with concepts of multiple reincarnations, but by the time the album had taken shape, his idea changed significantly to now be about Tommy's inner world of dark silence.

The first track on the album to feature Daltrey as lead vocalist, the song begins softly with guitar, piano and bass, but is given a psychedelic air by strange backwards noises throughout, along with reverse guitar parts that sound almost like bowed instruments. An orchestral air comes from Keith's drums that explode all around the track, bringing a heavy classical intensity to the piece, while Daltrey's vocals are melodic and tender as he sings of the protagonist trapped in his own world of sensory deprivation.

Once again, the acoustic guitar plays a huge role in the arrangement, with the electric guitars being used sparingly and the power of the song generated almost entirely by the drums.

As the song reaches its end, we enter the section that leads to 'Sparks'. Here, the groove slows and Townshend's acoustic guitar becomes the centrepiece, playing riffs similar to the Captain Walker section of 'Overture'. Keith lays down a mesmerizing beat while John roots it all with his simple pounding bass, showing great restraint, psychedelic backwards noises meanwhile really pulling the listener into a different world. Bizarrely, at around the 4.26 mark, there is an extremely noticeable cut, with the track seeming to fade just prior to this. John finally cuts loose on the bass, playing an upper-register pentatonic riff as Pete continues strumming away underneath.

5. 'SPARKS'

Written by Pete Townshend
Produced by Kit Lambert
Recorded at IBC Studios, London

The first instrumental on *Tommy* is another shameless, but also inspired, reuse of earlier Who material, and in this case a lot more blatant. Reusing a bit of the unreleased 'Glow Girl' was something no one outside the Who camp would have known about, but in this case, 'Sparks' features the music from 'Rael', the closing track from The Who's previous album. It is a bold move, but in hindsight a good one, as the piece fits *Tommy* perfectly, and in truth 'Rael' was hardly one of the band's most memorable tracks.

Here, Keith demonstrates an orchestral feel that sets him apart from any other pop drummer of the time. His drums are full of reverb and mixed fairly in the background so as to not overpower the delicate triad chord shapes played by Pete over a pedal tone of D.

6. 'THE HAWKER/EYESIGHT TO THE BLIND'

Written by Sonny Boy Williamson
Produced by Kit Lambert
Recorded at IBC Studios, London

Although The Who abandoned plans to include two Mose Allison covers on the album, one cover that did make the final cut was 'Eyesight To The Blind' by Sonny Boy Williamson. Its theme of a woman with the power to make the deaf hear, the blind see and the dumb talk was too perfect *not* to use, although the band changed the song musically, almost beyond recognition. Townshend also felt that the character of The Acid Queen needed a kind of pimp, someone to act as an influence upon her, so that she was not solely responsible for the actions of corrupting the innocent young Tommy. The character of The Hawker thus became part of the story and an effective set-up to Tommy's meeting with The Acid Queen.

Musically, Townshend rewrites the up-tempo blues progression of the original into a slow and tense song using more-typical Townshend progressions and based in a minor key. The song begins under the subterfuge of a pretty two-chord guitar arpeggio, before changing to muted, staccato two-note stabs, soon joined by another guitar, playing a full G minor chord. Soon, Entwistle's concrete slab-like bass figure enters, along with Keith's bludgeoning tom fills, and the song descends into an unsettling mood, as if a facade has been removed, revealing The Hawker as a conduit to a dark underworld of black-market voodoo rituals. Daltrey's pained howling vocal is a highlight, a watershed moment in his career as a singer.

The song does briefly lighten in mood with a simple guitar solo section, returning to the relative major of E flat, but it's a short respite before we are plunged back into the murky depths of The Hawker's underworld.

Narratively speaking, 'The Hawker' should have, and was meant to, come directly before 'The Acid Queen', but in order to fit the songs onto four sides of vinyl, some tracks had to be moved around. So 'The Hawker' is left here, somewhat out of place.

Although initial UK releases of *Tommy* credit this as 'The Hawker', US copies credit it as 'Eyesight To The Blind'. Over the years, subsequent international reissues have switched between the two, with the 2013 Deluxe version listing it as 'Eyesight to The Blind (The Hawker)'.

Bizarrely, at some time in the early 1970s, certain pressings of *Tommy* contained a version of 'Eyesight To The Blind' with an alternative vocal take from Daltrey. There is no way to identify which copies contain the alternative vocal without listening to them.

7. 'CHRISTMAS'

Written by Pete Townshend
Produced by Kit Lambert
Recorded at IBC Studios, London

Townshend was slightly inspired by his own memories of Christmas as a child, when his parents would leave him alone to go out on Christmas Eve before returning to put him to bed. 'Christmas' helps to set up Tommy's home life and the sense of frustration his parents feel at having a child who seems lost in another world. Even something as universally joyful and captivating for children as Christmas is rendered meaningless for Tommy, as he has no idea about religion, prayer or even who Jesus was. As his parents wonder if his soul can ever be saved, we hear Tommy's inner monologue, crying out to be seen, heard and healed, but unable to break through, just as his parents are unable to reach him. The 'See Me, Feel Me' refrain is introduced properly here, and this contrast between the parents' point of view and Tommy's was in fact a last-minute addition. As Pete worked on an ending for the album, it was decided to use the 'See Me, Feel Me' and 'Listening To You' sections from 'Go To The Mirror' in a reprise at the end of 'We're Not Gonna Take It'. At this point it was felt that it would be even better to use these sections in another song too, to reinforce the device of leitmotifs on the album. 'Christmas' was chosen and had to be rerecorded to include these sections.

The song also includes a jarring section where his parents repeatedly ask, 'Tommy can you hear me?' over Townshend's unconventional chord sequence, played on clean guitar, with him also taking the voice of the parents.

8. 'COUSIN KEVIN'

Written by John Entwistle
Produced by Kit Lambert
Recorded at IBC Studios, London

At this point in the story we encounter the first of Tommy's tormentors, the nasty and sadistic cousin Kevin. A song written by Entwistle at the behest of Townshend, wanting something dark but feeling unable to write it himself, Pete happily handed the task to John, who responded in impressive fashion, writing the song quickly after imagining a pleasant-sounding chopsticks-style piano part. Lyrically sadistic but at the same time believably childlike in its simplicity, it feels like the mind of an adolescent bully, complete with the most pointless and cruel pranks such as pins on a seat and glass in a dinner. Musically it's typically unconventional, as many Entwistle songs were. Its verse is incredibly pleasant, mirroring Kevin's mask of innocence and good-natured temperament, with soothing harmony vocals and a two-note guitar melody pattern, which is basic and calming, like a nursery rhyme. This drops down in semi-tones as Kevin unveils more and more methods of punishment for poor young Tommy, until we hit the pre-chorus. Here, Kevin fully unleashes his inner monster, the music intensifying as the chords change and the tension rises. The chorus section sees Kevin boasting about his savage nature as Moon's drums pound down, beating the listener over the head, while the 'Ahh Ahh' backing vocals further sum up the terror unfolding on Tommy.

Entwistle's vocals are beautiful in range, from the lower pleasant cooing on the verses to the crazed ego-driven hysteria of the chorus. With its theatrical leanings, unusual musical structure and dark lyrical content, 'Cousin Kevin' was a feather in the cap for Entwistle. Perhaps due to its complexity, 'Cousin Kevin' was not performed live until *Tommy* was played (almost) in full in 1989.

9. 'THE ACID QUEEN'

Written by Pete Townshend
Produced by Kit Lambert
Recorded at IBC Studios, London

Tommy is finally introduced to The Acid Queen, who attempts to cure him through means not disclosed within the song's lyrics, but sex and drugs are alluded to. After doing her work, she claims success, but of course Tommy remains deaf dumb and blind. Pete, taking the role of The Acid Queen, delivers another strong vocal. Partly arrogant, slightly unhinged, he would later say in the documentary *Sensation – The Story Of Tommy* that when performing it elements of his own mother would sometimes come into it. There is perhaps a trace of female arrogance hidden within, the idea that this woman can fix a deeply damaged boy, and Townshend described it as having an element of anger towards his own mother and all mothers.

The track begins with Pete's arpeggiated D suspended second chord, shifting into A for its chorus, while Keith's drums are hard-panned, something of a common early 1960s stereo technique which affected many popular records and sounds a little odd today. The reflective middle eight leads to a subtle change of key, up a tone to E. However, although the following chorus also moves up a tone to B, the E minor, D and A tail to it remains unchanged. Moving back to A, there is guitar solo/instrumental section, starting off soft and delicate and gradually building up, as Townshend's single guitar notes develop into chords, with him and Moon playing off each other in a dynamic battle of expression. Also listen out for the electric keyboard, which plays throughout the track but particularly comes to life here, as well as another Keith Moon scream during the last chorus, bleeding into his drum mic, hard-panned right.

10. 'UNDERTURE'

Written by Pete Townshend
Produced by Kit Lambert
Recorded at IBC Studios, London

'Underture' is essentially a reprise of 'Sparks', stretched out to ten minutes to fill out the second side of the album. There are some additional sections included which make this slightly different from 'Sparks', but as with that song, Keith's drumming is fantastic throughout as he adds to the orchestral feel of the piece, while Townshend's jarring chord work is innovative and fresh. The added length of this track allows the piece more time to breathe and make use of its dynamics, Entwistle's brass adding even more depth to the track, especially the dramatic ending. What the band delivers here is so mature and close to classical music that it's incredible to think this is the same punky lot that produced 'My Generation' less than four years previously.

11. 'DO YOU THINK IT'S ALRIGHT?'

Written by Pete Townshend
Produced by Kit Lambert
Recorded at IBC Studios, London

One of the very short songs designed to join the gaps and provide narrative content, 'Do You Think It's Alright?' is still catchy and could have possibly been developed into a longer track if Townshend wished. At this point in the story, we are about to be introduced to the second of Tommy's evil family abusers (presumably Kevin's father), the sexual predator Uncle Ernie. Tommy's parents obviously know something isn't right with Ernie, as they ponder if it's alright to leave him with Tommy, but they decide to anyway. The first section of the song is ostensibly in the key of C without ever visiting the home chord, but ends on the striking sequence of B flat, A flat and G, with the lovely harmonies suggesting G major seventh with the prominence of the F sharp note.

On the US release, this was credited without the question mark at the end.

12. 'FIDDLE ABOUT'

Written by John Entwistle
Produced by Kit Lambert
Recorded at IBC Studios, London

Like 'Cousin Kevin', 'Fiddle About' was a song written by Entwistle at Townshend's request. As a child, Townshend had been through experiences which he could not fully remember, these coming during a time when he lived with his grandmother Denny, who according to Townshend was highly disturbed and brought strange men home. Though Pete was unable to fully recall what had happened, it's clear this part of his life played a big role in the story of *Tommy*, and in essence this element of Tommy is Townshend. It is consequently understandable that being so close to the traumatic subject matter, he instead gave Entwistle the task of writing the song, one he grabbed with both hands.

The song starts with dramatic villain music, the descending chords instantly summing up childhood terror, enhanced by Entwistle's brass. Entwistle also uses descending and ascending chords to reinforce the lyrics dealing with pulling bedsheets down and nightclothes up. Although Keith Moon would play Ernie in the movie version of *Tommy*, perhaps over-comically, on the original version it is Entwistle himself taking lead vocals, and he does a great job.

13. 'PINBALL WIZARD'

Written by Pete Townshend
Produced by Kit Lambert
Recorded at Morgan Studios, London

The most famous song from *Tommy* and one of the biggest and well-known songs of their career, 'Pinball Wizard' had an unlikely genesis. During working on the album, Townshend was still apprehensive about the project and decided to talk about it to journalist and friend Nik Cohn. Cohn was a fan of the band, but upon hearing some of the early work on *Tommy*, he was in two minds. Although liking what Townshend had come up with so far, he felt the story was a bit 'po faced' and that it was a shame that in the story Tommy ended up as a guru. At this point, Townshend's story saw Tommy gaining followers through becoming a rock star of sorts, but Townshend, desperate for support, quickly began to rethink things.

As well as being a journalist and writer, Nik was an avid pinball fan and had written a book called *Arfur: Teenage Pinball Queen*, based on a real-life girl whom Pete had met and subsequently been slaughtered by at pinball. Pete asked Cohn, 'what if Tommy becomes a pinball champion?' What if he used vibrations to play pinball and became famous for that? Cohn, immediately pleased by the idea, told Townshend in that case he'd give it a five-star review.

Townshend went home to write what would be 'Pinball Wizard', but on completion was not at all sure about it. Bringing it in to the band, he was embarrassed, feeling it was ridiculous. However, the reaction was overwhelmingly positive, everyone instantly recognizing the hit they had on their hands, with engineer Damon Lyon-Shaw declaring it would be number one – something that unfortunately didn't happen but wasn't too far from the mark.

The song starts with just a reverb-drenched Gibson J-200 acoustic playing a series of baroque type chord changes that Pete had seen as in the same vein as the middle eight section of 'I'm A Boy'. The main riff switches from B suspended fourth to B, strummed with ferocity and vigour. The beginnings of this riff can be heard in the middle eight of 'Melancholia', which had been recorded in 1968 and left unreleased (available on several rereleases of *The Who Sell Out*), and even the fast-picking section of 'Sunrise' from *The Who Sell Out*. The guitar arrangement is bare, just an acoustic and one electric guitar which constantly changes through the verses. We initially hear the distinctive power-chord slides from the electric guitar, with Entwistle's undulating bass and Daltrey's powerful vocal joining. The riff following the verse is biting and heavy, much more so than the majority of electric guitar on the album. Keith's drums also enter, immediately lifting the song's energy, while the acoustic guitar thrashes away. In the second verse, Pete's electric guitar plays one-note harmonics instead of the famous chord stabs, while in the third verse he switches to muted staccato picked notes, almost summing up the energy of a pinball machine. After the last chorus, the song key changes to D (somewhat sneakily, as the chorus ends on the same chord) and the power chord slides return here, with Daltrey pushing his impassioned vocal even further, before the song fades out on some dreamy guitar picking.

'Pinball Wizard' was recorded in Morgan Studios in Willesden, London, and does have a slightly different feel to much of the rest of the album – more powerful than most other songs, with the electric guitar biting and much grittier. As a Who record, it is one of the best-produced, certainly of their Kit Lambert days, and even with its audible hiss during the acoustic intro, is overall very clean, something that wasn't always the case under Lambert's production.

'Pinball Wizard' was released as a single on 7 March in the UK, reaching number four, and 22 March in America, climbing to nineteen. Although the band had not scored the predicted number-one single, this was the hit they had been looking for and a huge change in fortunes after their last two singles. Ironically, whilst trying to move away from being a singles band and into the serious album market, they had managed to produce one of their most catchy and brilliant 45s to date. Though the public loved the song, the reaction was not so good elsewhere, former pirate radio DJ, now within the employ of the BBC, Tony Blackburn labelling it as 'sick'. Other negative press would also emerge, but after the album was released, the song made a bit more sense. Looking at 'Pinball Wizard' today, its subject matter seems utterly bizarre out of context (in fact even *within* context), never mind as a top-five single. Nonetheless, the music, arrangement and production were a huge leap forward for the band, and one that would lead to even greater heights.

After Pete wrote 'Pinball Wizard', the songs 'Christmas' and 'We're Not Gonna Take It' had lyrical alterations to include pinball as a theme of the story. Oh, and Nik Cohn loved the song and *did* give the album a great review.

14. 'THERE'S A DOCTOR'

Written by Pete Townshend
Produced by Kit Lambert
Recorded at IBC Studios, London

Another track that runs for less than half a minute, 'There's A Doctor' serves as a lead into the next song, as Tommy's parents seek out a doctor who can apparently cure Tommy. Breezy and bright, and founded on its elegant piano chords, it is one of the least-typical Who tracks on the record.

On the US release, this is credited as 'There's A Doctor I've Found'.

15. 'GO TO THE MIRROR!'

Written by Pete Townshend
Produced by Kit Lambert
Recorded at IBC Studios, London

At long last, Tommy is seen by a proper doctor (why this wasn't an option before The Acid Queen, we'll have to put down to artistic license), who confirms that Tommy's sensory deprivation is psychological rather than physical.

With Daltrey singing the role of the doctor, Townshend takes Tommy's inner voice for the 'See Me, Feel Me' interludes which originate from this song and were, along with the 'Listening To You' section, later adopted into 'Christmas' and as the rousing finale for 'We're Not Gonna Take It'.

On this track, Daltrey displays his inner actor and takes on a slightly official-sounding tone in his singing to reflect his role as the doctor, but also delivers some beautifully free singing in his upper range.

Once more, Keith delivers an outstanding performance, perfectly balancing a fairly slow, steady beat with grand drum fills, while the addition of piano to Townshend's mildly over-driven guitar adds texture. The 'See Me, Feel Me' interludes are a perfect counterpoint, showing Tommy once again trying to reach out as his parents and the doctor try to reach in, in a double act of futility. When the song finally reaches the 'Listening To You' section, it's a positively uplifting moment, made all the more powerful by the slow burn towards it.

On original American copies of the album, this song is titled 'Go To The Mirror, Boy'.

16. 'TOMMY CAN YOU HEAR ME?'

Written by Pete Townshend
Produced by Kit Lambert
Recorded at IBC Studios, London

A fairly short track, although much more an actual song than the sub-half-minute ones, 'Tommy Can You Hear Me?' is catchy enough, although with no middle eight it reaches the end of its interest after a minute-and-a-half. Unusually featuring no drums on it, the rhythm is provided by double-tracked acoustic guitars and Entwistle's lovely tight bassline, with the group singing in layered harmonies. The song doesn't really progress the story and could feature anywhere on the album prior to Tommy's cure, but placed where it is, it does help to press the point of his mother's frustrated attempts to reach her son, which will come to a head in the next track. On the original US release, this is credited without the question mark at the end. Perhaps punctuation was frowned upon by Decca?

17. 'SMASH THE MIRROR'

Written by Pete Townshend
Produced by Kit Lambert
Recorded at IBC Studios, London

On 'Smash The Mirror', The Who go funk, with Daltrey delivering one of his best vocals on the album, a sign of his burgeoning raw singing style. Keith opens the track with a great drum fill before Pete joins in with a series of sweet and fairly clean guitar licks. The song neatly emphasizes the word 'rise' with a rising chord sequence that feels more theatrical than the rest of the song, and features Pete's two younger brothers, Paul and Simon (at the time aged 11 and 9), singing backing vocals.

In this part of the story, Tommy's mother reaches breaking point (metaphorically) and breaks the mirror (literally), destroying the spell and effectively curing Tommy, her love and anguish managing to finally get through to her son.

18. 'SENSATION'

Written by Pete Townshend
Produced by Kit Lambert
Recorded at IBC Studios, London

'Sensation' is another track that Townshend wrote prior to the idea of *Tommy*, originally titled 'She's A Sensation' and written about a girl. Sung by Townshend, perhaps feeling his vocal worked better than Daltrey's, it is one of the more overlooked tracks on the album, probably due in part to the fact it wasn't a part of The Who's live shows until *Tommy* was revived in 1989. Nevertheless, it is a fairly strong song and could have possibly made a good single. Opening with a chord figure based around a D and suspended variations on it, it then moves to a rundown mimicked by Entwistle's horn lines. The chorus is in the key of A, while the exhilarating middle eight modulates to F sharp and then leads to one of Townshend's trademark sneaky key changes, placing the subsequent verse in the key of E.

At this point in the story, Tommy, having been freed from his internal prison, is starting to capture the imagination of the public, as more and more begin to see him as a messiah, his status growing and inspiring those around him.

19. 'MIRACLE CURE'

Written by Pete Townshend
Produced by Kit Lambert
Recorded at IBC Studios, London

Coming in at under twenty seconds, 'Miracle Cure' is the most throwaway moment on the album, the only purpose of which is to indicate that Tommy's cure has become front page news.

20. 'SALLY SIMPSON'

Written by Pete Townshend
Produced by Kit Lambert
Recorded at IBC Studios, London

As Tommy's fame spreads and he amasses a legion of fans, or even worshippers, we reach the point where he becomes a preacher of sorts, giving a sermon, but the adulation he receives is closer to that of a rock star. Meanwhile, the teenage Sally Simpson is forbidden to go to the 'meeting' by her father, but she sneaks out anyway to see Tommy, who is described as the new messiah. The character of Sally Simpson was inspired by a real-life incident during an American tour where The Who appeared on the same bill as The Doors. Townshend was witness to the moment where a girl who ran on stage to get close to Doors frontman Jim Morrison was brutally tackled by security. In real life she was brought backstage by the band, but in *Tommy* she is carried out by ambulance men. The irony at the end of the story is that her father, who disapproves of her obsession with Tommy, admonishes her, but Sally ends up married to a rock musician, seemingly trading the pursuit of enlightenment for the excess of rock and roll.

This song is another that features double-tracked acoustic guitar prominently, as well as the added colour of slightly bluesy piano from Pete. Keith is fairly restrained on the drums, sticking mainly to the toms, while Daltrey delivers another great vocal that hints at his development as a rock singer, especially on the final verse where he opens up in a way he hadn't really done since their debut album.

21. 'I'M FREE'

Written by Pete Townshend
Produced by Kit Lambert
Recorded at IBC Studios, London

The guitar riff from 'I'm Free' bears a resemblance to an earlier song of Townshend's called 'Glittering Girl', recorded in 1967 but not released. Here, the riff is given a more unusual timing, starting on the offbeat. Apparently, this timing caused some issues for Keith Moon; according to Entwistle, the main drumbeat ended up being recorded by him and Townshend, with Keith overdubbing the fills. Listening to it closely, you can definitely hear the main pattern continuing during the drum fills, especially the hi-hats, which would bear this story out. Once again, the piano plays a big part in the song, especially during the dark sections that shift to B minor.

At the end we hear a reprise of the 'Pinball Wizard' riff, this time with the piano delivering the distinctive power-chord hit.

22. 'WELCOME'

Written by Pete Townshend
Produced by Kit Lambert
Recorded at IBC Studios, London

Interestingly, 'Welcome' is apparently one of the tracks that predates the concept of *Tommy* and was worked into the plot. However, it's one of the songs that sounds furthest from popular music and closest to musical theatre, especially in its 'more at the door' segment, and it's hard to see the song existing in The Who's catalogue in any other way but within a concept album. At this point in the story, Tommy encourages all from far and wide to join him in his house and become part of the 'comfortable people'.

The song's languid acoustic feel in the key of G, with Daltrey's mellow vocal, picks up in the middle section as the song key changes to E and adds haphazard harmonica, before a new section leads back to the verse, now in the key of A. The song has another sneaky key change back to the original key of G before it ends with a pretty trail of piano notes and the whispered 'Welcome'. One of the album's most theatrical songs, this was not played live by The Who until 2017, having been omitted from even their 1989 *Tommy* set.

23. 'TOMMY'S HOLIDAY CAMP'

Written by Keith Moon
Produced by Kit Lambert
Recorded at IBC Studios, London

By now, Tommy has a following of disciples who wish to learn from him. Credited to Keith Moon, this track was in fact written by Townshend, based on Moon's suggestion that instead of building a temple, the gathering place for Tommy's followers should be a traditional English holiday camp, an idea that Townshend loved and decided to include. Keith was pleased and said he would write the song, but Pete avoided this by insisting he had already written it. Moon, taking the hint, left Townshend to it, but Pete credited him anyway, composing something so quirky it could well have been written by the eccentric drummer.

The song starts with a chromatic line played on organ and banjo creating a screwball feel, before Pete's cheery cry of 'Good morning campers!', and soon sets off on its jolly pace.

Pete says Kit used his demo for the recording, which is why it's Pete who sings the role of Ernie on the record, and not John, who actually plays Ernie, or Keith, who is the credited writer. The end of the track hits a rather eerie feel with its unsettling organ, foreshadowing that not everything might be as wonderful as it first seems.

24. 'WE'RE NOT GONNA TAKE IT'

Written by Pete Townshend
Produced by Kit Lambert
Recorded at IBC Studios, London

Written as an anti-fascist statement, before the project began, Townshend found this would make the perfect ending to *Tommy* and could be reworked to fit the album's story. In the song we find Tommy telling his followers what they must do to follow in his footsteps. Simply, they must experience what he has and so they must be deaf, dumb and blind, which involves the use of eyeshades, earplugs and a mouth gag, as well as playing pinball and rejecting alcohol and drugs. The lines about pinball were hastily worked into the song after the writing of 'Pinball Wizard' introduced this aspect into the plot, though the fact that the abuser Uncle Ernie is there to guide the followers to their own pinball machine is rather unsettling. Thankfully, the abuse Tommy receives from both Ernie and Kevin is not mentioned anywhere as a requirement of becoming like him.

Alas, the disciples quickly revolt, turning on Tommy and rejecting his leadership, ideals and power over them. The change is rather quick and feels a tad condensed story-wise, but the song stands up as a great ending to the album. Pete and Kit debated the musical ending many times, feeling that something should be reprised from earlier on. At first there were ideas to write words to 'Sparks' (which in itself was an instrumental version of a section of 'Rael' from *The Who Sell Out)* or reprise something from 'Amazing Journey', but in the end it was decided that the 'See Me, Feel Me' and 'Listening To You' sections from 'Go To The Mirror!' would be used.

Keith once again pulls off a fantastic performance, alternating between a steady beat and explosive, tight fills. His drums being hard-panned into one speaker removes some of the power from the track, but does also highlight his playing. The vocals are another standout, with Daltrey once again beginning to tap into his raw voice, while the backing vocals offer support, particularly Entwistle, whose part in the chorus is essentially a lead vocal, being mixed so high. As the song reaches what appears to be the end, an interesting change occurs, with the guitar playing E to D but the bass playing the reverse. This then leads to the 'See Me, Feel Me' refrain, sung with tenderness and vulnerability by Daltrey, the high backing harmonies giving a hymn-like quality to the section. We finally reach the crowning glory of *Tommy* as we get to the 'Listening To You' section, a hugely uplifting end which rides high on the dynamic chord sequence, making use of the semi-tone rise from B to C, and the typically rich harmonies that The Who had become so adept at producing both in the studio and live.

Chapter 5

Who's Next (1971)

Produced by The Who
Associate Producer – Glyn Johns
Released in the UK on 27 August 1971 as Track 2408 102
Released in the USA on 14 August 1971 as Decca DL 79182
Chart position – UK = 1, USA = 4
Recorded at Olympic Studios in London and Stargroves in Hampshire, using The Rolling Stones Mobile Studio
Pete Townshend – Guitars, Vocals, VCS3 and ARP Synthesizers, Lowrey Organ and Piano on 'Baba O'Riley'
Roger Daltrey – Vocals
John Entwistle – Bass, Vocals, Brass and Piano on 'My Wife'
Keith Moon – Drums, Percussion and Vocals
Nicky Hopkins – Piano on 'Song Is Over' and 'Getting In Tune'
Dave Arbus – Violin on 'Baba O'Riley', produced by Keith Moon

Although *Tommy* and *Quadrophenia* are often voted as The Who's best albums, many people are of the belief that *Who's Next* was by far the greatest LP they ever recorded. Of course, much of this is down to the collection of brilliant songs, the performances captured and the expert production by Glyn Johns. But part of it can perhaps be attributed to the straightforward nature of the record. Double albums can be polarizing, by nature dense and complex listens, and while some people will enjoy the intricacies and depth of them, others can be put off by their vastness and length. Complicate things further with a story concept and you can divide the listener even more.

Who's Next has none of that; it's a straightforward nine-track rock record, lean, mean, with seemingly no underlying concept; 'seemingly' being the operative word. For although few listeners would have known at the time (unless they had been following Townshend's various interviews and columns for *Melody Maker*), *Who's Next* sprang from the most complex idea Townshend would ever have, one that ultimately proved too hard to understand by anyone but its author and in the end too complex to realize.

In the short time between the release of *Tommy* and *Who's Next*, much had changed. *Tommy* had been a huge international success and The Who had taken it out on the road in extensive tours across the UK, Europe and USA. During this time, the album was developed as a live piece, the band honing their skills in the process, morphing from a pop band to rock giants.

In February 1970, The Who performed two concerts, at Leeds University and Hull, the purpose of which was to tape a live album. During 1969, the band had recorded a run of American shows, with the intention to release their first live LP comprised from these recordings. However, upon returning to the UK, it emerged that sound man Bob Pridden hadn't made any notes on which shows were best, and Townshend decided to have him burn the lot rather than go through each show himself. The distraught Pridden was allowed to keep one show, although several others seem to have survived.

In March, the band released their first new music since *Tommy*, a non-album single 'The Seeker', which only reached number nineteen in the UK charts. The band were still overshadowed by *Tommy* at this point and 'The Seeker', though indicative of where the group would be heading musically, was barely played in concert at the time. Daltrey was not fond of it, later describing it as pretentious and like 'trying to push an elephant up the stairs', the spiritual quest at the heart of its lyrics (which also name-checked Bob Dylan, The Beatles and Timothy Leary) not landing in the same way that *Tommy* had. Effectively, The Who had now become an album band, and a single like 'The Seeker' wasn't going to do much for their reputation in the minds of the public. The bottom line was they needed a new album to compete with *Tommy*. Early ideas that floated around included a double album with each member having one side to curate, but this seems to have been dropped fairly soon.

Also in March 1970, in an interview with *Music Now*, Townshend talked about the abandonment of a proposed *Tommy* film for another idea altogether, describing *Tommy* as stale and explaining it would be difficult to put any genuine effort into such a project. Instead, he spoke of a new film idea which was somewhat vague, as even Townshend admitted, but would be unscripted and more along the lines of a documentary, featuring other artists besides The Who. This new idea would be an effort to keep a finger on the pulse of music, as Pete remarked that rock films always seemed to be late to what was happening; he hoped to avoid this. This would be the first hint of *Lifehouse*.

In August 1970, appearing at the Isle Of Wight Festival for the second straight year, The Who played new songs such as 'Water', 'I Don't Even Know Myself' and 'Naked Eye', which were earmarked for release on their next record, Daltrey even announcing 'I Don't Even Know Myself' (referred to as 'I Don't Know Myself') as appearing on their next album, which he stated they were halfway through recording. The band had indeed been recording at Pete's home studio for an intended fifth album, before downsizing the planned release to a maxi-single (a three- or four-track single) and ultimately shelving the whole idea, some of the tracks later appearing on *Odds And Sods* in 1974.

Shortly after the Isle Of Wight Festival, Townshend wrote in the second of his columns for *Melody Maker* about his idea for a musical note that forms the basis of existence, being careful to acknowledge the idea of the Hindu 'Om', but differentiating this as a separate idea. Once again, he was talking out his ideas in a public forum to consolidate them in his head. Townshend had perhaps begun a column for *Melody Maker* as a vehicle to help him connect more to the public and get valuable feedback. This was more vital now than ever, as Pete's usual sounding board, Kit Lambert, was growing increasingly preoccupied and absent.

After *Tommy*, Townshend felt the need to come up with something new to replace it in concert and provide the band with a new hit album. His idea went beyond just an album, being conceived as both a record and a movie. The movie would incorporate live performance into its script and the music would seek to dissolve the line between the band and audience by incorporating them into the music itself, using personal data from them to generate synthesized music.

Townshend wrote the basis for *Lifehouse* in three days, from 28–30 September 1970. He then sent the idea, as well as a full breakdown of all the technical aspects needed to record the album, the details of how to collate the data of audience members and how the movie would be filmed, to Chris Stamp. Soon after, he explained the ideas to the band, but found everyone confused. His idea was broken down into three sections, or acts, these being titled 'Overture', 'Lifehouse' and 'Glorification'. The song which formed the centre of *Lifehouse* (just as 'Amazing Journey' had formed the centre of *Tommy*) was 'The Note', the working title for 'Pure And Easy'.

In October 1970's issue of in *Disc And Music Echo*, Townshend would reveal details of the upcoming *Lifehouse* idea, which at this time centred on a band based on The Who and a roadie of theirs obsessed with finding The One Note. The unnamed roadie spends his time looking at ancient charts and writings, and converting them into electronic circuitry. Pete also mentioned that they manage to produce a note which destroys everything, leaving behind only the true note. This seems to link to the lyrics of 'Pure and Easy' about the note also being able to destroy.

At a meeting with Universal Pictures in November, Townshend was able to secure $2 million for the proposed film, a huge fee at that time for a novice film maker and quite astounding when apparently no one but Pete even understood the script. However, a high budget was needed for the technical aspects of the project, including the quadrophonic sound that Pete planned.

Pete initially had a working title of 'Barrel One' and 'Barrel Two', the idea being the former would be the fictional story and the latter would feature documentary-style filmmaking and live performances. However, the project soon came to be known as *Lifehouse*, the pursuit of realizing which would drive Townshend almost to breaking point.

The basic story centred on a dystopian future in which pollution had become so bad that people spend most of their time indoors. The government provides them with 'Experience Suits' which allow them to live artificial lives that placate them but offer no real spiritual fulfilment. They are also connected to something called The Grid, a kind of internet, and within this world they become consumed by a bland, couch-potato life and are cut off from physical interaction with other humans. In this scenario, The Grid is penetrated by a hacker who plays the people the now long-forgotten rock music of the past and seeks to draw them towards a place called The Lifehouse, where a concert will take place. Part of the story centres on a girl called Mary, who escapes and goes on a quest to find The Lifehouse, and her parents, who try to find her. Also at the heart of the story is the idea that the meaning of life is a single note. The story ends with the audience at The Lifehouse and the band coming together to produce The One Note, which makes them all vanish, presumably into a higher plane of existence. Townshend admitted in a *Classic Albums* programme that at the heart of it he was trying to produce a story in which the protagonist was in a sense deaf, dumb and blind again, except this time technology was being used to metaphorically dull the senses and prevent true spiritual fulfilment. He was partly inspired by *The Mysticism Of Sound*, a book written by Sufi spiritual teacher Inayat Khan, but the story was in the same sort of dystopian science fiction vein as *Brave New World*, *1984*, *Fahrenheit 451* and *A Clockwork Orange*.

Townshend's idea was to incorporate the band's own live performances into the film, and the band began rehearsing the songs at the Young Vic Theatre as early as November 1970 following a positive meeting with its director, Frank Dunlop, eventually inviting audiences along, and by doing so essentially turning the theatre into The Lifehouse contained within the story. Daltrey thought the idea about the meaning of life being a musical note to be a great starting point for a project, but couldn't work out how the rest of the plot fitted into anything.

The idea for the band to branch into film was not a new one, of course. Universal Pictures had expressed interest in a cinematic version of *Tommy*, offering up a deal, and even during the recording of that album, Kit Lambert had begun work on a script for a film adaptation, sensing even in the early stages the potential to adapt it for the silver screen. Presenting it to Townshend at dinner one night, the story's creator was not forthcoming with his approval, feeling the work too personal to simply hand over, especially when his attentions were occupied with the busy touring required to promote the album. There was also a fear that he might effectively lose to Hollywood the man who was not only his manager, but his confidant and co-conspirator. Alas, this rejection would help to sow a seed of divide between Lambert and Townshend that would lead to an inevitable estrangement over the next few years.

When Townshend, who was not experienced at script writing, showed his managers what he had for *Lifehouse*, he was not given the help that he perhaps expected, at least not compared to the unwavering belief and support he had been shown with *Tommy*. In retrospect, it must have been difficult for Lambert to put aside the rejection of his own film script and jump into a project in which Townshend was now writing a movie. Lambert had originally only stumbled upon The Who in the pursuit of making a film, and though this had never happened, Kit had glimpsed with *Tommy* the real prospect of finally doing so, only for his protege to snatch it away and instead offer up his own cinematic ambitions. Kit had been vital to Pete in the years of the band so far. The songwriter was a well of brilliant ideas, but he needed someone to help shape them, and often to help explain them. Lambert was the sort of confident, dynamic character that the often shy and self-doubting Townshend needed to bring out the best in him, and as a right-hand man there could be no better. But Kit was increasingly absent, and without his presence and full backing, Townshend was struggling to pull together the pieces of *Lifehouse* in the same way that *Tommy* had been crafted from a collection of part-formed notions and elements. Pete knew that even if no one outside of himself understood the idea, they would have full faith in the project if Kit was there to sell it. Unfortunately, this wasn't the case this time.

During early 1971, Pete set about recording a set of demos of the songs he had written for a new album, playing all instruments, including his newly acquired synthesizers. Like the songs themselves, the demos were of high quality, leaving the eventual producer of *Who's Next*, Glyn Johns, to ponder how he could better them. Whilst he was no Moon or Entwistle, Townshend nonetheless was an impressive multi-instrumentalist and was able to convey the brilliance of the proposed new material far better than he could the concept which would bind them.

In January 1971, at a press conference at the Young Vic, Townshend announced the band's intentions with *Lifehouse*, including their concerts at the theatre. The premise of the shows was a sort of rock workshop format, with the band taking up residency at the Young Vic, performing a series of concerts to a small crowd, who would become pivotal in the creative process. Data would be collected from audience members and fed into a synthesizer, which would produce electronic music unique to the person and then incorporate it into The Who's music. This idea never came to pass at the time, but many years later, in 2007, Townshend launched *The Lifehouse Method* website, which allowed users to generate synthesized music from data they inputted. After the material had been developed through multiple shows, it was then planned to film performances which would be incorporated into the *Lifehouse* film to go alongside scripted scenes depicting the story. As a multimedia concept, it was light years ahead of its time.

For the concerts, passers-by were invited in for free to watch The Who rehearse new material, as well as old hits, but the shows weren't as regular as hoped for by Townshend due to the theatre's schedule of events. These shows started in February 1971 but were abandoned for the group to record in America, with additional concerts taking place in April. The results at the Young Vic were not quite what was desired, as the people attending were an unpredictable rag bag. According to Townshend, at an early concert the group found themselves playing to a group of rowdy skinheads, while another individual was a drug-crazed hippie who hurled abuse at the band and rushed the stage, prompting an altercation. Although the group had experienced golden moments of connection between band and audience before, they were elusively difficult to manufacture, especially when the people were not a typical Who audience. These concerts had been announced but intentionally not mass-publicized, so they attracted the proverbial man in the street, lured in through bored curiosity rather than a heartfelt appreciation of the evolving rock music scene.

In March, the deal with Universal fell through, a massive blow that made the realization of the entire *Lifehouse* project virtually impossible. It seems that Kit Lambert had all the while been selling the film deal as an adaptation of *Tommy*, the confusion causing the film studio to pull the plug. But progress was to be made on the recording side of things.

That same month, the band travelled to New York to begin recording at The Record Plant, a state-of-the-art studio that Kit had found whilst co-producing girl band Labelle's debut LP. Townshend was elated at the apparent renewed interest from his manager and friend, and became excited about the sessions. These early sessions also included Leslie West from the band Mountain, who provided extra lead guitar on some recordings. West was responsible for providing Pete with a Gibson Les Paul Junior guitar, which would feature on some tracks on *Who's Next*. The inclusion of a second guitarist might seem rather bizarre, as Townshend had been The Who's sole guitarist since the days when they were called The Detours and Daltrey had vacated his role as lead guitarist to concentrate on singing. Townshend had developed as a lead player through the years and hundreds of gigs, and by this point certainly needed no help. However, according to West, the band were keen to record as live as possible, with little or no overdubs, so Pete was interested in focusing on rhythm with someone else handling lead duties, and West's band happened to be in The Record Plant's second studio at the time. The studio was fairly new but one of the most advanced, and had already been used for much of *Electric Ladyland* by Jimi Hendrix as well as by John Lennon for *Imagine*. According to Townshend, The Who were the first band to use the brand-new Studio One, and while Lambert was a no-show for the first couple of days, the band pressed on recording Pete's new songs with engineer Jack Adams. When Kit did eventually turn up with his assistant Anya Butler, his presence didn't have quite the desired effect. At one point, as the band were performing 'Getting In Tune' live in the studio, Lambert approached them during its outro section jam, carrying a piece of paper with a badly scrawled message on it. Struggling to read the illegible note and still play, Townshend eventually made out the writing as 'This is great, keep playing!' Of course, the pointless note was extremely counterproductive and completely disturbed the groove the band had got into. The fact that Kit Lambert was now using heroin didn't help matters either, but the excess wasn't confined to just him. Keith was using more drugs too, Pete was drinking, and according to engineer Jimmy Robertson, Jack Adams would often disappear with a bottle of scotch. Despite all this, some good work was being made, Townshend largely being the one in control rather than Lambert, but things were about to come to a head. Pete called a meeting in the Navarro Hotel, his intention being to possibly pull the plug on the movie portion of *Lifehouse* but get Kit onside to help him structure the album in a more cohesive way. Walking past Lambert's room, Pete heard his manager raging about him and his frustration at being, in his opinion, opposed. Perhaps agitated by Townshend becoming more forceful in his creative endeavours and not simply allowing Lambert to use The Who and their music as he best saw fit, Kit was animated, and especially hurtful for Townshend was hearing Lambert call him by his surname, something which had never happened before, indicative of the change in their relationship. With that, something inside Townshend snapped. During the following meeting, he had an episode which he would later describe as an alcoholic anxiety attack, in which the people in the room morphed into frogs. Losing his mental grip and feeling panicked, he moved towards the tenth-floor window with the intention of jumping. Fortunately, Anya Butler spotted Pete's growing crisis and gently took him by the arm, guiding him away from the window, but Townshend was left shaken up and confused. Mixing reality with delusions, he believed his life was under threat from the mafia and Universal Studios, and that Kit was behind it all. A friend of Roger's, a girl called Devon, attempted to calm him down, but although he came out of his episode, it spelled the end for the Record Plant sessions, as once again The Who abandoned recording.

With the *Lifehouse* concept proving frustratingly difficult to nail, the focus shifted towards the songs. Although Townshend was struggling to convey his ideas, he had not struggled with the music and had produced his most deep and well-crafted compositions to date. The idea was now to simply record the material and worry about the concept later. So The Who returned to England and began again in April with Glyn Johns, who had famously worked with The Beatles on the *Let It Be* sessions but had also been the engineer on The Who's debut album. They first worked at Mick Jagger's Hampshire home, Stargroves, using The Rolling Stones' sixteen-track mobile studio, before finally moving to Olympic Studios shortly afterwards. At first Townshend hoped to still involve Lambert, but Glyn Johns was not willing to work on the album with his interference. Listening to the Record Plant tapes, Johns heard great potential, but although the plan had been to use the work made so far, with Johns overseeing the mixing and additional overdubs, the producer was adamant that he could achieve better results if they started from scratch. Johns would prove true to his promise, but somewhat unfairly would only receive an associate producer credit for his efforts. Another important person from their first album sessions who would return was pianist Nicky Hopkins, who would end up providing beautiful work on several songs.

On *Who's Next*, Townshend would sacrifice spelling out the narrative for the benefit of the material. Unlike on *Tommy*, where some tracks seemed written specifically to fill in parts of the story, this time the songs written for *Lifehouse* were looser in the way they advanced the plot, thus they still form a cohesive album when the concept is removed. Nevertheless, many songs were left on the cutting room floor, including – inconceivably – the very song that formed the centre point of the story, 'Pure And Easy'. Glyn Johns felt, however, that without any concept, the band would be better off releasing a single album rather than the proposed double, even though plans for the two-disc release were in place until relatively late on. Townshend had hoped that at very least he could arrange the songs in a sequence that served the plot of *Lifehouse*, with the story written out in the gatefold sleeve, but Johns was intent on arranging the running order in a way that best served the flow of the music and provided the optimal audio experience for the listener. As Townshend and Johns reached an impasse over the track listing, the former attempted to explain the concept of *Lifehouse* to the latter, but the producer could not grasp anything about the story and it was finally ditched from the album. As an upside to this, Entwistle was now given the opportunity to contribute one of his own songs, picking the hard-rocking 'My Wife', which would become a live favourite amongst fans and provide the bassist with a new solo vocal showcase at concerts.

In April, the band returned to the Young Vic to play more concerts, using The Rolling Stones' mobile studio as they had at Stargroves, this time with Andy Johns (Glyn's brother) overseeing the recording. Here, the band tested out playing 'Won't Get Fooled Again', with the synthesizer on backing tape.

Previously they had attempted to use a live synth part, but the result was not quite satisfactory. Despite being labelled as a wild drummer with erratic timing, Keith could play to the tapes remarkably well, a skill that is often overlooked. Though the live performances had kept the band sharp and allowed them to quickly produce live takes in the studio, Pete became disillusioned with the Young Vic rehearsals and, finding it impossible to perform there as often as he would like, scrapped the idea. In his opinion, the band should have been there all week, but this was impossible, with weekly gigs on a Monday being the best that was offered. In December 1972, in an interview for *Creem* magazine, Townshend, looking back on the *Lifehouse* idea, revealed he had foreseen a six-month-long residency. During a Young Vic concert on 26 April, Townshend's uncertainty regarding the new material was also revealed when he said some of it was 'sounding a bit lame', but despite these misgivings, the new songs were some of the band's strongest to date. Sadly, none of the shows were filmed as intended, but an audio recording of the 26 April gig survived, with parts of it available on the Deluxe edition of *Who's Next* in 2003, followed by a full release as part of the Super Deluxe boxset in September 2023.

As recording continued in May and June, the band were suitably impressed by the sound Glyn Johns was achieving, feeling for the first time that they were working with a producer more interested in their sound than their image. In May, Daltrey also gave an interview in *Record Mirror*, still talking of a double album and the possibility of filming one of the upcoming shows. During July, the band played a small series of UK shows, showcasing some of the new tracks, including the ill-fated 'Pure And Easy', as well as other tracks that would not make the final cut, such as 'Water', 'Too Much Of Anything', 'Time Is Passing' and 'I Don't Even Know Myself', ironically often playing more tracks that didn't end up on *Who's Next* than those that did.

Who's Next marks the moment The Who change from boys to men. This change had happened during the process of touring *Tommy*, but this is the moment it is made apparent on record. For a start, Townshend's songwriting had hugely matured. There were still moments of naivety on *Tommy*, songs that seemed hurried together to join the plot, tracks that still found The Who in quirky, playful mood not far removed from the vibe of *A Quick One* and *The Who Sell Out*. On *Who's Next*, however, every track is superbly crafted. Townshend was now a master songwriter, and there are no weak songs or goofy moments. As a guitarist as well, Pete had improved markedly, thanks to the vast number of gigs played. Having often been insecure and critical about his lead guitar abilities, he had developed his skills through improvisational jams within many songs such as 'Young Man Blues', 'Shaking All Over' and 'Sparks', and this new-found fluidity as a lead player shines through, even with his restrained approach to the task. Entwistle also reaches new heights on this record, his playing more complex and melodic than ever before, creating hugely memorable bass runs on 'Won't Get Fooled Again' as well as producing many other sublime moments throughout the nine tracks. Moon had pretty much always been a phenomenon, but even he raises the level once more, with outstanding expression from beginning to end. But perhaps the biggest and most striking change is Daltrey, whose voice is transformed into a rock powerhouse, capable of going toe-to-toe with any frontman of the era. The real catalyst was the process of performing *Tommy* live, where Roger discovered an inner power and passion that elevated him to a 1970s classic rock icon.

The sound of the record as a whole is also an important step forwards, Glyn Johns producing a rich sound that allows the instruments to breathe, and is full of life. An important part of the record's instrumentation is Pete's use of acoustic guitar as a foundation for many of the tracks. This, along with the synth, provides much of the songs' rhythmic pulse, allowing Entwistle and Moon to be more expressive in their own playing. In fact, although it's arguably Moon and Entwistle who had the biggest impact on the signature sound of The Who, on *Who's Next*, two of the most key sonic elements would be provided by Townshend, namely the synth and the Gretsch guitar rig used for most of the songs. More than just an interesting new sound, the synth parts that Townshend used were perfect for the 1970s sci-fi that was his *Lifehouse* concept. That same year, the film adaptation of another dystopian tale, *A Clockwork Orange*, made use of synthesizer in its soundtrack by Wendy (at the time Walter) Carlos, who arranged a synth version of 'Music For The Funeral Of Queen Mary' by Henry Purcell, the composer who had inspired Townshend's use of suspensions within his songs. At a time in which most of his guitarist contemporaries were busy growing their six-string hero credentials, Pete was honing his skills as a composer and multi-instrumentalist, embracing the altogether alien concept of the synthesizer in its infancy. While onstage he was the ultimate showman, inspiring multiple generations of guitarists, behind the scenes he was working with a broader palate of sounds than just the ones a guitar could offer him. Synth sounds were very new in the world of popular music. George Harrison had brought in a Moog on the *Abbey Road* sessions, where it had been used sparingly on songs such as 'Here Comes The Sun', 'Maxwell's Silver Hammer' and 'Because', but this was superficial in comparison to the way Pete would use it on *Who's Next*. Pete would first use a VCS3 MK 1 model, before moving onto an ARP 2500 and later an ARP 2600. For some of the tracks, he would feed his 1968 Lowrey Berkshire organ into a synthesizer, utilizing sweep filters and a sample and hold feature to create a unique sound.

Pete's Gretsch guitar, a 1959 Chet Atkins 6120 with Bigsby vibrato, was a gift from Eagles guitarist Joe Walsh. Townshend hated it on first sight, but plugging it in he discovered a sound that would be a go-to for the bulk of *Who's Next*, as well as the majority of *Quadrophenia* and many recordings after that. His exact rig was the Gretsch, an Edwards volume pedal, a Fender Bandmaster amp and a Whirlwind lead, Townshend insisting that every part – even the lead – was vital in the resulting sound. The Gretsch has the right amount of grit as well as a shimmering quality, which along with the subtle Bigsby vibrato wobbles provide a quality that separates *Who's Next* from other classic rock guitar tones of the time. Gretsch guitars had been popular in the mid-Sixties, due in part to their prominent use by George Harrison, who primarily used both a Country Gentleman and a Tennessean. But in the late Sixties, as bands got louder and heavier, guitarists sought out something more suitable, with the British blues boom giving rise to popularity of the Gibson Les Paul. By 1971, Townshend had himself been using a Gibson SG Special, which unlike the generally humbucker-fitted Les Pauls, had two P90 pickups, which were large single coils. But the Gretsch was essentially a country guitar, and although fitted with Gretsch's own humbuckers, the 'Filtertron', produced a very different sound. Thus, the guitar tone on *Who's Next* is entirely different from other rock bands of the time such as Led Zeppelin and Free, who favoured Les Pauls, or the Stratocaster tones of artists like Jimi Hendrix and Deep Purple. On *Who's Next*, Townshend exploits the guitar's strengths for a slightly rockabilly sound, and rather than just being heavy it has a character and texture, which comes through both the driving rhythmic and wiry lead parts.

The cover of the LP happened by chance. Driving across England the day after a gig, they happened upon a slag heap with a monolith-type stone jutting out. Photographer Ethan A. Russell decided to take pictures while the band urinated on it, though in fact only Townshend was able to do so on command, the others' trails being made by pouring rainwater out of a film cannister. The sky was added in later, apparently from a photograph of Townshend's mobile home that had been rejected for the cover. The location of the shoot has long been debated, with it often being reported as Sheffield or Easington. However, in June 2024, whilst making a documentary on Ethan Russell, the production crew met with John Hirst, who was able to confirm the location as a patch of land in Temple Normanton, Derbyshire, having been to the site in question, and taken pictures, soon after the album's release. Townshend was unimpressed with both the title and the cover and somewhat perplexed by the positive reaction to both by many people – including fans, friends and respected colleagues – even as late as 2023 expressing his dislike for it in an interview with Johnnie Walker on BBC Radio Two. However, he was at least happier with it than one of the other ideas which would have made the naked women cover of Jimi Hendrix's *Electric Ladyland* look positively tame in comparison. Dave King, who had been involved in the aforementioned *Electric Ladyland* as well as The Who's own *The Who Sell Out* record, had originally been commissioned and came up with a photograph of a large naked woman, legs spread, with an image of the band placed over her genitalia. Had the band gone with that cover, it's hard to imagine the LP having quite the same reverence, despite the undeniably incredible music contained within. King refutes that he had anything to do with it, though an image like this does exist which seems to have been used in some marketing for the record.

The album was preceded by the release of the single 'Won't Get Fooled Again' in June 1971, which had to be mercilessly hacked down from its eight-and-a-half-minute running time to just under four minutes. The song perfectly summed up the current feel of The Who and just cracked the top ten, boosting the band in the singles market even as they began to move fully into their period as an albums band.

Townshend's feelings on the record itself were perhaps clouded by what might have been. For him, the album was in a way their biggest failure, as it was a collected best of what could be achieved at the time. Unlike *Tommy*, they hadn't managed to redefine what a rock band could accomplish, and thus the sense of disappointment left a bitter taste. Daltrey would go on to feel that The Who had lost some of their power on the album, and after the recording of their next LP, *Quadrophenia*, he would liken *Who's Next* to 'missing one bollock'. However, by the time of the *Classic Albums* documentary on *Who's Next* in 1999, he would call it the best album they ever made.

The Who took to the road across America in late July 1971, playing several songs from the new album and also, interestingly, still performing 'Pure And Easy' up until at least the day before the album's Stateside release, even though the song had not made the cut and would not even end up as a B-side. It was eventually released as a Townshend solo track on his *Who Came First* album the following year, before finally getting a release as a Who version on the 1974 outtakes compilation, *Odds and Sods*.

Who's Next was released first in America on 14 August, with its UK release coming on 27 August. Reaching number one in their home territory – the only Who album to hit the top spot in the UK – it was a commercial and critical success, for many the high point of their entire career. Though Townshend's concept might have failed, most people were unaware that one ever existed. Indeed, many listeners today would still have no idea of the intended storyline that runs through *Who's Next*.

If *Tommy* was the curtain call for the 1960s, with its idealized youth movements and rebellious optimism, *Who's Next* is the beginning of the 1970s, with a more realistic and grounded outlook. It is a comedown from the free love and carefree spirit of the previous decade; the kids have grown up, and now the band sing of teenage wastelands and the world-weary realization that the new boss is the same as the old boss. The band had finally got rich. Keith had now purchased his own pub, the Crown And Cushion, and could at last descend into the full-blown, larger-than-life rock existence that he had always been destined to attain. Townshend was a married man with two young daughters (Emma, born in 1969, and Aminta, born in 1971, just prior to the April Young Vic gigs), and this family life had a huge influence in the story of *Lifehouse*, evident in songs like 'Won't Get Fooled Again' and 'Going Mobile'. The revolution had happened, but it had simply left a lot of confusion and anger at the lies and broken ideals of the previous decade.

Who's Next had been a roller-coaster ride, particularly for Townshend, but there's no doubt all members had felt the strain. Daltrey claimed that the band had never been nearer to splitting up than they had been at points during its creation – a bold claim given how many times The Who had already flirted with dissolution. *Lifehouse* would also cast a long shadow, and Townshend was by no means done with it or the material that had been trimmed off *Who's Next*. In October 1971, the band released 'Let's See Action' as a single, a song which had been recorded as part of the *Who's Next* sessions, backed with Entwistle's sublime 'When I Was A Boy'. The following year, the band would go on to release as singles two more songs linked to *Lifehouse*, 'Join Together' and 'Relay', though these were probably written after the release of *Who's Next*. Pete's demos of 'Pure and Easy' and another song recorded for *Who's Next* but not released, 'Time Is Passing', ended up on his solo album *Who Came First* the following year. In addition to these songs, Pete would over the years continue writing tracks he based on *Lifehouse*, perhaps hoping to one day combine them all into a film adaptation.

In 1995, *Who's Next* was given a reissue, containing bonus tracks such as the abandoned 'Pure And Easy' recorded at The Record Plant, 'Too Much of Anything' and a couple of live tracks from the Young Vic in April 1971. The reissue also remixed several tracks, but some multi-tracks were missing. In 1999, Townshend released a boxset entitled *The Lifehouse Chronicles*, which sought to bring together the various demos for songs that had been mooted for inclusion on, or inspired by, *Lifehouse*, including later Who tracks such as 'Slip Kid' and 'Who Are You'. The set also included a radio play of *Lifehouse* featuring actors such as David Trelfall and including snippets of Townshend's demos. At this time there was also a highly interesting retrospective documentary *Classic Albums – The Who: Who's Next* – in which the surviving members of the band, producer Glyn Johns and others looked back on the creation of the album. In 2003, a Deluxe edition was released, which contained a bonus disc featuring most of the

Young Vic concert from 26 April, before finally a ten-disc Super Deluxe *Who's Next/Life House* ('*Lifehouse*' now being spelled as two separate words) boxset was made available in September 2023. This set included the entire Young Vic concert as well as one from San Fransisco 1971, and a *Lifehouse* graphic novel. This release also used de-mixing technology to remix the album for 5.1 surround sound. This was performed by Steven Wilson, who managed to separate and reconstruct the mixes of all songs apart from 'Bargain'.

TRACK BY TRACK

1. 'BABA O'RILEY'

Written by Pete Townshend
Produced by The Who, associate producer Glyn Johns
Recorded at Olympic Studios, London, May 1971

One of The Who's most popular and often-played songs, 'Baba O'Riley' is often mistakenly called 'Teenage Wasteland' after its anthemic refrain. In fact, Pete had written another track called 'Teenage Wasteland', a mournful piano-led ballad containing parts of 'Baba O'Riley', which was abandoned at the demo stage but is available on the 2023 *Who's Next/Life House* Super Deluxe boxset and Pete's *Lifehouse Chronicles* set. The unusual title, which appears nowhere in the lyrics, comes from combining the names of Meha Baba and composer Terry Riley, of whom Townshend was a fan and whose 1969 work 'A Rainbow In Curved Air' was an obvious inspiration for this song's organ part.

'Baba O'Riley' makes significant use of Townshend's Lowrey Berkshire organ and was edited down from a demo of around nine minutes. According to Townshend, the end result was made up of thousands of physical tape edits to prune the length.

For a popular rock song, its structure is highly unorthodox. Containing no real chorus, it elects instead to make its powerful three-chord hook the mainstay for almost the entire track, using dynamics to prevent it from getting monotonous.

The distinctive pattern of organ notes was achieved by using the Lowrey on a setting called 'marimba repeat', whereby keys held down would repeat themselves. The opening burst of this is still striking today, but must have been a curious sound back in 1971 when electronic-sounding music in general was barely heard by the music-buying public. The hypnotic, bubbling series of notes are at first very simply played root, fifth and octave, before opening up with further cascades of notes rippling like water. This part continues for half a minute, teasing the audience with anticipation and sounding very different from The Who we know. Just at the point where this fluttering, random part might get tiresome, the piano (played by Townshend) arrives, playing the three-chord riff of F, C and B flat. Keith comes thundering in, his drums having more punch and depth than on any previous Who album thanks to Glyn Johns, with a micing technique that is often named after him. The warm and rich bass enters with the vocal – and what a vocal it is. In the period between the release of *Tommy* and the recording of *Who's Next*, Roger Daltrey had blossomed as a singer, finally finding his truest voice. Like a lion let out of cage, his range and power is evident on the whole of the record, but as an opening gambit, it is especially powerful. The guitar doesn't enter until after the first verse, Townshend saving the sublime power chords to provide greater impact, but not long after that we reach the mellow middle eight as all instruments drop out, save for the organ, which continues to play throughout the entire track. Here, the song rests on C, as Pete takes the vocal, his pure tone contrasting perfectly with Roger's rough-hewn style. The band comes roaring back in for another verse before a very short guitar break, leading to the 'Teenage wasteland' refrain, which is as close to a chorus as the song gets. Daltrey's scream of 'We're all wasted!' brings the song to a halt again as Townshend's power-chord stabs crash home. The song breaks away here from its three chords, introducing an E flat to provide added interest, as the lead guitar plays a repeating three-note pattern. Towards the end, the song pulls another trick in the form of a violin solo played by Dave Arbus. Arbus was a friend of Moon's, and Keith sometimes sat in with Arbus' band, East Of Eden. Arbus was asked by Keith to contribute to the song, this alone earning the drummer a violin production credit. The violin, part eastern and part Irish in flavour, takes the place of a guitar solo, as the song picks up the pace into something resembling an Irish jig, the music becoming mesmerizing as the song reaches an energetic frenzy before its sudden stop.

The lyrics of 'Baba O'Riley' point to the *Lifehouse* concept, the song being possibly sung from the point of view of the farmer, fighting for his meals in an area of countryside ravaged but just about able to yield crops. The inspiration for the 'teenage wasteland' line is said to have been a reference to the Isle Of Wight Festival in 1969, where the audience left the grounds in a state of littered destruction, which The Who's road crew helped to clean up. Later, a photographer sent a picture of the devastation to Townshend, entitling it 'Teenage Wasteland'. In the 1999 *Classic Albums* documentary, Townshend explained that the 'teenage wasteland' refrain wasn't about getting wasted, but the wasting of youth. Within the context of the story, this could be looked at as the wasted potential of youth, trapped in experience suits, devoid of real human interaction.

Having edited it down from a lengthy organ track, Pete perhaps later felt it would have been better as an instrumental, and maybe if *Lifehouse* had been made there would have been room to have it as a separate instrumental too. Thankfully, it was released in its eventual form, as there is no doubt the song is one of the best in The Who's entire catalogue. A full nine-minute demo of this song would feature on the album *I Am*, released in 1972 as a celebration of Meher Baba.

'Baba O'Riley' is one of classic rock's most played and recognizable tracks (even if it is often erroneously titled) and has one of rock's most distinct intros, in part because it simply doesn't sound like anything else. The song has been featured in countless films and adverts, and gained a new audience when it became the theme of TV show *CSI: New York* in the 2000s.

Interestingly, on the 1995 reissue of the album, the version of 'Baba O'Riley' features a slightly longer synth intro which has not been on any subsequent reissues.

2. 'BARGAIN'

Written by Pete Townshend
Produced by The Who, associate producer Glyn Johns
Recorded at Olympic Studios, London, 12 April 1971, mixed 5 and 18 June 1971

Although 'Bargain' may seem like a typical love song to a partner, the subject really deals with Pete's devotion to Meha Baba and his teachings, believing that to find God and enlightenment was worth losing oneself. The track makes use of Pete's synthesizer, providing the melodic line at the start, which plays over the bright twelve-string acoustic.

'Bargain' bears a passing resemblance to the previously written and subsequently abandoned 'I Don't Even Know Myself', both in its sense of melody and guitar riffs. Especially around this time, Townshend would begin to use and reuse variations of the same sort of riffs, usually built around the chords of A, G and D, sometimes transposed into different keys. This had been the case on their most recent single, 'The Seeker', and here this is used again but shifted up a semi-tone, with Pete playing B, A and E chord-shapes on a guitar tuned down a semi-tone to put it in the key of B flat. This chord riff technique would also be used in 'Won't Get Fooled Again', the coda of 'Pure And Easy' as well as in future on 'The Real Me' and other portions of *Quadrophenia*.

Another key element, as with much of the album, is Pete's guitar work on his Gretsch guitar, given to him as a gift by Joe Walsh. The electric parts on 'Bargain' possess just the right amount of rawness, but with a shimmer and a country-laced twang that is a signature sound of Gretsch Filtertron pickups.

Keith once again delivers an outstanding performance of solid beats combined with shotgun fills. Townshend's original demo had the song sitting in a laid-back half-time groove, but Keith turns the song into an upbeat rocker (some early live versions of the track would find Keith switching between half-time and regular time) of ferocious onslaught.

Like with the opening track, 'Bargain' has a mellower middle eight sung by Townshend, backed by John's tastefully melodic bass, plus Pete's twelve-string and sparing use of synth.

As the song picks up again, the synth plays arpeggiated figures while a second synth part brings back in the opening melody. The song has another quiet section at the end before gathering momentum once more, with Keith's double bass drum thundering away like a herd of stampeding elephants.

Though not as well-known as 'Baba O'Riley', 'Won't Get Fooled Again' and 'Behind Blue Eyes', 'Bargain' would be a well-loved track, featuring an outstanding high note from Daltrey at the end of each chorus, and would feature extensively in concerts in 1971 and be a regular addition to set lists for the rest of The Who's career.

Pete would reveal in the 2023 Super Deluxe reissue that the song had never really been intended as part of the *Lifehouse* story, leaving one to wonder if the track would have been released at the time had the project not collapsed.

3. 'LOVE AIN'T FOR KEEPING'

Written by Pete Townshend
Produced by The Who, associate producer Glyn Johns
Recorded at Olympic Studios, London, April–May 1971

'Love Ain't For Keeping' underwent something of a 360-degree journey before ending up on *Who's Next*. Townshend's original demo had been fairly similar, although it also featured swirling synth through its extremely short duration, which was essentially only one verse and chorus. Inevitably, when the entire band got hold of it, it changed. During the Record Plant sessions, they recorded a blistering electric version featuring Pete on lead vocals and Mountain's Leslie West on searing lead guitar. This version was a good deal longer, featuring a false ending and a jammed-out end section, with West wailing away and Townshend demonstrating more of a rock edge to his voice than usual. This version can be found on various reissues as a bonus track. However, in the end the group went back to basics, returning it to a more sedate acoustic arrangement which does allow us to once more appreciate Pete's acoustic prowess. Daltrey would also assume the lead vocals, dialling back from his grittier rock performances on the album but still managing to demonstrate power in the purity of his voice. The track is another one that is built around an A, G and D chord progression, with the only deviation being a C chord thrown in.

As stated, the highlight of the track is Townshend's crisp acoustic guitars, two parts panned left and right, the left part playing tight rhythm, with the right supplying nifty improvised lead runs which blend blues and country in some delightful phrases.

Roger does a fine job of providing just enough rawness in his vocal without overpowering things, while Keith also takes more of a backseat on this one, playing the type of groove that featured on many Townshend home demos, including 'Bargain', 'Won't Get Fooled Again' and, in the future, 'The Real Me'. Whereas on all those songs Moon ended up doubling the pace, for 'Love Ain't For Keeping' he would adopt Pete's more languid feel.

As well as having an additional verse to make the song longer than the demo's minute and a half, we also get Pete's understated but perfectly executed guitar solo, again played on acoustic.

According to Pete, the song was set to be a love story between Ray and Sally, the parents of the young girl Mary, although whether this was written with that in mind or simply adopted into the story, as many songs from Townshend's concepts were, is hard to tell. Townshend has also talked of the lyrics referring to people wanting to make love while the world goes to hell, as alluded to with lines about black ash.

In concert, the band would revert to a heavier electric approach like they had at the Record Plant sessions, with Roger taking lead vocals as he had done on the album. The band would open their shows with the song for a short time in 1971 and keep it in the set for much of that year. The song would reappear live in 1982 before being played a few times in the 2000s.

4. 'MY WIFE'

Written by John Entwistle
Produced by The Who, associate producer Glyn Johns
Recorded at Olympic Studios, London, May 1971

With the abandonment of the *Lifehouse* project and the resolution to make *Who's Next* simply a collection of songs, the track selection was opened up to allow John Entwistle to contribute. Entwistle, who had released his debut solo album, *Smash Your Head Against The Wall*, earlier that year, had 'My Wife' left over, a typically comic tale about the perils of a scary spouse. Written after storming out with his two large dogs following an argument with his less-than-intimidating wife, the track came to John quickly as he began imagining what would happen were she more threatening. Upon returning home, he rushed upstairs to work on it. According to Entwistle, his wife Alison found the result very funny and joked of one day getting up onstage with a rolling pin during its performance.

The song, whose working title during recording was 'Give Me A Bodyguard', is a fairly slow-paced rocker, with piano, played by Entwistle, adding a touch of old-school rock and roll to it. John would still be a little dissatisfied with the result, feeling it didn't quite swing in the way he wanted it to, and he would end up releasing his own version in 1973. Another addition to the instrumentation is brass from John, which renders the track as something more interesting than standard stadium rock and takes the place of a guitar solo in the middle section. John's double-tracked vocal displays a bit more of a deep bluesy tinge than he had showed on previous Who records; he sounds barely recognizable as the same man who sang 'Fiddle About' and 'Cousin Kevin' on their preceding album.

On this track, though Moon is forced to keep a slower pace than usual, he makes up for it by expressing himself wonderfully on the pounding fills, so manic that you can practically feel him making faces at you through the speakers. Perhaps anticipating playing it live, Entwistle's bass part is unusually simple for him, playing mainly root notes in contrast to his rapidly developing lead bass style. Towards the end he adds another brass part, playing a mournful minor third-to-second phrase, adding an interestingly gloomy feeling to the mix.

'My Wife' would become a live favourite with fans, John's solo vocal of choice over the years, where it was often played at a swifter pace, usually becoming more of a heavy rocker with plenty of room for Pete to solo, as well as giving John a chance to let fly on the bass towards the end.

As revealed on the 2023 Super Deluxe boxset, the unedited take was in fact longer, featuring each middle eight repeating itself.

5. 'THE SONG IS OVER'

Written by Pete Townshend
Produced by The Who, associate producer Glyn Johns
Recorded at Olympic Studios, London, May 1971

'The Song Is Over' closes side one of the original vinyl, but more likely would have been the very last track of a *Lifehouse* album. It is a little strange to think of 'Won't Get Fooled Again' not being the grand finale, but theme-wise 'The Song Is Over' would seem to fit at the end of the story, especially with its call back to the unused 'Pure And Easy'. Opening with a beautiful piano part played by Nicky Hopkins, subtle synth and sparse, sparkling guitar lines from Pete, it instantly sets up a wistful mood. The song is harmonically and structurally the most complex on *Who's Next*, one which shifts the listener from key to key and from one mood to another. A major part of its light and shade comes again in the form of featuring the contrast between Daltrey's and Townshend's vocals. Here, the song starts with Pete's high and tender singing, up until the song changes to a more upbeat and driving feel with the whole band joining in. At this point Roger takes over on double-tracked lead vocals, delivering another strong performance. The song shifts up from C sharp to D sharp, Nicky Hopkins' piano notes cascading and Entwistle delivering yet more melodic, upper-register bass runs. The song again shifts key for a short instrumental break led by Pete's restrained lead lines. Another section in E features Pete taking the lead vocal once again, and interestingly the third line of lyrics in this section, 'She was the first song I ever sang', appears to have originated from an unreleased song of Townshend's called 'Party Theme From Rael', whose lyrics were published in *Eye* magazine in September 1968 and which was presumably from the unreleased full-length *Rael* opera.

There is so much going on in this song between the usual bass, drums, guitar and vocals, plus the added piano and synth, that it's an impressive achievement in the arrangement and production that the mix never becomes messy or overcrowded. At the end of the song, the piano notes double up, Moon's drums mirroring them for added energy, and we hear the refrain from 'Pure And Easy', providing the perfect ending.

'The Song Is Over' was never played live by The Who, owing to its complexity. However, Roger Daltrey would play it in 1994 as part of a birthday concert at New York's Carnegie Hall, in which he sang many Townshend-written songs, both Who and solo, as well as being played by Townshend at a few *Lifehouse* concerts in 2000.

6. 'GETTING IN TUNE'

Written by Pete Townshend
Produced by The Who, associate producer Glyn Johns
Recorded at Olympic Studios, London, 28 May 1971, mixed 18 June 1971

Like 'The Song Is Over', 'Getting In Tune' opens with Nicky Hopkins' piano, here playing a typical Townshend chord change utilizing suspensions. John then enters proceedings with a characteristically melodic bass run, before playing single root notes and sitting out the second half of the verse, just leaving the piano and Roger's vocal. At the end of the verse, Moon makes his grand entrance and the whole band kicks in as Daltrey's vocals open up, revealing his harder and more powerful edge. The song has a neat trick of having the piano chords change, moving to G and F minor, whilst the bass and guitar riff stay rooted in F, for a slightly unsettling effect. Townshend's guitar doesn't sound like his

Gretsch setup, so is most likely the Les Paul Jr, given to him by Leslie West. This guitar was equipped with a single P90 pickup, the same type that featured on Pete's live guitar of choice at the time, the Gibson SG Special, and his tone on this song is fairly close to his live sound of the day.

As the song moves back into its verse, we are treated to Entwistle's fantastic bass lines, both rhythmic and melodic, as he leaves the space required for the song to breathe. Townshend also delivers some sparkling fills, while his acoustic guitar is subtly mixed in the left-hand speaker. The song moves to G minor for its middle eight before settling into a groove in C, Roger's voice being answered by backing vocals, which switch from left to right, while the acoustic guitar also plays a more prominent role throughout this section. At the end of this we hit another trademark Who key change as the song moves into G, Keith dropping out and Townshend adding a beautiful harmony vocal. The song winds up in a groove which then switches to double time, where Keith and John are allowed to let loose in a wonderful jam that fades out.

The working title of this track was 'I'm In Tune', and the band had worked on it in New York, thus by the time of the Olympic sessions they were tight and the performance captured here is brilliantly live-sounding and dynamic. The words, on the surface, seem to deal with music, but with lots of underlying metaphors that could be derived. Within the *Lifehouse* story itself, it could have provided a strong link to the theme of The One Note and everyone having their own particular note that would create it.

7. 'GOING MOBILE'

Written by Pete Townshend
Produced by The Who, associate producer Glyn Johns
Recorded (most likely at Olympic Studios, London, possibly Stargroves, Hampshire) April–May 1971

'Going Mobile', which would have been a key song in *Lifehouse*, found a place on *Who's Next* despite there being several stronger songs on offer during the sessions, perhaps due to it being a very suitable vehicle (no pun intended) for Townshend as a lead vocalist. It was partly inspired by Pete's own family adventures in his American Airstream motorhome, nicknamed 'Maxine', which he had bought while on tour in Maryland and had later taken to the Isle Of Wight Festival. As Townshend travelled in the air-conditioned motorhome, he began to imagine a future in which the world was polluted and one might survive inside such a vehicle, its air conditioning purifying the oxygen inside.

The song is built on Townshend's snappy acoustic guitar, with a capo at the seventh fret so that the home chord of A becomes D. During the verse, Keith plays in his usual expressive way before dragging back the beat at the end of each line. In the middle section, which forms a guitar solo of sorts, Townshend's guitar was plugged into a synthesizer for a highly unique spluttering sound, with him also vocally ad-libbing over the top. The second middle eight provides a moment of calm before the song sets off again, like a caravan hurtling full speed down a highway, Keith's drums pounding away, with the synthesized guitar providing added electronic chaos. 'Going Mobile' is one of two songs from the album to have never been played live by the band.

8. 'BEHIND BLUE EYES'

Written by Pete Townshend
Produced by The Who, associate producer Glyn Johns
Recorded at Olympic Studios, London, April–May 1971

Sometimes referred to as The Who's only ballad (a claim which isn't really true), 'Behind Blue Eyes' does, however, provide a relative moment of calm before the storm of the closing 'Won't Get Fooled Again', even if it veers into rockier territory itself towards the end. Within the *Lifehouse* story, this song was to be sung from the point of view of a villain called Brick, though details of this character are practically non-existent from reports at the time, and the character did not appear in the radio play from 1999. Later, in the 2023 Super Deluxe reissue, the character would take a central role in the graphic novel, while in the accompanying notes for the album, Townshend details the character further, painting him as a go-between for Jumbo, the head of the government, even describing him as a double agent working for both the government and the rebels.

The song starts with a gloriously rich, reverb-soaked acoustic guitar arpeggiating an E suspended fourth chord, before shifting sombrely to E minor, at which point Daltrey enters with one of his most chilling vocals in the band's discography, joined on the title line by harmonies from Pete and John. According to Daltrey, his first pet, a dog called Nellie, had been run over and killed that day, which added to the emotion he put into the song.

In the chorus, the bass finally makes an appearance and Daltrey's vocal is double-tracked, adding weight and power to it. We also hit a striking chord change when, at the end of the second progression, we land on an E major, instead of the E minor home chord, providing a more defiant tone. In the second verse there is the addition of beautifully ethereal backing harmonies which provide high 'Ooohs' before harmonizing the lyrics in the first part of the following chorus. After over two minutes of run time, with seemingly nowhere else to go, the song pulls the rug from under the listener and enters a totally different section as the pace picks up, Keith finally joining in and making up for his absence in barely a minute's worth of frenetic assault. Unusually, he plays the breaks between vocals fairly straight but accentuates the rhythms of the vocals throughout the singing. Pete's Gretsch guitar is bitingly fierce in tone, with a short, almost slap-back delay, adding to the slight rockabilly sound as he switches from power chords to country fills. Daltrey's vocal is tough, angry and weathered, joined on the second set of lines by Pete's harmony. The song winds up with a series of classic Townshend power chord stabs, the Bigsby vibrato providing subtle chord wobbles while the acoustic guitar flourishes in the background, before the melee dies down, leading us back to the familiar verse of the song.

The track was apparently written on tour in Denver, where two things are said to have happened. Firstly, Townshend became angry with a fan at a gig, which he later regretted, perhaps prompting the line about his first clenching. He would write this as a sort of poem to Meher Baba, genuinely looking for his anger to be dissolved. He was also approached by a groupie who attempted to seduce him, but he ended up retreating to his hotel room, where he wrote the song.

'Behind Blue Eyes' would instantly become a stand-out track on *Who's Next* and a firm fan favourite, played for much of the band's career. At the Young Vic in April 1971, before the album's release, Townshend announced the song as probably soon being released as a single, noting that it was untypical of the old Who but one that they felt right about. Although it was never released as such in the UK, it did get a single release in the USA, reaching number thirty-four.

9. 'WON'T GET FOOLED AGAIN'

Written by Pete Townshend
Produced by The Who, associate producer Glyn Johns
Recorded at Stargroves, Berkshire, 6–7 April 1971
Mixed at Island Studios, London, 28 May 1971

Few rock albums are bookended by two such iconic tracks as the opening and closing cuts on *Who's Next*, and to match the brilliant opener we get this eight-and-a-half-minute rock landmark as a finale to the LP. The track manages to turn a synthesizer into a vital sonic tool in a rock band's arsenal, even if its sound is close to an organ, because in fact it *is* an organ which is simply fed through a synth.

Part of the inspiration for the song was a hippie commune near where Pete and his family lived, on Eel Pie Island. These seemingly friendly lot would sometimes visit Pete looking for food and other items, and Townshend would explain later that they became increasingly demanding. He had to draw the line when they apparently began to talk about 'liberating' his children. Some of the people were, in Townshend's recollection, 'whackos'; according to him, when one refused to leave, he ended up hitting him with a hammer. Scary times!

Townshend had recorded a demo of the song which featured a more laid-back half-time groove for a very different feel. It did, however, include the signature synth part which in the end would be lifted from the demo for the band's version. The effect was achieved by plugging his Lowrey Berkshire organ into a synthesizer, which was an EMS VCS3, instead of the more famous ARP 2500, which Townshend would only acquire later. The synth was set to a sample and hold feature, which would give a random frequency sweep, revealing incredible harmonic complexity in quite simple chords being held down, as well as providing the rhythmic pulse.

The band attempted to record the song at The Record Plant in New York, using a live organ part instead of a pre-recorded track, an idea that Daltrey was keen on as he didn't like the idea of the band being locked into backing tapes. This version is available on various reissues as a bonus track, but it's a curious listen. Maybe it's the effect of hearing the familiar synth part for so many years, but the live rendition, with a more improvised pattern of notes, doesn't have anywhere near the same beauty or power. Another potential issue was that the synth had a rhythmic pulse which would be almost impossible to match to the band's tempo in concert. For these reasons, perhaps, it was decided to record the band playing to the pre-recorded synth track from Pete's demo. This would also be the way they would perform the song live, since synthesizers were tricky pieces of equipment that took time to program, offered no way to recall patches, and the idea of hauling around a synth and organ to every venue was not really a practical one.

Though it is the thrilling climax to the record, it was in fact the first song to be recorded, and possibly the only track on the record from the Stargroves sessions. Here, in the reception hall of the lavish home of Mick Jagger, the band came up trumps and captured a flawless performance, playing live along to Pete's original synth part, Keith Moon following the song perfectly with the synthesizer in his headphones.

The song opens with guitar and organ blending into one, the latter then taking over before the whole band steams in. The chord changes are really made by Townshend's acoustic guitar (still playing in a half-time feel) and the synth, while the electric guitar mostly plays A power chords and single open A string hits, even over the D chord. However, it's still the oft-used Townshend chord patterns built around A, G and D that dominate the song's riffs. Meanwhile, the bass plays chromatic figures throughout the verses, shifting to higher-register melodic phrases in the choruses, that somehow work, though operating independently from the chords underneath.

Townshend's guitar parts on his Gretsch are fuzzy in tone but with a real ring to them, while the drums represent one of Moon's masterclasses on record, playing to a synth track but not holding back one inch from creatively filling the space with deft fills and accents.

The chorus sees Daltrey's vocals joined by the usual tight harmonies, while the middle eight key changes to B and then essentially repeats the same Townshend three-chord riffs a tone up from the home key. Townshend's shout of 'Do yer?' is followed by a guitar solo, featuring two guitars playing slightly different things, but working together nicely. The first break-down introduces Daltrey's scream, fairly mild the first time around, but just a taster of the earthshattering one to come later. That only occurs after a riotous passage following the final chorus, with Townshend, Moon and Entwistle jamming the song out until a power chord cues the band to a halt, a still lingering acoustic playing on for a moment. Here, the organ becomes a solo, hypnotically weaving away, at first dark as it changes to minor before resolving back to major, and carrying on for almost a minute on its own. Finally, reaching a point of urgency as a synth note rises like an alarm, Moon takes his cue and unleashes a short drum solo that is a defining moment in rock history. As the band come roaring back in, Daltrey produces one of the most iconic and hair-raising screams ever committed to tape. Roger would later talk in his biography about going for the scream and alarming others in the studio, as, such was its ferocity, it sounded like someone being murdered! He would mention that on Pete's demo there was a smooth 'Yeeah', but in fact on the demo it is still a scream, only a shorter one, guttural but not blood-curdling like Daltrey's.

Years later, Townshend talked of the song's place in the *Lifehouse* story, where the rebels were offered amnesty if they became part of the system, although how much of this was in place at the time in 1971 is not known. The song, though, works just as well as a political statement away from the rock opera it was intended for, relevant as much now as it was in 1971.

Though its message was powerful, it has also been contentious as the song can be seen to be an anti-revolution track. In July 1971, at a house-warming party for Keith, at his newly acquired property, named 'Tara', several members of the press were invited, including people from *International Times*, a publication dedicated to counterculture and one that counted Mike McInnerney (Pete's friend, who had provided artwork for *Tommy*) as a designer. At this joint house-warming party/album press launch, certain people were heavily critical of the perceived message of the song, and Townshend found himself under fire. Later, in 1987, Townshend would call it the dumbest song he'd ever written, going so far as calling it irresponsible and claiming it was wrong to deny people a political stance, although it is probably unfair to suggest that the song advocates this. In the *Classic Albums* documentary in 1999, he described it as a plea to not install him as the new boss, not to make the rock star the role model, but for people to take control over their own lives. At its core, the song can be taken as not an anti-revolution song, but a warning against repeating the same mistakes and believing that simply taking a stand will inherently make things better.

'Won't Get Fooled Again' was released on 25 June 1971 in an edited form. Although it was not as successful as 'Pinball Wizard' had been, it did reach a respectable number nine in the charts, a perhaps unexpected hit for a band that were now steadily focusing on albums rather than singles chart success. In America, the record label jumped the gun, advertising the song on the record sleeve as being from the upcoming motion picture *Lifehouse*.

The song would forever be one of the band's most iconic and well-known songs, played live in concert for almost every gig henceforth. In 2023, Townshend said that he felt Daltrey wanted to drop the song from live performances, but that he (Townshend) could not see what they would replace it with. Of course, it *is* irreplaceable. Epic and grand, it showcases The Who not only as individual musicians, but also as a unit, as well as Townshend as a writer, perhaps better than any other song in their catalogue. It is the perfect distillation of 1970s Who.

The song would also find a whole new audience in 2002 as the theme tune of TV show *CSI: Miami*.

Chapter 6

Quadrophenia (1973)

Produced by The Who
Associate Producer on 'Love Reign O'er Me' and 'Is It In My Head?' – Glyn Johns
Released in the UK on 2 November 1973 as Track 2657 013
Released in the USA on 27 October 1973 as MCA2 10004
Chart position – UK = 2, USA = 2
Note – Some sources offer slightly different release dates, but these are the most up-to-date and official ones
Recorded at Ramport Studios in London, using Ronnie Lane's Mobile Studio, and Olympic Studios in London
Roger Daltrey – Vocals
John Entwistle – Bass, Vocals and Horns
Keith Moon – Drums, Percussion and Vocals
Pete Townshend – remainder (including Guitar, Vocals, Synthesizer, Piano and Banjo)

Even though 1972 would be a relatively quiet year for the group, there was still plenty going on for the individual members, including three of them releasing or recording solo albums, an orchestral production of *Tommy*, a film role and of course a smattering of gigs, although by no means the amount that the band had usually found themselves performing. The most significant activity would be the early work on songs that would become part of the group's next album, *Quadrophenia*.

In May and June, The Who began work on sessions at Olympic Studios with Glyn Johns for a project called *Rock Is Dead – Long Live Rock*. According to Townshend, an early idea had been for each member to curate a side of a double album, although this is also a notion that seemed to have been floating around prior to *Who's Next*. Pete was determined to put *Tommy* to rest and felt the band needed a new piece to replace it onstage, something which *Who's Next*, with its lack of a fully realized concept, hadn't achieved. This was to be a collection of songs looking back at the band's own past, and songs taped during the sessions included 'Relay', 'Join Together', 'Put The Money Down' and 'Long Live Rock', before Pete curtailed recording.

Journalist friend Nik Cohn, who had influenced the writing of 'Pinball Wizard', wrote a movie treatment based on this idea, but the script was much too lengthy, with an estimated running time of eight hours, so he proposed the idea of four separate films, each from the perspective of a different member of The Who. Although the film seems to have been an attempt to present a kind of biography of the band, detailing each individual member from birth through to present day, Cohn mixed the characters of the child versions of The Who into one central character called (of all names) Tommy. Townshend would find Cohn's treatment whilst compiling his Director's Cut boxset, released in 2011, and realized the important role Cohn played in the genesis of *Quadrophenia.* According to Pete, in this treatment, John was portrayed as a good kisser with a conventional home life, Roger a sex machine, Keith a kind of dethroned prince and Pete as torn between his devotion to Meher Baba, his life as an artist and his role as a family man. Ultimately, although Pete rejected Cohn's treatment, the idea of a character made up of the members of The Who was a seed that would ultimately bear fruit.

'Join Together' and 'Relay', recorded in the 1972 Olympic sessions, were no doubt inspired by *Lifehouse*, and Townshend still hoped he might be able to work some ideas for that project into the new album. Both songs were almost certainly not written until after the completion of *Who's Next*, but fitted in with the story and themes of *Lifehouse* better than some of the songs originally intended as part of it. Perhaps Pete had attempted to shoehorn in several previously composed songs, but given more time was able to write material more strongly linked with the central concept. However, maybe this was part of the reason the sessions were abandoned, as Townshend soon began to feel that what was being recorded sounded like *Who's Next* part two. 'Relay' and 'Join Together' would be released that year as standalone singles (the latter being a relative hit, reaching number nine in the UK charts), while two other tracks, 'Put The Money Down' and 'Long Live Rock', were unreleased until the compilation album *Odds and Sods* in 1974. A couple of other tracks recorded during the sessions would find their way onto their next album, these being 'Is It In My Head?' and the crucial 'Love Reign O'er Me'.

Townshend wrote and recorded demos through 1972, and in August of that year, speaking to *NME*, he unveiled more plans, revealing that the new Who album would not just deal with their history, thematically, but musically as well, with several songs being more reminiscent of their earlier sound, akin to material like 'Tattoo', 'I'm A Boy' and 'Odorono'. No evidence exists for any songs written at this time that really sound anything like this early-period Who, so perhaps Pete was planning to finally use several songs that had gone unreleased from around 1967–1968. Whatever the case, nothing came of the idea.

By 1973, the *Rock Is Dead – Long Live Rock* project had evolved into something else. The idea to look back at The Who's own history was still retained, but Townshend found a more interesting way to achieve this. The band would no longer be the main focus of the story, but would play cameo roles as seen through the eyes of a central character – a mod in the 1960s. Not only this, but the main character's personality was to be made up of four identities, each based on the individual members of The Who, and each represented by a musical theme.

Pete had given an interview for *Rolling Stone* in 1972 where the idea seemed to have pretty much gained its final concept. In it, Townshend bemoaned the fact that the band had stopped progressing, feeling that they were not experimenting and were losing ground to acts like David Bowie, Roxy Music and the Electric Light Orchestra. Townshend explained that these groups were like The Beatles, in that they were always pushing, and that he hoped to do some crazy things the next time The Who were in the studio. Townshend also spelled out the idea that the record would look at the history of The Who but also centre around a kid with personalities based on the band, Pete himself representing good, Daltrey representing bad, Entwistle as a romantic and Moon as insane. He summed it up as a kid becoming 'spiritually desperate' but finding the secret to life. He also described the still-unnamed hero of the piece as suffering from 'Quadrophonia' (*sic*) and stressed the album would be in quadrophonic sound.

The inspiration for the story of *Quadrophenia* is attributed by Townshend to a flashback he had in early 1973, possibly caused by a lack of amyl nitrate, which he had taken to using. This flashback was of a night after a Who gig in Brighton in 1964, when a 19-year-old Townshend and his friend, Liz Reid, missed their train home and ended up under the pier with a load of mod boys in parkas, with the tide rising around their feet. In early 1973, in the midst of a cold and blustery day, as Townshend sat in his second home – a creaky, falling-apart cottage in Cleve Lock near Goring-on-Thames – he began to feel the way he had on that day aged 19, depressed and lost. Quickly grabbing a pen and paper, he scrawled out the basics for the story which would feature on the inside cover of *Quadrophenia*. The nostalgia of that night, not only the time under the pier but the romance of the ride back on a milk train in the early hours, was a powerful reminder of a time merely a decade ago but so far removed from the present that it was almost another world. That juxtaposition would be key; this project would be like a time machine ride back to those days, but viewed and musically presented in a very different way.

As the project came together, Townshend found he had songs which would fit loosely enough into the story, such as 'Drowned', another song based on spirituality. Many of these songs had been written in the previous year as Townshend was still trying to find the right concept on which to base a new Who album. Unlike *Tommy*, where he had called on Entwistle to contribute songs, this would be a Townshend shut-out, with him writing every track, the sleeve notes declaring, 'Quadrophenia in its entirety by Pete Townshend'. Likewise, while the other three members are listed for their individual contributions instrument-wise, Townshend is simply listed as 'remainder'. This not only includes acoustic and electric guitars, vocals and synth, but piano, banjo and apparently even some cello, which Townshend learnt to play well enough over the course of a couple of weeks to include on the record. This, of course, was a total reversal from early notions of allowing each band member to write or curate a side of vinyl. The concept of each member representing a side of the hero's personality was now firmly in place, but with Roger deemed as the tough guy rather than 'bad' and Pete as a 'hypocrite, a beggar' rather than 'good'. Aside from this, early fan and friend 'Irish' Jack Lyons provided much inspiration for the character who was now called Jimmy.

Pete began assembling a studio in Cleve which would be capable of quadrophonic production (something that had been a consideration during the making of *Who's Next*), but although progress was good, he realized that while fine for mixing, it was not an ideal solution for actually recording a band. As he discussed this with John 'Wiggy' Wolf, who was The Who's production manager and former driver for John and Keith, Wolf had an idea and invited Townshend down to the band's storage facility in Battersea, South London. This was an old church hall where much of the band's equipment was stored. Townshend immediately recognized the great acoustics of the building and knew it would make a fantastic recording studio, but there was scarcely time to transform the place into what was needed. Wolf, however, insisted it could be done, and work started with the help of John Alcock from a company called Trackplan. Specializing in building home studios for musicians, including Daltrey, Cat Stevens and others, Trackplan was a company in which Pete was a shareholder. Six weeks later, the hall had been transformed with hardwood floors and soundproofing, a booth for acoustic guitar, another for a grand piano as well as a vocal booth. However, despite their best efforts, the equipment wasn't quite ready and the band hired Ronnie Lane's mobile studio to use, which had been equipped by Ron Nevison, who would also become the engineer for the record. Further work on the studio continued even while the record was being produced. Ronnie's studio was set up in a 'silver bullet' Airstream mobile home that was parked outside the new studio (which Pete referred to as 'The Kitchen' but which became better known as Ramport) along with a huge generator – a necessary part of the equipment due to a government-imposed three-day week restriction on commercial electricity use. The motor home acted as a control room while Ramport was being finished, Nevison keeping contact with the band via a video link. Townshend, who had lost his driving licence in late 1972, travelled from Twickenham to Battersea in a speed boat each day, a commute he found enjoyable.

The band would record in the live room, with Pete and John placed left and right, as on stage, the studio's arrangement meaning the band could simultaneously record drums, bass, piano and a guide vocal as well as acoustic guitar. At the time, no other studio in London offered this option. One thing that wasn't recorded at Ramport was the synth tracks, as Pete's synthesizers took time to program and sounds couldn't be saved, meaning that moving them to Ramport was impractical. Instead, Townshend worked on this at his own studio, bringing these in, with the band cutting live tracks playing along to them, Keith playing to a click track as he would do at concerts. Another piece of the sonic tapestry recorded outside of Ramport was John's horn parts, which he would lay down at his own studio and bring in, Nevison recalling that he had nothing to do with engineering these parts.

Chris Stainton provided addition piano parts on 'Dirty Jobs', '5.15' and 'Drowned', subbing for the unavailable Nicky Hopkins, who had traditionally provided keys when more tricky piano work than Townshend could provide was needed. Of course, Pete himself would still play some piano, including the stunning intro to 'Love Reign O'er Me', taken straight from his home demo. Pete had seen Stainton play with Joe Cocker, and, remembering him, decided to invite him to the sessions, even basing 'Drowned' around a piano riff he had played on the song 'Hitchcock Railway'.

When the control room was complete it was an advanced system employing twenty-four-track, sixteen-track and eight-track Studer tape machines. Whereas most studios employed a pair, or at most four, studio monitor speakers, Ramport had twelve of them, four pairs at the front and two pairs at the back, making it capable of monstrous volume. A huge objective of building the studio was to allow quadrophonic mixing, something that no current studio in the UK offered. In the end, though, Townshend was unsatisfied by the attempts to make quadrophonic sound work, and without the time to further develop the technology, it was decided to concentrate on making a great stereo mix. For the Director's Cut edition in 2011, Townshend oversaw the quadrophonic remixing of eight tracks for Dolby 5.1, before once again abandoning this idea. These eight tracks, mixed by Bob Pridden and Richard Whittaker, appear on disc five of the release. In 2023, it was announced that a full Dolby Atmos mix would be released for streaming.

Aside from studio work, Nevison and Townshend would also record sound effects to link the songs, including crashing waves, train whistles and brass bands, Pete using a mobile studio to record the sea noises at Perranporth beach in Cornwall. With the vast number of brass parts and synth, as well as a full band, they found that sometimes they didn't have enough tracks to add the sound effects and ended up playing them off cartridge machines used to play radio adverts.

For the horn parts, Entwistle brought twenty or thirty brass instruments and spent time writing out parts on manuscript paper. Townshend would praise his work in *Melody Maker* in October 1973, explaining that whereas John had previously been a fairly quiet member of the band in the studio, for *Quadrophenia* he had spent many hours arranging horn parts, attributing this new dedication to the work he had done on his own solo albums.

Though the group had attempted to record the follow-up to *Who's Next* with Glyn Johns, and two of the songs made with him as producer would end up on *Quadrophenia*, The Who ultimately decided against having him produce the whole record, initially going back to Kit Lambert. This may seem a strange decision given the sheer quality of Johns' production and the erratic and disruptive behaviour of Lambert, plus the ill feeling caused during the Record Plant sessions in 1971. But perhaps a reason for this was the failure of *Lifehouse* to be carried off as Townshend wished. Johns had been unable to see the concept Pete was so passionately trying to create and had been insistent on making a straightforward single album, unlinked by any discernible story. On the other hand, Kit was a great sounding board and a vital part of helping Pete to achieve his creative visions. Thus, the production path taken makes a lot of sense given that this time Pete really had to pull off an idea that could outstrip *Tommy*. Lambert attempted to co-produce with Pete for the first week or two, but had become even more lost and unstable than he had been during initial production for *Who's Next*. Showing up drunk and disrupting work, he was, according to Daltrey, eventually fired by Townshend after turning up with a feast of expensive and delicious but unwanted food. This enraged Townshend, who might have still been feeling hurt over the experience in New York, and he ended up so agitated that he became physically threatening towards his manager, until, ironically, Roger had to step in to quell his fury. The argument was ended without any physical harm, but this would effectively be the end of the road for the relationship between Townshend and Lambert. With Lambert out of the picture, this left Townshend as sole producer, adding to his near total control of the project, though Daltrey reminds us in the documentary *Quadrophenia: Can You See The Real Me* that Pete never produced his vocals as Roger would not allow him to be present when he was recording them; instead, Ron Nevison would produce. Nevertheless, Daltrey would remain unhappy with how his voice was produced and mixed on the record and would also state that the studio hadn't been built properly, saying that though the mixes sounded great at Ramport, they sounded vastly inferior played back at any other studio. He put this down to the fact it had been built by people who didn't really know what they were doing.

For the artwork, Townshend decided to include a lavish booklet which would feature pictures of Jimmy. This and a story synopsis written in the first person, printed on the inside of the gatefold cover, would greatly help to explain the plot of the album, whose songs were often thinly linked to the story. For this booklet, Pete enlisted Ethan A. Russell, who had shot the cover of *Who's Next*. Long-time friend Richard Barnes was tasked with helping make the photos as authentic as possible. He immediately sought out Lydon Kirby, who had been a dedicated mod of the time and still remembered much about the prevailing fashions of the era. As well as local kids, Pete's brother, Paul, was also recruited to be in some shots. These photo sessions lasted around five weeks and included a trip to Brighton to get the iconic photos of the pier as well as the Grand Hotel. A couple of local Battersea girls, Julie Emson and Maxine Isenman, were enlisted to appear in shots and recommended a local lad, Terry Kennett, who went by the name of Chad, for the role of Jimmy. Chad would make a good choice for Jimmy; however, a problem arose when he had to appear in court after stealing a bus. Standing in front of the judge, he told him that he was a male model for The Who, a fact that Ethan Russell confirmed, and thankfully Chad was let off so that shooting for the booklet could continue. The photographs contained in it are evocative and striking, like a British kitchen sink drama film. Rendered in gritty black and white, they show Jimmy's life, including greasy spoon cafe breakfasts, his smashed scooter and a ride out in front of the famous Battersea Power Station, and help to put images to the songs. In one especially arresting image, he stands outside the Hammersmith Odeon as the venue plays host to The Who, who are themselves pictured exiting the building as Jimmy looks on. However, The Who in the picture are not the 1960s mods, but the Who of 1973, appearing like ghosts from the future. Here is Jimmy, a boy out of place within his family, within his friends and the mod scene, and now out of place in *time*. This stark representation of Jimmy's misplacement in life helps to ram home the fact that Jimmy is very much on his own, and acts as a foreshadowing of the end of the mod scene. Interestingly, it appears that at the time The Who had never in fact played Hammersmith Odeon, and would not do so until 1975. For the actual album cover, though, it would be Roger Daltrey's cousin, Graham Hughes, who would be the photographer. According to Richard Barnes, this was largely down to Roger feeling everything had become about what Pete wanted, so as well as having the idea for the cover with the band's name painted on the back of Jimmy's parka coat, Roger also chose the photographer.

Quadrophenia is a remarkably bold concept. The only other band that could have as effectively revisited their past nearly a decade into their recording career would have been The Beatles. The effect is striking, a story about the mod days of The Who told with their most progressive music to date, a juxtaposition that perhaps shouldn't work, but brilliantly does. The songs call back to previous Who material, right back to their High Numbers days, including 'Zoot Suit', 'I'm The Face', 'My Generation', 'I Can't Explain' and 'The Kids Are Alright'. What's more, none of these feel forced or out of place, each reference (mostly lyrical excerpts or song titles) finding a natural place within a new context on the record, nearly a decade after first being used.

The story has been accused of being murky and not fleshed out, but this is part of the charm. This is meant to be a distorted memory from an unreliable narrator. Let's not forget, Jimmy is mentally ill – he has four different personalities, and he is often on mind-altering substances. This story is told first-person by him – how can it be anything but confused and a roller-coaster ride of emotions? Townshend would speak of removing specifics when dealing with Jimmy, allowing him to be a cipher rather than a well-rounded character. The story allows space for people to find themselves, the vagueness in some parts allowing the listener to connect with the emotion without the need to be fed the plot in careful detail. The story would lose its realism and credibility if it wasn't a bit fuzzy around the edges, for this was not a concept album driven by story, so much as emotion, with the songs acting as mood pieces and vignettes rather than as a means to move the plot forward. As a story it's pretty thin, but as a study in adolescence, and the confusion and frustrations in life, it finds great depth and is a subject that was not being explored in popular music.

Quadrophenia is a vital piece of youth culture, as important within the medium of music as *The Catcher In The Rye* is within literature. The story is set within the 1960s but deals with themes – such as loneliness, the struggle to fit in and mental illness – which have spoken to generations of youth since its release, and probably always will. As well as these themes, there is the recurrence of water, which is not surprising as part of the story revolves around Brighton beach, but here water becomes an analogy. Water is used as a cleansing metaphor, but the sea also represents God, with droplets of water being us as individuals, longing to return to the source. Much of this comes from Meher Baba, who would also say the rain was a blessing from God, and this water metaphor for humans returning to the source would crop up again in other Townshend-penned songs such as 'The Sea Refuses No River' from his 1982 solo album *All The Best Cowboys Have Chinese Eyes*.

Quadrophenia is also starkly different to *Tommy*, the latter being mystical and fantastic, whereas the former is gritty and realistic. Where *Tommy*'s songs had explicitly spelled out the story and *Lifehouse* had been loose with it, *Quadrophenia* sits somewhat in the middle, with some songs more abstract than others. Several tracks were also dropped from the album, including 'Joker James', a song which dated back to around 1967 and whose lyrics were published in *Eye* magazine in 1968. 'We Close Tonight', a breezier song, featuring a fantastic vocal by John with a chorus sung by Keith, was also dropped, leaving John with no lead vocal apart from the chorus of 'Is It In My Head?'. It's true that these songs don't fit the tone of the album, and there probably wouldn't have been room on it anyway, but 'Joker James' as well as two more abandoned songs, 'Get Out And Stay Out' and 'Four Faces', would feature on the movie soundtrack album in 1979, while 'We Close Tonight' would be released on the expanded reissue of *Odds And Sods*.

On *Quadrophenia*, The Who as a band were never better. John Entwistle, not permitted any songwriting contributions, turns the album into a bass solo, as well as supplying wonderful brass arrangements. If Entwistle had shown his skills on their previous record, it was a mere warm-up for his playing on this one. Throughout the album, his playing is both rhythmic and melodic, redefining the role of bass within a rock band as he weaves in and out of the other instruments like an Olympic skier on a gold medal-winning slalom run. In November 1973, Entwistle, talking to *Beat Instrumental*, revealed that he had been given more freedom than ever before to play what he wanted on bass, explaining that he had never been told what to play, but the songs this time around had allowed for more embellishments. Entwistle would talk about the complex brass arrangements he was assigned, sometimes tracking fourteen parts on a single song to get the desired effect, also noting Pete's more classical influence with the material.

Daltrey would state that the album contained Townshend's best songs, far surpassing anything he had done so far, without becoming overindulgent. Roger also felt that *Who's Next* had lacked some of The Who's usual firepower, but that *Quadrophenia* had restored it. Journalist Dave Marsh, on the other hand, would write that *Quadrophenia* wasn't rock, while also saying it was a deep album that grew on you. He's not wrong about the latter at least, as *Quadrophenia* may be the group's greatest album but it's also one that rewards repeat listening, through which more and more emerges, and songs that didn't grab you at first listen burrow their way into your soul.

Richard Barnes would comment that when sent demos, he felt it was very Wagnerian in its heavy approach, and it's certainly true that it's a much more serious album than the at times playful *Tommy*.

Charles Shaar Murray of the *NME* described the album as perhaps the most rewarding musical experience of 1973, high praise in a year that saw the release of albums such as *Dark Side Of The Moon* (Pink Floyd), *Band On The Run* (Paul McCartney & Wings), *Sabbath Bloody Sabbath* (Black Sabbath), *Houses Of The*

Holy (Led Zeppelin) and *Aladdin Sane* (David Bowie), although he did long for less synthesizers.

Quadrophenia was released on 27 October 1973 in the US and 2 November in the UK (although some sources offer slightly different dates), reaching number two in both territories. It was preceded on 5 October by the release of '5.15' as a single in the UK. Unlike *Tommy*, *Quadrophenia* had no obvious choice for a sure-fire hit single (though it is perhaps strange that the group didn't go with 'The Real Me' as first choice), and '5.15' only just broke into the top twenty. The album was an undoubted success, but ironically it failed to achieve what Townshend had originally set out to do – replace *Tommy* on stage. In an interview in *Melody Maker* in October 1973, Pete saw the main hurdle with playing *Quadrophenia* as Keith Moon, commenting that Keith kept on forgetting how to play drums and joking that they'd need to rebuild him with a new set of legs. But while Keith would prove a problem for at least one gig, he wasn't the only, or main, issue. In typical Who fashion, no sooner was mixing done on the album than a tour was booked. With barely any time to rest after the monumental effort of building a studio and producing one of the finest and most ambitious albums in rock history, the band's management were again shipping them out on the road, and The Who had mere weeks to arrange and rehearse the new material for the stage. The band started rehearsals, joined by a camera crew who were tasked with filming them, but during this time tensions arose, and Pete and Roger came to a physical altercation. Roger, frustrated that the hired crew were sitting around and not filming anything, informed them that he'd only be singing through the songs once, as it was a hugely demanding piece. For some reason, Townshend took exception to this and rounded on Daltrey. As crew members sensed a possible fight, they grabbed Roger to hold him back, while Townshend tried to hit the singer with his guitar, this thankfully glancing off his shoulder. Townshend told the crew to let go of Daltrey, but after they did, Pete – who wasn't much of a fighter – aimed two haphazard blows at him before walking straight onto an uppercut, resulting in him being lifted off his feet and knocked out cold after hitting his head on the ground. To make matters worse, their PR agent, Keith Altham, had just picked up a representative from The Who's new record label, MCA, who walked in on the fight and asked in horror, 'Is it always like this?' Altham replied, 'No, this is a good day.' Roger was distraught and held Pete's hand in the ambulance on the way to hospital, where he was treated for concussion.

The subsequent shows were at best passable and at worst a disaster. The *Quadrophenia* songs were some of The Who's strongest yet, but were intricate and much more precise than *Tommy*, an album whose material had allowed for huge reinvention in a live setting and, crucially, didn't require any backing tracks.

Whether, given more time, The Who could have reworked the *Quadrophenia* material in a different way for live performance is uncertain, but they had used tapes for 'Won't Get Fooled Again' and 'Baba O'Riley' so in theory things should have been fine. In practice, however, playing to the tapes would be trickier. At a show in Newcastle in November, the tapes malfunctioned badly, sending Townshend into a fury against sound man Bob Pridden, who he dragged across the stage before ripping the tapes out and storming off. The audience remained and the band returned to the stage, playing a selection of oldies.

In truth, even with a glitch-free performance, *Quadrophenia* didn't capture the average fan's imagination in the same way as *Tommy* had, particularly in America, where the story was not as instantly relatable. Roger took to explaining the plot between songs, a valid idea, but one which stymied the flow of the concert and irritated Townshend. Part of the problem was the plot of *Quadrophenia*, told out loud, didn't sound that interesting, because unlike *Tommy* there barely *is* a plot. Even with this narration, it was likely most audience members were really none-the-wiser without studying the booklet contained in the album. When the tour reached America, they played to audiences who wouldn't know what a mod was if one ran over them on a Lambretta, but things really turned to disaster at the Cow Palace in San Francisco, where Keith Moon collapsed after taking animal tranquillizers, forcing the band to recruit audience member Scott Halpin on drums.

Quadrophenia would in the end be elevated beyond simply an album by the 1979 film, which transformed it into a cultural phenomenon. In a way, the movie would overshadow the album. Indeed, when many people hear the name now, the movie is often the first thing that comes to mind. The film kickstarted a mod revival at the end of the 1970s, which saw new groups and fashion that harkened back to the day, and there are many fans of the film who wouldn't claim to be fans of The Who in general. But the songs on *Quadrophenia* do more than provide a loose structure for the plot of the film; they feature as the backbone of the soundtrack, along with a selection of contemporary tracks from artists such as The Kingsmen, Booker T and The MGs and James Brown. The Who tracks that appeared were remixed, and in some cases featured additional overdubs, with John Entwistle taking the opportunity to completely unnecessarily redo the bass part for 'The Real Me'.

Quadrophenia is The Who's towering achievement as a band, an opinion shared by Townshend himself. It does have its faults, though. For instance, it does feel a slight oversight that while Roger and Keith sing at least part of their themes, John and Pete do not. This seems especially odd in the case of Townshend, who after all wrote the entire record and had the right to decide who sang what. It's not a surprise that the song 'Love Reign O'er Me', which is Pete's theme, was sung by Roger, as his performance is breathtakingly powerful, but given the fact the theme crops up elsewhere, it seems a shame that at no point is it sung by Townshend. Also, while the themes of 'Bell Boy', 'Love Reign O'er Me' and 'Helpless Dancer' combine at points and musically fit together, 'Is It Me?' never joins in at the same time, simply not fitting with them musically.

Given that Townshend had no help from Lambert or really anyone in terms of plotting the album, and considering the near-nervous breakdown he had experienced trying to make *Lifehouse*, the result in the album *Quadrophenia* is a remarkable achievement for him. Flying solo in the director's chair, with a studio to build, Townshend more than lived up to the task. Despite it being a huge achievement, Townshend had been driven to breaking point, and before the album had even been released he penned a letter to the band's lawyer, asking for advice. Much of the reason was the destructive behaviour of Keith Moon and the mismanagement from Kit Lambert, as well as the overworking that had built up over the years. In his mind, he already had one foot out of the door, announcing this would be the last album and tour he would undertake. In the end, he never sent the letter and The Who continued.

Quadrophenia would eventually be played in concert much more successfully at a gig in Hyde Park in 1996. Subsequently, it would then be taken out on tour during 1996 and 1997. In 2010, it would again be revived for a one-off gig for the Teenage Cancer Trust at London's Royal Albert Hall, before again being toured in 2012 and 2013. In 2015, the album would receive an orchestral adaptation, scored by Townshend's partner, Rachel Fuller. This was performed at the Royal Albert Hall and featured opera singer Alfie Boe, with Townshend as a guest along with Billy Idol and Phil Daniels, who played Jimmy in the movie version, and then taken on a short tour.

TRACK BY TRACK

1. 'I AM THE SEA'

Written by Pete Townshend
Produced by The Who
Recorded at Ramport Studios, London, 1973

The opening track on the album isn't really a song but instead a cinematic soundscape, like the opening credits of a film. Indeed, six years later, when *Quadrophenia* was adapted into a movie, this very track provided the audio for its opening, though somehow, stripped of any visuals, the collection of sound effects, such as crashing waves and, bizarrely, a cat's meow (we're all still puzzled by it now), seem even more evocative than the film. In an interview in the *NME* in November 1973, Townshend talked about being inspired to make a film without any pictures, like a 'Frank Zappa thing', partly due to the failure of making a conventional film. In amongst the sound effects, we hear voices and musical motifs from the main body of the album, like a series of thoughts and memories from the mind of the album's protagonist, Jimmy, including the four themes, 'Love Reign O'er Me', 'Is It Me?', 'Bell Boy' and 'Helpless Dancer', as well as the whispered words 'I Am The Sea'. This leads to the first full song on the album.

2. 'THE REAL ME'

Written by Pete Townshend
Produced by The Who
Recorded at Ramport Studios, London, 1973

The first proper song on the album, the angst-ridden and thunderous 'The Real Me', is based on a classic Townshend-style riff, utilizing A, G and D chords in much the same way as 'Won't Get Fooled Again', 'Let's See Action' and 'The Seeker'. Here, it is transposed to the key of C by use of a capo on the third fret, with Pete driving his Gretsch solely as a rhythm instrument. Indeed, the arrangement is stark and lacking in guitar overdubs or leadwork, with Pete leaving the rhythm section to own the song. Keith's drums are a masterclass of power and dexterity, but even he is outshone by the virtuosic bass playing of Entwistle, who manages to set a new high watermark in terms of his playing. The story is that he simply sat down and went through a warmup take on his Thunderbird bass, only to be told he had nailed it in one. Listening to Townshend's demo (available on the Director's Cut version), it appears that John had taken a simple, repeated three-note phrase played by Pete in-between the first chorus and second verse, and used this as his opening statement, before veering off into an audacious bass lesson, stretching the length of the fretboard. On the verses, John plays in the gaps between the vocal and the guitar, while Keith keeps a deft beat going as the constant driving force.

Another classic Townshend trick is employed on the chorus, which features changing guitar chords over a droning C root, with John switching between a phrase in C Dorian and pentatonic runs. Another key element that arrives in the chorus is John's brass, adding intensity and sonic colour to an otherwise stripped-back rock arrangement.

'The Real Me' contains no guitar solo, and as we reach the penultimate verse, the guitar drops out altogether, leaving Keith's incredibly expressive drums,

John's intricate bass and Roger's vocals to play off each other. The song then lurches back into the chorus before Pete introduces another riff, a variation of the main one, as a segue into the final verse. Interestingly, at this point, instead of playing the riff along with Pete, John instead lays down a bass run over the first two bars before synchronizing with the guitar. It's my theory that Entwistle, still unfamiliar with the song, and in his mind jamming to the track, just forgot that this section was approaching and missed the beginning of it. Years later, when *Quadrophenia* was being turned into a film, John decided to rerecord his bass for 'The Real Me' for the accompanying soundtrack album. This redone version gives credence to this speculation, as John proceeds to play the riff from its beginning.

Lyrically, the song perfectly sets up Jimmy's life and mental state as he seeks answers from his psychiatrist, mother and even a preacher. Jimmy gets no joy from the doctor, who asks about the trivialities of his weekend without ever offering any real opinion or insight, while his mother (who struggles with mental health too, as alluded to by Jimmy's father in the story printed in the inside cover) admits that she knows how he feels, as it runs in the family. The song contains the wonderful poetic imagery of the cracks between paving stones resembling rivers of flowing veins, and you can feel the sense of paranoia as Daltrey sings of strange people peeping from behind window panes. As the song comes to a crashing end, Daltrey's voice rings out again and again, leading us into the title track and first of two instrumentals.

3. 'QUADROPHENIA'

Written by Pete Townshend
Produced by The Who
Recorded at Ramport Studios, London, 1973

Serving as an overture, the title track introduces us fully to the four main themes that represent the four sides of Jimmy's personality. First up, we hear Townshend's rhythmic, strummed acoustic octaves, as the piano beneath it plays the chord sequence we will later hear forming a significant part of the song 'Bell Boy'. Then the lead guitar enters (most likely a Stratocaster plugged directly into the mixing desk), clean and crystal clear in tone, with another guitar, likely to be his Gretsch, playing rhythm.

The song then enters the 'Is It Me?' section, the soundscape backed by carefully orchestrated synth.

The next section of the song is 'Helpless Dancer', where synthesized strings weave the song's melody, soon joined by the duelling bass and guitar of Entwistle and Townshend. As the section picks up pace it gains tension, with the drums resembling a bolero.

The song then simmers down, and we hear the three-note piano refrain that is the introduction to 'Love Reign O'er Me', followed by its synth string figure and Pete's wiry lead guitar, with the end of the song featuring additional lead from the clean Stratocaster.

Pete told *NME*'s Charles Shaar Murray that the instrumentals were incredibly hard to put together without sounding like he was on a 'Keith Emerson trip'. However, they were certainly worth the effort, displaying an impressive classical majesty.

4. 'CUT MY HAIR'

Written by Pete Townshend
Produced by The Who
Recorded at Ramport Studios, London, 1973

'Cut My Hair' begins with the piano chords that are more associated with '5.15', in a familiar Townshend technique where the chords are played over the same bass note, in this case C. Over these chords, we hear Moon's light cymbal work and Pete's subtle guitar phrases, John also adding a melodic bass line.

This is also Townshend's first lead vocal on the album, though the chorus is taken over by Daltrey, who harmonizes with himself.

Where the verse is melancholy and relaxing, the chorus is much more typical Who, with John's bass providing some typically slick runs in the gaps between the trademark power-chord guitar stabs.

The song also makes use of the Edwards volume pedal that was an essential part of Pete's Gretsch guitar rig given to him by Joe Walsh, as he plays some nice volume swells with it. Moon's pounding drums in the chorus are another highlight; listen out for more screams from him, particularly just before the second chorus.

Lyrically, the song borrows lines from the band's High Numbers days, namely the song 'Zoot Suit', repurposing these lines perfectly.

The rousing middle eight with added brass is triumphant-sounding, sung by Townshend and featuring a key change halfway through, which further lifts the song, before plunging back down into a verse that is far gloomier than the previous ones. In a way this sums up an amphetamine comedown; the effect enhanced by a descending brass note at the end of the middle eight. On the last verse there is an addition of synth, and though the chords largely remain the same, they resolve to A minor instead of C major seventh as before, John's bass in fact rooting the chords in A. This changes the whole tone of the song, and as Jimmy talks of coming down, you really feel it.

For the news story that features at the end of the track, newsreader John Curle was persuaded to read it live on air, so that an accurate taping of it could be captured, as Nevison had struggled to simulate a real radio broadcast. Curle would follow the announcement with an explanation informing people that the riot was not in fact real.

5. 'PUNK AND THE GODFATHER'

Written by Pete Townshend
Produced by The Who
Recorded at Ramport Studios, London, 1973

Another classic Townshend chord riff opens 'Punk And The Godfather', in the Who-friendly key of A. The acoustic guitar here is a solid foundation, but the star of the show has to be the bass, which bubbles, thunders and provides delightful answers to Townshend's own rhythms. Before the end of the intro, it's already caught the ear, while on the verse it continues to stand out, interestingly playing phrases in A, rather than following the chord changes.

That's not to say the rest of the band don't pull their weight. Daltrey gives a stunning performance, down to his Wilhelm-type scream of 'Whoaa yeah!' at around 4.21, and again provides a harmony to himself on verses. Moon also emphasizes the rhythms of the riffs, whilst laying back in sections that contrast with his more manic drumming.

The middle eight is given to Pete's more wistful voice, with a very faint delayed vocal in the opposite channel, at the end of which we hear audience applause, before launching back into the verse.

A point to note is the stuttered 'My generation' lines at the end of the chorus, which are fed through an Eventide flanger and are actually hard to decipher.

'Punk And The Godfather' deals with the distance between artist and audience, as the former eventually ends up out of reach and possibly out of touch with the fan. At this point in the story, Jimmy goes to see The Who, whom he used to watch in their early days, but none of them recognize him and he leaves with a feeling of disappointment.

On the American release of the album, the song was titled 'The Punk Meets The Godfather'.

The author with Roger Daltrey after a show at Wembley Arena, June 2007. (*Dante DiCarlo*)

Roger Daltrey onstage as The Who play live at London's Wembley Arena during a *Quadrophenia* tour, July 8, 2013. (*Dante DiCarlo*)

Pete Townshend onstage as The Who play live at London's Wembley Arena during a *Quadrophenia* tour, July 8, 2013. (*Dante DiCarlo*)

Roger Daltrey onstage as The Who play live at London's Wembley Arena during a *Quadrophenia* tour, July 8, 2013. (*Dante DiCarlo*)

A Gretsch 6120 'Chet Atkins' model, owned by Justin Harris. similar to Pete Townshend's 1959 Gretsch 6120, played extensively on *Who's Next* and *Quadrophenia*. (*Justin Harris*)

The author with Pete Townshend at a book signing, November 2019. (*Dante DiCarlo*)

The former Ramport Studios in Battersea, London, now a doctor's surgery. The studio had been a church hall and was turned into a studio for the recording of *Quadrophenia* in 1973. (*Dante DiCarlo*)

A green plaque outside the former home of The Who's Ramport studios. (*Dante DiCarlo*)

Olympic Studios in Barnes, London, where The Who recorded *Who's Next*. The building is now a cinema. (*Dante DiCarlo*)

The Who live at London's Wembley Arena during a *Quadrophenia* tour, July 8, 2013. Roger Daltrey looks up at video footage of Keith Moon, from their Charlton 1974 concert. (*Dante DiCarlo*)

Roger Daltrey and Pete Townshend onstage with The Who, live at London's Wembley Arena during a *Quadrophenia* tour, July 8, 2013. (*Dante DiCarlo*)

Roger Daltrey onstage as The Who play live at London's Wembley Arena during a *Quadrophenia* tour, July 8, 2013. (*Dante DiCarlo*)

Pete Townshend onstage as The Who play live at London's Wembley Arena during a *Quadrophenia* tour, July 8, 2013. (*Dante DiCarlo*)

Pete Townshend onstage as The Who play live at London's Wembley Arena during a *Quadrophenia* tour, July 8, 2013. (*Dante DiCarlo*)

Simon Townshend performing with The Who, live at London's Wembley Arena during a *Quadrophenia* tour, July 8, 2013. (*Dante DiCarlo*)

Pete Townshend onstage as The Who play live at London's Wembley Arena during a *Quadrophenia* tour, July 8, 2013. (*Dante DiCarlo*)

The author with Pete Townshend before the *Classic Quadrophenia* show at London's Royal Albert Hall on July 5, 2015. (*Dante DiCarlo*)

Pete Townshend's ARP 2500 synthesiser, used on *Who's Next* and other recordings, pictured here at The Townshend Studio, at The University of West London. (*Horace Austin*)

An ARP 2600 synthesiser, similar to one used by Pete Townshend in the 1970s on such songs as 'Relay'. (*Daniel Spills with modifications by VortBot CC BY 2.0: https://creativecommons.org/licenses/by/2.0/deed.en*)

Pete Townshend's EMS VCS3 synthesiser, and Lowrey Berkshire organ, used on *Who's Next*, pictured here at The Townshend Studio, at The University of West London. (*Horace Austin*)

John Entwistle's 1965 Jazz bass, used to record the song 'My Generation' and others, at the Play It Loud: Instruments Of Rock & Roll exhibition at the Metropolitan Museum Of Art in New York in 2019. The bass was loaned to the exhibition by David Swartz. (*Eden, Janine and Jim with modifications by Clusternote. Wikimedia Commons, CC BY 2.0: https://creativecommons.org/licenses/by/2.0/deed.en*)

John Entwistle's 1964 Thunderbird IV, alongside one of Pete Townshend's 1969 SG Special guitars, at the Play It Loud: Instruments Of Rock & Roll exhibition at the Metropolitan Museum Of Art in New York in 2019. The Thunderbird IV was used onstage as well as during the recording of *Quadrophenia* and *The Who By Numbers*, while the SG was used in concert. Both instruments were loaned to the exhibition by David Swartz. (*Eden, Janine and Jim with modifications by Clusternote. Wikimedia Commons, CC BY 2.0: https://creativecommons.org/licenses/by/2.0/deed.en*)

John Entwistle's 1976 eight-string Alembic Explorer bass, at the Play It Loud: Instruments Of Rock & Roll exhibition at the Metropolitan Museum Of Art in New York in 2019. The bass, pictured alongside a guitar of Steve Miller's, was loaned to the exhibition by David Swartz. (*Eden, Janine and Jim with modifications by Clusternote. Wikimedia Commons, CC BY 2.0: https://creativecommons.org/licenses/by/2.0/deed.en*)

The Who live in concert in Hamburg 1972. (*Gladstone-dewiki with modifications by GladstoneHH. Wikimedia Commons, CC BY 4.0 https://creativecommons.org/licenses/by-sa/4.0/deed.en*)

Pete Townshend onstage as The Who play live at London's Wembley Arena during a *Quadrophenia* tour, July 8, 2013. (*Dante DiCarlo*)

Roger Daltrey and Kenney Jones onstage during the Rock N Horsepower gig, June 14, 2014. A special gig organised by Jones at his Hurtwood Park polo club, for prostate cancer, this night saw The Who reunite with their old drummer who played on *Face Dances* and *It's Hard*, for the first time since 1988. (*Dante DiCarlo*)

The Who pictured circa 1966. (*Alamy, Pictorial Press*)

The Who in 1971, at Keith Moon's house Tara in Chertsey, Surrey, for the album launch of *Who's Next*. (*Alamy, Gijsbert Hanekroot*)

John Entwistle pictured in 1998 at his home, Quarwood, with friend Craig Addecott. (*Craig Addecott*)

Zak Starkey pictured with the author and author's friend, Brooke Valverde outside The Phoenix pub in London's Cavendish Square, October 2014. (*Dante DiCarlo*)

Pete Townshend onstage as The Who play live at Liverpool's Echo Arena during their *The Who Hits 50* tour, December 11, 2014. (*Dante DiCarlo*)

Pete Townshend onstage during the *Classic Quadrophenia* show at London's Royal Albert Hall on July 5, 2015. (*Dante DiCarlo*)

Roger Daltrey onstage as The Who play live at London's Wembley Arena, February 13, 2016. (*Dante DiCarlo*)

Pete Townshend onstage as The Who play live at Liverpool's Echo Arena during their *The Who Hits 50* tour, December 11, 2014. (*Dante DiCarlo*)

Roger Daltrey onstage with an image of Keith Moon behind him, as The Who play live at Liverpool's Echo Arena during their *The Who Hits 50* tour, December 11, 2014. (*Dante DiCarlo*)

6. 'I'M ONE'

Written by Pete Townshend
Produced by The Who
Recorded at Ramport Studios, London, 1973

Though it may be one of the shortest songs on the album, 'I'm One' has some of the largest and most profound impact. Opening with a beautiful, fingerpicked acoustic guitar, Townshend again takes lead vocals, lending the song the required emotion, although on the 1973 tour Roger would sing the middle verse, perhaps only to give him something to do.

On the second verse, the full band kicks in, Townshend's rockabilly slap-back delayed Gretsch contributing sharp fills and adding to the country feel. Keith's groove is a joy here, staying reserved but letting fly at the end of the chorus with a series of inventive fills.

On the final verse, Pete harmonizes with himself, and at the end of the last chorus displays more power and range.

'I'm One' is one of the best-loved songs from *Quadrophenia*, offering a more introspective moment that reveals Jimmy's sense of dejection and inferiority, and one of the few tracks without synth. It also feels like a more autobiographical song, especially the line about having a Gibson without a case, which seems purely to relate to its author, as at no time in the story is it ever implied Jimmy even plays guitar. In this song, perhaps we get the closest glimpse at Townshend himself, but there will be many listeners who feel a connection with the awkward character who blends in a crowd.

The song has often been played live by Townshend as a solo acoustic piece, working just as well in this arrangement.

7. 'THE DIRTY JOBS'

Written by Pete Townshend
Produced by The Who
Recorded at Ramport Studios, London, 1973

In the story, the day after Jimmy goes to see The Who, he gets a job as a binman. 'The Dirty Jobs' relates to this, though really it seems to be sung first-person from the working man in general, and in fact never mentions the binman job specifically. The first verse references a farmer, the second a driver taking miners to work, and the third possibly finally Jimmy himself, as it is sung from the point of view of simply 'a young man'.

The song uses the familiar Townshend method of playing a series of chords over a root note which remains the same, Entwistle strengthening this and offering chromatic runs. It also makes use of prominent synth, simulating violins, while the guitar is mixed pretty low and plays an understated role in the arrangement, except in the middle eight where there is the addition of some nice harmonized lines.

Though the song has a fairly slow pace, the band doubles the time at the end and we get the addition of piano, which does raise the energy.

'The Dirty Jobs' is perhaps one of the more obscure songs on *Quadrophenia*, but in a way one of the most progressive, with its lack of prominent guitar and use of synth strings.

The song's commentary on modern life and the struggles of the man in the street have a weight and importance outside of *Quadrophenia*, and probably would work just as well on its own, but within the story it becomes a key point of showing Jimmy's frustrations with life.

This song is also one of the clearest examples of Keith Moon screaming, which can be heard several times during the song, usually in the choruses.

For the end of the track, Nevison surreptitiously recorded a marching band in London's Regent's Park, which was not allowed.

8. 'HELPLESS DANCER'

Written by Pete Townshend
Produced by The Who
Recorded at Ramport Studios, London, 1973

'Helpless Dancer' is Roger's theme, another song about the everyday man in the street, which is somewhat tenuously linked to the story.

Sparsely arranged, it is opened by the fanfare of Entwistle's majestic brass over the top of a rumbling piano, with an acoustic guitar joining for a repeated three-chord progression. Daltrey delivers vocals that alternate between left and right channels, while in the second verse, Townshend throws in some flamenco flourishes on acoustic guitar, Roger raising his voice by an octave to add more passion. The song comes in at barely two minutes, serving as a brief piece to flesh out the album, but unlike some of the shorter tracks on *Tommy*, is not really essential to the story.

The end features a snippet from 'The Kids Are Alright', a choice which shows just how much the band had changed in the mere eight years since its recording.

'Helpless Dancer' was played live briefly in 1973 before being dropped, these live performances featuring John playing live brass over a backing tape of piano and acoustic guitar, with Pete not actually playing any live guitar at all. The vocals were also sung in turns, with Roger, Pete and John all taking lead lines, greatly helping to replicate the almost overlapping vocal lines.

9. 'IS IT IN MY HEAD?'

Written by Pete Townshend
Produced by The Who, associate producer Glyn Johns
Recorded at Olympic Studios, London, May–June 1972

Barely linked to the plot of *Quadrophenia*, 'Is It In My Head?' had been written before the idea had materialized, and was recorded in 1972 with Glyn Johns, along with 'Love Reign O'er Me'. Once again, the song doesn't really advance the story, but does fit in with the spirit of the album and Jimmy's confused search, though the line about hearing his history could perhaps point to the *Rock Is Dead – Long Live Rock* project that preceded *Quadrophenia*, which would have dealt with the history of the band itself.

Enriched by piano, the opening also features acoustic guitar, low subtle synth and a nice melodic bass run from Entwistle. John also gets his only lead vocal on the album, on the song's chorus, which makes a pleasing contrast, and we hear further use of Townshend's signature Gretsch sound, complete with volume swells on some of his lead lines. For once, Keith is relatively restrained, not playing at all on the verse, save for some crashes and mild fills, and then keeping a steady beat on the chorus, for one of his most stripped-back parts on record.

The middle eight changes from half-time to full-time, but is still minimalist for Keith, while Daltrey relishes the chance to go for more on his vocal.

'Is It In My Head?' is a great song in its own right, but again, becomes greater as part of *Quadrophenia*.

10. 'I'VE HAD ENOUGH'

Written by Pete Townshend
Produced by The Who
Recorded at Ramport Studios, London, 1973

'I've Had Enough' is one of the fundamental tracks on *Quadrophenia*, which manages to combine sections from other key songs and really sell the rock opera format. Starting with an energetic drum roll from Keith, an instant statement is made. Townshend then keeps a D pedal tone going on his acoustic guitar as he shifts chords on top of it in an unnerving fashion. Daltrey's voice is rough and powerful on a vocal line that's unusual and barely melodic, the aggression in his delivery adding to the tension of the sustained D pedal tone, which is supported by Entwistle's single-note bass. At the end of the verse, we finally get a sense of release as the song breaks into a G, D and A sequence, and then plays on a trademark Townshend riff, with Pete also taking over lead vocals for this part, as well as delivering some nice rock and roll guitar lines. At the end of this section, we get a preview of 'Love Reign O'er Me', this time in the key of A instead of its usual E flat. In this key, Daltrey's voice is more relaxed and mellow, but the section is just as powerful, Townshend's acoustic guitar arpeggios chiming in alongside the piano and synth. As Roger reaches for a higher note, the song resolves into D again and gets to what is effectively its chorus, which takes the form of a country-style ditty, with Pete playing some fine banjo in the right channel and tasteful electric guitar in the left. Soon the vocals are joined by harmonies for another round, before the song thunderously sends us back to the start. The effect is a brilliantly wild ride of emotions, much like the roller-coaster Jimmy is going through, the different moods and personalities summed up and shifted through seamlessly. Again, we go round the sections, the 'Love Reign O'er Me' part having additional brass for a sorrowful atmosphere. The song ends with a gut-wrenching scream from Daltrey which rings out nakedly as the music crashes to a halt behind it, a moment of pure commitment from him that sums up his dedication to the material. We then hear sound effects, the song leaving the listener as shaken up as the protagonist.

11. '5.15'

Written by Pete Townshend
Produced by The Who
Recorded at Ramport Studios, London, 1973

The song '5.15' was written out of a soundcheck jam, and as such is one of the few tracks on the album for which there is no demo. Perhaps because of its creation coming during production of the record, its lyrics have a far stronger link to the story than many of the other tracks. At this point in the narrative, Jimmy, feeling fed up and yearning for better times, jumps on board a train to Brighton, the place he has fond memories of. Contained in the song are some notable lyrics. As well as referencing 'My Generation', the line about ushers Eau-de-cologning is about The Beatles, whose concerts would provide such excitement that some of the girls would literally wet themselves, leading to ushers employing perfume to cover up the smell.

The song starts off with atmospheric sounds of train doors slamming before the actual music intro begins, which is a reprise of the chords from 'Cut My

Hair', this time played on guitar, while the piano plays octaves. Pete again sings "Why should I care?', followed by a nice descending harmony guitar line, then a bass fill before the introduction of the whole band. As they all enter, we hear a train whistle, which was recorded at Waterloo station when a driver was bribed £5 to let it off, which was against regulations, although this appears to have been omitted from the remixed versions.

The song is built off a guitar riff which is in E but transposed to G by use of a capo. This riff is also doubled by Entwistle's brass, which almost drowns out the guitar, leaving some sparse power-chord hits at the forefront of the guitar mix. Another key feature is the call-and-response vocals between Daltrey and the three-part harmony of him, Entwistle and Townshend in the verse. The chorus of the song changes key to B flat and brings the energy down with Townshend's country picking. Again, there is a call-and-response, this time Pete harmonizing with himself and Daltrey answering.

The song grooves at a steady pace, with piano also adding to the mix, especially during the outro guitar solo where it seems to rise in volume, and at one point becomes doubled up in both sides of the mix. Townshend's Gretsch guitar also growls and splutters during this section, and you can feel the fun the band are having jamming this song out.

In the UK, '5.15' would be released as the only single from *Quadrophenia.* Although a great song and one of the most popular in concert, it isn't the most commercial and it is perhaps not surprising it only reached number twenty. On *Top Of The Pops*, the band performed the song to a recorded backing tape, Townshend becoming angry and smashing his prized Gretsch guitar at the end of the performance, earning the group a ban from the BBC. Thankfully, the guitar was later repaired and the ban was also overturned.

The song would be a regular live set choice throughout the band's career, and in later years would feature a virtuoso bass solo from John Entwistle.

12. 'SEA AND SAND'

Written by Pete Townshend
Produced by The Who
Recorded at Ramport Studios, London, 1973

Having arrived in Brighton, Jimmy takes a walk on his own by the sea and reflects on life, finding it quieter in the off-season without the large gathering of mods. One of the more story-connected songs on the record, 'Sea And Sand' makes use of three separate sections, starting with its opening, which mostly forms a I–IV–V chord progression in A, almost similar to a classic 1950s pop song in its simple but melodic nature. Out of the sea noises we hear an acoustic guitar joined by Roger on vocals and John's simple but melodic bassline, with the song then using the dynamic shift between this sparse arrangement and the whole band kicking in over the IV and V chords.

The second section of the song moves to C major and drops the tempo as Jimmy thinks about the girl he loves, whom he describes as the perfect dresser, and how he must match her to stand a chance of attaining her. The next section is a reprise of music heard in 'I've Had Enough', sung again by Townshend and once more repeating the lyrics borrowed from 'Zoot Suit', another clever musical device which helps tie the album together.

The song also has a couple of false endings, most notably the last one, after which we get a trademark Townshend riff consisting of A, G and D chords, with Townshend singing 'I'm the face, if you want it', another call back to their mod days. The outro section jam also features some lovely 1950s-inspired lead lines from Pete on his trusty Gretsch. All in all, one of the album's highlights.

13. 'DROWNED'

Written by Pete Townshend
Produced by The Who
Recorded at Ramport Studios, London, 1973

According to Townshend, 'Drowned' was written in 1970 and had been scrawled on various pieces of paper. The song is another one that is rooted in Pete's devotion to Meher Baba and his spiritual search. Here, the idea of getting back to the sea can be seen as returning to God, and although this is external to the *Quadrophenia* story, it does fit in with Jimmy's own search for meaning in his life. The water theme also connects it nicely to *Quadrophenia*, a story that deals with the sea both as a physical element and a metaphor.

The piano part on the track was based on the piano from 'Hitchcock Railway' by Joe Cocker, which was played by Chris Stainton, who also plays on 'Drowned'. This is no coincidence, Pete having sought out Stainton to replicate his piano part for this song.

During the recording of the track, a particularly heavy downpour started, which unfortunately came through the roof of Ramport and began to leak into the booth with the piano. Nevison watched from the mobile studio outside as the water poured through the roof, but Stainton carried on playing. At the end of the take, the door of the booth was opened and water came pouring out, Townshend exaggerating that it was about 500 gallons. Had it continued, perhaps Stainton would have ironically drowned!

'Drowned' is easily one of the standout cuts on *Quadrophenia* and one of the most successful as an individual song. Dominated by the upbeat groove, which is enhanced by Entwistle's chromatic basslines, it manages to be optimistic in feel on an album that is often more downbeat in tone. The song starts with the borrowed piano riff and Townshend's biting guitars, with a capo at the fifth fret, duelling left and right in the mix. Daltrey also does a fine job vocally, using his falsetto range in places as well as his full-bodied chest voice.

After the middle eight we get a key change and enter an instrumental section which could be deemed a guitar solo but is as much a showcase for Entwistle's rapid-fire bass, featuring a dizzying alternation of fretted and open notes played on the D string.

At the end of the solo section, the band breaks into a reprise of the riff from '5.15', John slightly altering the pattern of notes, leading us back into the verse and chorus, with an energetic jam to fade out the song. After the fade out we hear sea noises and Pete singing 'Sea And Sand', which he had recorded walking along the beach.

In part thanks to the lack of synthesizer, but also down to its sheer energy, 'Drowned' was one of the more successful live *Quadrophrenia* songs, being retained in the set into 1975 when many other songs had been dropped. After not being played in 1976, it was revived on stage as a regular choice in 1979, this time sung by Townshend, with Daltrey providing harmonica, as well as John 'Rabbit' Bundrick facilitating a live piano part at last. The change in lead vocalist probably stems back to the Secret Policeman's Ball concert in June 1979, where Pete played an especially beautiful solo acoustic version of the song. The new Townshend-fronted full band version would be played through to and including their 1982 farewell tour. Ever since, Townshend has often performed the solo acoustic version at Who concerts, although it would eventually be revived as a full band version with Townshend on vocals for the *Quadrophenia* tours in 2012 and 2013.

14. 'BELL BOY'

Written by Pete Townshend
Produced by The Who
Recorded at Ramport Studios, London, 1973

At this point in the story, Jimmy discovers that the Ace Face, the popular mod he looked up to, is working as a bell boy in a hotel. Seeing a figure of power and independence now being subservient and ordinary has a profound effect on Jimmy, who feels disillusioned, almost like a child discovering Santa Claus is really his dad in a costume. Playing the part of the bell boy is Keith, a role he evidently has a lot of fun with, although Pete didn't want the song to become a comedy number as *Quadrophenia* was a serious album, and this would be the only time the Ace Face sings. As it is, Keith does a wonderful job of not just singing the song but acting the role, and it is perhaps the one true moment of light relief on an otherwise heavy album. Keith makes an instant impression on the song with his barnstorming drum fill that begins it, Pete joining in with power-chord strums before his acoustic guitar takes over. The song starts off in E flat but moves up to F for the signature riff, which also forms a vital part of the title track and 'The Rock'. Here, Townshend's electric guitar cuts in like a serrated knife before dropping out when the vocals enter, once again leaving the acoustic to take over. At this point Keith assumes lead vocal duties, delivering a charmingly rough cockney voice, dripping with roguish character. As we reach another section of the song, Keith's voice changes to a softer tone, almost childlike, as we see a more tender side of the Ace Face. Keith again leads the song back in with a pounding fill, before a longer verse with an instrumental gap in-between, during which we can clearly hear the 'Helpless Dancer' theme playing out on synth, another nice touch arrangement-wise that links the songs and thus the album as a whole.

'Bell Boy' would become a favourite amongst Who fans, largely thanks to the spotlight it gave Keith, and they would often request the song live. Though the backing track made it complex to perform, it was kept in the set throughout 1974, a video performance of it even being captured at Charlton Athletic football ground. This footage was later used in concerts in The Who's revival of the album in 2012 and 2013.

15. 'DOCTOR JIMMY'

Written by Pete Townshend
Produced by The Who
Recorded at Ramport Studios, London, 1973

Although the character of Jimmy has four different sides, 'Doctor Jimmy' seems to deal with a kind of duality, summed up as a Dr Jekyll and Mr Hyde-type dynamic. Here, the key to unlocking Jimmy's wilder, more aggressive side is alcohol rather than the uppers (amphetamine pills) that are usually favoured by him. One wonders if this was possibly inspired by Keith Moon, whose alcohol intake and subsequent unpredictability were well known. Indeed, Entwistle had previously written the Who B-side 'Dr Jekyll And Mr Hyde', which was apparently partly based on Keith.

At this point in the story, Jimmy is a man on the edge, let down by everything in life and now, most hurtful of all, feeling let down by being a mod. Out of this bitter state of dejection arise desires of defiance, violence and sexual conquest. On this track, Daltrey does an incredible job of summing up just how wired and desperate Jimmy is. At one point, as he sings the word 'hold' during the last verse, his voice brilliantly cracks, something that today would have probably been rerecorded, but actually is the icing on the cake of an impassioned performance. Of course, the tough guy, macho, 'I'll fight anyone' emotion of the song is the part of the character that's inspired by Roger, so it's no surprise he does such a great job. But 'Doctor Jimmy' also contains John's theme, 'Is It Me?', representing Jimmy's romantic side, which is also sung by Roger, a part he handles equally as well.

Musically, the song is another roller-coaster ride that switches moods and energy levels several times. The song starts with a triumphant fanfare before kicking into a brisk pace, again Townshend using moving chords over a static root. Despite displaying some of his busiest and most virtuosic bass playing on this album, Entwistle takes a minimalistic approach here, sticking to the root and octave, showing that he never played more than what was required. Chord-wise it's a simple sequence of A, E and D inversions over an A bass until the dissonance of the A sharp over A chord, which raises the tension and injects a sense of unease. The song's pre-chorus almost feels like a chorus, with its more upbeat feel. This also modulates to the key of F and contains more triumphant brass, but the chorus itself changes to the darker A minor, which contrasts with the A major home key of the verse.

After the second chorus the song switches to A flat for the 'Is It Me?' section, which is a beautiful and calm reprieve amongst the testosterone-fuelled bravado of the rest of the track. Here, for a brief moment, the tone is more reflective as Jimmy's romantic side emerges. Towards the end we get a little organ-led instrumental interlude that breaks up the repeating pre-chorus, another interesting addition to the song.

'Doctor Jimmy', more than most songs on *Quadrophenia*, displays a classical influence in its music and structure. Keith's drums are often orchestral-sounding and sections of the song possess a huge sense of drama and dynamics, with several themes played on brass and synthesizer. 'Doctor Jimmy' would be kept in The Who's live sets longer than many other songs from the album, which is perhaps surprising due to its complex nature and length. Of course, some of the lyrics are controversial today, with mentions of rape as a macho statement of power from Jimmy – though not, I feel, in a literal sense. However, in a way they indicate a part of male ego that still exists in society today as much as it ever did, and the song takes a brutally honest look at this.

Townshend did write and demo a complete song called 'Is It Me?' but would only end up using part of it, inserted into 'Doctor Jimmy', the full song appearing on the Director's Cut edition.

16. 'THE ROCK'

Written by Pete Townshend
Produced by The Who
Recorded at Ramport Studios, London, 1973

The second instrumental on *Quadrophenia* basically contains all the same themes as the first, but arranged differently, both in structure and instrumentation.

In the story, Jimmy has reached the end of his tether and steals a boat, in which he rows out to sea and winds up sitting on a rock, hence the title of the song. This time we begin with the octave, fifth and root piano figure from 'Love Reign O'er Me', and the 'Bell Boy' riff being played on synth. Keith's drum fills pound away, almost like his famous drum break on 'Won't Get Fooled Again', here doing the same job of building anticipation before the whole band comes in, Pete delivering a pick-scrape just before. We go around the 'Bell Boy' riff a few times before the onslaught dies down and we enter the 'Is It Me?' theme, Pete playing the melody on clean DI'd (Direct Injection – plugged straight into the mixing desk) guitar. There is more orchestral drumming from Keith and then the introduction of the 'Helpless Dancer' theme, played again by Pete on electric guitar while the piano sticks to a one-note vamp. When the drums enter, so does the bass, but here it keeps to the root note instead of following the guitar part. The section then key changes, not up but down a semi-tone, and the guitar is joined by a harmony part. These harmonies build up over successive passes, the band coming in and out of proceedings to keep the dynamics shifting. At the end of the section, we are left swimming in a dizzying array of guitars until another pick-scrape cues in the 'Love Reign O'er Me' section, Pete delivering some tasteful and emotionally wrought lead lines. The track comes to a crescendo finish, but it's a false ending; as the piano part lingers on, the 'Bell Boy' theme starts up again, joined by a vocal-sounding synth part. The song gathers pace again before an abrupt finish, complete with crashing thunder sounds. Again, it's another intricate and clever piece that sees the band bringing rock music close to classical composition in a striking way.

'The Rock' would feature as an unlikely set addition from 2016 right up to 2024, where it was included in a short *Quadrophenia* section, perhaps chosen to give Daltrey a vocal rest.

17. 'LOVE REIGN O'ER ME'

Written by Pete Townshend
Produced by The Who, associate producer Glyn Johns
Recorded at Olympic Studios, London, May–June 1972

The grand finale of *Quadrophenia* was written before the album's conception and recorded in 1972 in sessions with Glyn Johns.

One of The Who's most majestic and moving songs, the closing track again uses water as a metaphor but also mixes the use of the words 'rain' and 'reign'. Here, once more, the song has little to do with the actual story, but as an emotional piece it helps to sum up the feelings of Jimmy.

The song begins with the sound of rain and a stunning piano part, played by Pete and taken straight from his demo. This starts in the key of E flat major, but quickly shifts to E flat minor, allowing him to play the black keys, the notes falling like rain. Over this, Keith plays orchestrally on timpani, finishing the rumble by hitting a gong. As this intro ends, we get to the three-note piano figure that has already been played throughout the album in various places, and the verse begins with an added synth part over the strummed acoustic guitar. Daltrey's voice, which instantly draws you in, complete with its blues note on the word 'laying', is mellow and restrained, but as Keith Moon's fill comes in, he unleashes, producing a soul-wrenching plea. Over this chorus, Townshend plays a simple but effective descending guitar line, harmonized by another guitar, while Entwistle holds back, allowing the song to breathe without complicated basslines cluttering things. On the second verse, Roger alters the vocal melody, reaching for higher notes, including a falsetto leap to an E flat five on the word 'tears' that catches the ear, and in the following chorus he is even more savage than the first. The middle eight strikes a more positive tone as it switches to F sharp major, and then alternates between this and E flat major, the synth orchestration adding a sense of excitement which carries on throughout Pete's solo. As we return to the verse chords, we don't get vocals but instead melancholic, reverb-soaked blues guitar lines by Townshend that sound like they have been dragged from the waters beneath Brighton pier. On the final chorus, Daltrey reaches within himself and blasts us with a primal scream from the blackness of the universe, a moment of visceral abandon that rivals his scream on 'Won't Get Fooled Again' two years previously. Daltrey would describe it as a scream from the streets, one of the ultimate anger, passion and every emotion we have. He continues to wail away like his life depends on it as the song reaches it thrilling conclusion, with Keith pounding the drums and the addition of a whole host of percussion instruments that were kicked over by him to provide extra chaos to the finale. The song leaves Jimmy's fate uncertain, and it's best left this way, with the listener left to make up their minds.

Though 'Love Reign O'er Me' is not strictly linked to the story, it somehow fits with the spirit of the album. As a conclusion, it feels like Jimmy calling out for some sort of spiritual answer to all that has gone on before. He may be a working-class teenager, but deep down his soul is yearning for something beyond the mundane, something beyond the fried egg breakfast, the mod scene which he had believed would give him what he was looking for, the girl he used to love and the other kids with whom he tries to fit in. Jimmy is a more spiritually switched-on soul than many around him, looking for meaning in a world where he has never been given the intellectual development to even understand what he's looking for. In him we find the seeker that existed in Jimmy's creator, Pete Townshend.

'Love Reign O'er Me' is the perfect end for *Quadrophenia*, but Townshend almost gave the song away to Lou Reizner's 1972 orchestral version of *Tommy* as an addition song for Maggie Bell, who was playing Tommy's mother. One can see that it probably would have worked as a song about a mother's love, but ultimately it fits in much better as a part of *Quadrophenia*, and Townshend had to go back on his offer.

'Love Reign O'er Me' was released as the first single from the album in America, where it only reached number fifty-four.

The song was played live in 1973, but then inexplicably dropped until 1982. The song has been played more often since, both as part of *Quadrophenia* tours and regular shows.

Chapter 7

Odds and Sods (1974)

Produced by The Who, Pete Townshend, Glyn Johns, Kit Lambert, Pete Meaden and Chris Parmeinter
Released in the UK on 4 October 1974 as Track 2406 116 SUPER
Released in the USA on 12 October 1974 as MCA 2126
Chart position – UK = 10, USA = 15
Recorded at various studios
Pete Townshend – Guitars, Vocals, Synth and Keyboards
Roger Daltrey – Vocals
John Entwistle – Bass, Vocals and Horns
Keith Moon – Drums and Percussion

Over the years, The Who had amassed a fairly substantial collection of unreleased songs, and plans for a compilation of abandoned gems came to pass in 1974 with the stop-gap album *Odds And Sods*. There were two main reasons for the release. Firstly, the band had some seriously good material in the can, going unused. The second reason was illegal bootlegs, as unfortunately (though fortunately for fans) many songs had managed to escape and find their way on to unauthorized albums. With these songs circulating, Track Records decided to do something about it and tasked John Entwistle with compiling a track listing. The band had many unreleased songs from throughout their career, but most were recorded during three different periods. The first was in 1968, when several songs were taped and intended for release on a record to be titled *Who's For Tennis?*, earmarked for summer 1968 to cash in on the British phenomenon of the Wimbledon tennis championships. The second period was in 1970 (although the original release of *Odds And Sods* credits these recordings as being 1969, most sources seem to agree these sessions were in fact March to May 1970), when the band made a series of recordings at Pete Townshend's home studio, Eel Pie, in Twickenham. The idea was that rather than spend money in expensive studios, they could make use of Pete's production prowess and fairly advanced home-recording setup. These songs were mooted for their next album, then considered for a maxi-single (which were singles with more than two tracks), before being abandoned altogether. The third period came during sessions at the Record Plant and Olympic Studios for the band's *Who's Next* album. This record of course started out as the *Lifehouse* project and had been intended as a double album, before it was trimmed back to a nine-track single LP, leaving many quality songs on the cutting room floor. There were also tracks left over from the aborted sessions with Glyn Johns in 1972, which are credited on *Odds And Sods* as produced by The Who with Glyn as associate producer, similarly to the *Who's Next* credits.

Between August and September 1973, even as *Quadrophenia* was being mixed by Ron Nevison at Pete's own studio in Goring-on-Thames (confusingly also called Eel Pie, just like his studio in Twickenham), John Entwistle was remixing and adding overdubs to songs for *Odds And Sods* at Ramport, with the sleeve noting final mixing at Nova Sound on 4 July 1974. What was released was a great indication of just how prolific the band really were, for it was easy to think of them as not especially speedy at putting out records. The record could have even been a double album with all the quality discarded songs they had floating about, and there were rumours of an *Odds And Sods* part two which would contain some of these, including an unedited version of 'Join Together' which would eventually be released on the *Who's Next/Life House* Super Deluxe release. Though a follow-up to *Odds And Sods* never materialized, a whole host of bonus tracks were added on the 1990s reissue, with the track order being completely rejigged, and a special two-LP edition was released in 2020 for Record Store Day, containing extra tracks, including two unreleased mixes – a remix of 'Zoot Suit' and an unedited version of 'The Seeker' which would later be released on the *Who's Next/Life House* Super Deluxe boxset.

For the cover, Daltrey's cousin, Graham Hughes, who had shot the cover of *Quadrophenia*, was once again employed. He stayed up the night before the photo shoot applying the band member's names to American football helmets, but when they went to put them on, it was found Pete's and Roger's didn't fit properly and they had to swap, hence why the helmets are wrongly named on the cover. During the US *Quadrophenia* tour, Hughes showed the resulting image to Townshend, who was in a bad mood and responded unfavourably. Hughes was frustrated and began ripping it up, but Townshend changed his mind, which prompted Hughes to use the pieced-together photo as the final artwork. This would become another interesting idea for album packaging, which ended up with cut-out sections, through which the inside could be glimpsed. The album would also include a poster of a live shot of the band and a booklet with complete lyrics and liner notes from Pete. Added to this, the original UK copies had the song titles embossed on the back cover in Braille.

TRACK BY TRACK

1. 'POSTCARD'

Written by John Entwistle
Produced by Pete Townshend and The Who
Recorded at Eel Pie Sound, London, March–May 1970, overdubs in 1974

In spring 1970, the band regrouped at Pete Townshend's Twickenham home studio, referred to as Eel Pie Sound, to record a group of songs they had floating around. The main reason they decided to use Pete's own studio was the money it saved, as well as being somewhere that was always available. Townshend had achieved good results on his demos and knew enough about recording to be a good producer, so although space was a slight issue, the band found the situation more than acceptable. Townshend would later laugh, imagining people going by the river and hearing Moon's incredibly loud drumming, explaining that soundproofing was not perfect.

'Postcard' is a John Entwistle song detailing life on the road and containing sound effects that, according to Pete's liner notes, were recorded in the actual countries they're meant to represent.

The track starts with a chromatic ascending line running from F sharp to C, played on brass by Entwistle, which is a main feature of the song. Aside from this there is also some nice electric piano played by Pete in addition to his fuzz guitar, while Entwistle, as well as providing a good lead vocal, comes up with great bubbling bass lines. The track's lyrics are pretty straightforward but highly amusing as Entwistle talks of perils almost everywhere they go, as well as running out of money and being thrown off long-haul flights to Australia for drinking, alluding to a disastrous tour 'down under' with the Small Faces in which both bands were not warmly received. As each country is mentioned, we get various sound effects, including Pete strumming a mandolin to give us an Italian vibe, as well as some wobble board and spring noises for Australia. The middle eight is a nice change musically as John sums up the business of touring, explaining 'Next week I'll try and phone'.

The band are tight and the arrangement is full without being cluttered, and as on all the tracks recorded at Eel Pie Sound, Pete shows himself to be an excellent producer, making the band sound better than many Kit Lambert-produced records. Put simply, these sessions are outstanding for home studio recordings in the early 1970s, Pete even achieving the elusive 'great drum sound' which fully showcases Keith's wonderful playing.

Some overdubs were made in 1974 to prepare the song for release, but the original 1970 mix is available as a bonus track on the *Who's Next/Life House* Super Deluxe boxset released in 2023. Comparing the two mixes, the notorious perfectionist Entwistle recorded more brass and redid his bass. The track was also slowed down very slightly.

The 1990s reissue of *Odds And Sods* erroneously credits this as having been produced at Eel Pie on 14 August 1973, though this is possibly the date that John remixed it at Ramport, while the original recording was indeed at Eel Pie. The original album credits it as having been recorded at Eel Pie in 1969 and finished at Ramport in 1974.

2. 'NOW I'M A FARMER'

Written by Pete Townshend
Produced by Pete Townshend
Recorded at Eel Pie Sound, London, March–May 1970

One of the strangest songs written by Townshend, this track seems like it would have fitted on a concept album, and one wonders if Pete could have somehow reworked it into *Lifehouse*. The track starts with an acoustic guitar playing changing chords over a pedal tone (classic Townshend) and some wonderful drumming from Keith Moon in an intro that seems to foreshadow 'I've Had Enough' from *Quadrophenia*. The song comes to a stop before Daltrey leads us into the verse, showing signs of his matured voice that would be fully revealed on 1971's *Who's Next*, the band also sounding powerful and dynamic, with deep throbbing bass, exuberant drums and lively acoustic guitar. The chorus is ridiculous but catchy nonetheless, while the post-chorus section, with Pete singing lyrics that sound as though they're from a classic stage musical, somehow works better than it should. As the song seems to come to an end, it becomes even crazier as a country and western section springs from nowhere, Keith playing a block of wood and Pete offering his best yodelling country twang on the lead vocals. The song's verse comes storming back in and then we get yet another section, a variation on the 'Alarming how charming' part, which cuts in rather abruptly and ends with Daltrey's rough 'When you grow what I grow', suggesting for a second that he might just being talking about something one might smoke. However, the end of the song, which goes back to the country and western part, gives us a list of what's being grown in amusingly accented spoken vocals, while in the background someone whistles. The track pretty much grinds to a halt with the final 'Pineapples', suggesting this was probably meant to be faded out but was too funny not to be played in full.

'Now I'm A Farmer' is an off-the-wall track that seems too weird to have ever been released, but too well written and recorded not to have been. The whole group performs with impressive energy and the mix is further complimented by some nifty piano playing from Pete.

Apparently demoed in 1968 and considered for *Who's For Tennis*, it was eventually recorded at Eel Pie in Twickenham from March–May 1970, even though the original album says 1969.

3. 'PUT THE MONEY DOWN'

Written by Pete Townshend
Produced by The Who, associate producer Glyn Johns
Recorded at Olympic Studios, London, 6 June 1972, overdubs 1974

'Put The Money Down' is one of a handful of songs recorded in 1972 at sessions intended for producing the follow-up to *Who's Next*. Again, the band worked with Glyn Johns at Olympic Studios before Pete called an end to recording, feeling that what they were producing sounded too similar to their previous album, and 'Put The Money Down' wouldn't see the light of day until it was exhumed for *Odds And Sods*. It's a fine song, but the biggest issue with it is that it perhaps sounds too close in style to 'Join Together', and while it's the more complex of the two songs, it's the lesser of the two in terms of catchiness.

The song starts with piano and subtle synth before the rest of the band comes in, the slow pace of it constraining Keith to a basic beat, while Pete plays a rudimentary riff that lends the song much of its similarity with 'Join Together'. Roger is in as fine a voice as ever, and certainly puts every ounce into things, especially on the chorus, where Keith is also allowed to display more of his trademark finesse and power.

The line about bands killing chickens might relate to the Toronto Rock 'n' Roll Festival in 1969, where a chicken thrown into the crowd by Alice Cooper was torn to shreds by them.

While compiling *Odds And Sods*, Entwistle says he found it impossible to get Roger back in the studio to redo his vocal, something that was necessary since he had only ever put down guide takes, and what was available didn't show him in his best light. Eventually, John told Roger that he himself would sing lead on the finished track, to which Daltrey responded, 'Fine, and I'll do the bass'. The next day, the singer turned up at the studio. A mix with the original vocal can be found on the 2023 *Who's Next/Life House* Super Deluxe boxset.

4. 'LITTLE BILLY'

Written by Pete Townshend
Produced by Kit Lambert
Recorded at IBC Studios, London, February 1968

Perhaps due in part to The Who's foray into advertising of sorts on their 1967 album *The Who Sell Out*, as well as several other jingles they had recorded, Townshend was approached by the American Cancer Society with the aim of writing an anti-smoking song. The idea of a major rock band writing such a song might seem a little unlikely, and certainly if a band were to do such a thing, there were far more clean-cut acts than The Who that might have been considered. However, Townshend was never one to turn down an assignment and ended up composing this surprisingly good track, which in the end was never even used for its original purpose.

The story is about a boy called Billy who is rather overweight and thus becomes the butt of children's jokes, and is told, due to his obesity, he will more than likely die an early death. In contrast, the rest of the children smoke, a habit which Billy does not share, and he eventually winds up looking after the children of his schoolmates as they all pass away from cancer. On the surface, the story may be a little too simplistic and far-fetched, but the beauty of its anthemic music allows the song to get away with it.

The track starts with single acoustic and electric guitar strums, a little similar in feel to the opening of 'Overture' from *Tommy*. Keith enters on drums and is soon joined by Roger's double-tracked vocal, but John doesn't enter until the short chorus, which is basic but thoroughly uplifting with some delightful fills from Keith and catchy harmony vocals. Throughout the second verse, John plays a great melodic line, spelling out the chord changes with a tight picked sound that really stands out. The two-chord middle eight lifts things further before we get a third verse, this time sung by Pete, and then a final fourth verse which switches back to Roger.

A prime example of The Who as a power-pop band, writing catchy melodies without losing any of their punch, 'Little Billy' is a bit of an oddity in their catalogue due to its subject matter, but it's a topic that Townshend handles with his typical idiosyncratic touch of storytelling. As well as containing fantastic melodies, it has some of Keith's most joyous drumming and some of John's most inventive bass playing. Add to the mix Nicky Hopkins on piano and you have a special Who recording that absolutely deserved to be rescued from the archives.

Despite never receiving a release at the time, the band thought enough of it to play it live in concert at a handful of American dates in March and April

1968, one such performance at The Fillmore East in Manhattan being captured and released officially in 2018 after many years of being bootlegged.

Called a masterpiece by Townshend in the liner notes for the album, the working title of this was 'Little Billy's Doing Fine'.

5. 'TOO MUCH OF ANYTHING'

Written by Pete Townshend
Produced by The Who, associate producer Glyn Johns
Recorded at Olympic Studios, London, April 1971, overdubs 1974

'Too Much Of Anything' was another song from the *Lifehouse* project, having been played at the Young Vic shows in April 1971 and also tackled in the studio at Olympic. Although the back cover of *Odds And Sods* seems to put this down as being from the May–June 1972 sessions with Glyn Johns, most other information, including the *Who's Next /Life House* Super Deluxe boxset, do confirm the recording as being a part of the Olympic sessions for *Who's Next*, in 1971, although Roger rerecorded his vocal in 1974 for the album.

The track, a perfect example of Pete's country-tinged ballad writing, starts with two twelve-string guitars strumming a suspended chord motif that is typical Townshend, before being joined by Nicky Hopkins' piano and then the rest of the band. Keith relaxes into the sort of half-time groove that often adorned Pete's demos, and it's a satisfying one which fits in nicely with John's funky bass. Roger's vocal is a standout performance and is nicely aided in the choruses by Pete and John. The second verse changes dynamics dramatically as everything stops, save for the vocals and Pete's acoustic guitar, with what sounds like a cross between another high capoed guitar and a mandolin being furiously strummed in one side of the mix. At the very end, Keith and John come storming back in, now joined by a distorted electric guitar, a switch-up which packs a punch and reminds you of the range The Who had. The band have another trick up their sleeves before the song is done, and they key change up a tone to B, as Moon also switches from half-time to full-time. Townshend also wrestles dirty rhythmic riffs out of his guitar, the overall effect immediately giving the listener an adrenaline rush, before we return to half-time on the second half of the verse, allowing the song to return to a more sedate pace to ease us towards its end.

Like many songs of the time, 'Too Much Of Anything' showcases the band at their best, and *Who's Next*'s loss would be *Odds And Sods*' gain. The original mix with Daltrey's 1971 vocal (which in my opinion is superior to the rerecording) is also available on several *Who's Next* reissues.

6. 'GLOW GIRL'

Written by Pete Townshend
Produced by Kit Lambert
Recorded at De Lane Lea Studios, London, January 1968

Hot on the heels of *The Who Sell Out*, The Who were back in the studio in January 1968, where they set about recording one of Pete's latest tracks, a strange but brilliant song dealing with a couple on a doomed flight. The genesis of the track came on a 1967 tour supporting Herman's Hermits, when they were forced to make an unplanned stop in Tennessee on a DC7 chartered plane as they ran into difficulties. Townshend recalled that the incident shook him up enough that for the next few months, he found himself writing songs about plane crashes. 'Glow Girl' was obviously a keeper, and the same month they recorded the song. Townshend mentioned both this song and 'Faith In Something Bigger', as reported to the *NME* by Keith Altham, mooting 'Glow Girl' as their next single. The song was recorded in De Lane Lea Studios, but the band must have been unsatisfied with the recording as they attempted a remake of it in February at CBS while putting down 'Little Billy'. However, for *Odds And Sods*, the original recording was used (the remake is available on *The Who Sell Out* Super Deluxe boxset).

As stated, the song's subject is a plane about to crash, with a girl (sometimes said to be in fact a couple) going through the contents of her bag, seeing photographs and personal items that recall memories of her life. As the song ends, the plane crashes and the girl (or couple) are immediately reincarnated into a newborn girl. As a subject matter, it's unlike anything else being written at the time, and it contains some notable themes and links to future Who work. The theme of reincarnation is something that seems to have been of interest to Pete at that time; when writing *Tommy*, the early stages of the story would feature the idea of a soul being reincarnated many times before reaching its highest level. Musically, the end of the song would also crop up in *Tommy*.

The song begins with a suspended chord riff by Townshend that also forms the verse, the whole band leaping in on the two-chord turnaround. The first verse has lovely harmony vocals, with the voices blending seamlessly into one, while John sits things out on the bass until the two-chord turn-around appears again. From this point, Entwistle makes his mark, his galloping bassline raising the pulse, and he plays a fantastic descending slide down at one point. Keith's drumming is light and explosive, and his cymbal work and rat-a-tat fills before the verse turn-around and going into the chorus are a real delight. The chorus of the song has a chord sequence which rises before plunging back down, expressing the feeling of the plane falling from the sky. After the second chorus, we reach an instrumental section which serves as the plane crash, Townshend turning guitar string pick-scrapes from mere noise into a technique of its own, varying the rhythms so that he's actually playing something musical. Here, the song resolves into its outro section, with the band singing 'It's a girl Mrs Walker'. Townshend takes a lovely high counter vocal in a section which tells of instant reincarnation, something that probably would have escaped most listeners, had this not been explained. This section would of course be repurposed for the song 'It's A Boy' from *Tommy*.

The title of the song is never mentioned in the lyrics but did feature in one of two Pete Townshend home demos of the song (both available on *The Who Sell Out* Super Deluxe edition) in which he sings the title over the beginning and end of the track.

It's hard to say whether 'Glow Girl' would have been a hit if released as a single as originally planned, but one feels it would have been a better bet than 'Dogs' or 'Magic Bus'. The song represents The Who at their power-pop best, combining gorgeous melodies and harmonies with dynamic drums and bass, a pop art concept that showed Townshend developing even more as a composer of great originality, far better expressed here than on their chosen singles of 1968. Unjustly left on the cutting room floor, thankfully *Odds And Sods* rescued it, one of the biggest justifications for the album's much-needed release.

7. 'PURE AND EASY'

Written by Pete Townshend
Produced by The Who, associate producer Glyn Johns
Recorded at Olympic Studios, London, April–May 1971

'Pure And Easy' is possibly the biggest casualty from any Who recording session, it being almost unthinkable that it was a studio outtake. Not only was the song the central point of the *Lifehouse* story that *Who's Next* was based around, but it is one of the finest songs in the Who's discography. The song, which was originally titled 'The Note', was very much intended to be a part of The Who's 1971 album and was recorded at both the Record Plant in New York and Olympic Studios in Barnes, with *Odds And Sods* using the latter version.

Starting with a great drum fill intro from Keith, the song then settles into its mid-paced verse with sparse acoustic guitar, allowing the organ to carry its repeating three-chord phrase. Roger's vocal is a rerecorded take from 1974 and displays him in his melodic upper range, pushing just enough to break into grittiness where needed. The chorus consists of three sections. The first, in C, sees Townshend introduce an electric guitar riff which runs through the chords and finishes up with some lovely Entwistle bass licks. The second is in D, before the third turns to the dark A minor. The song then skips the verse entirely and goes back to repeat the chorus sections, before changing to a middle eight. This middle eight features Moon pounding away throughout, as Townshend lets single-chord strums ring out, later veering into a solo. As the solo ends we get another chorus, which is cut short and we at last return to the verse, which is itself curtailed as we head to the coda, this being another typical Townshend A, G and D riff, over which we hear Pete's vocal.

The full unedited version of this with the original vocal is available on the *Who's Next/Life House* Super Deluxe boxset, as well as the Record Plant version which in my opinion is superior in many, though not all, ways.

'Pure And Easy' was one of Townshend's best songs and its non-inclusion on *Who's Next* was a painful loss and a perhaps bizarre choice, considering it is stronger than several tracks that made the cut. Apparently, Glyn Johns felt there was no point including it, since 'The Song Is Over' repeated the 'Pure And Easy' verse lyrics at the end, and as this now wasn't a concept album, this reprise would be confusing to the listener. It's hard to fault *Who's Next* as an album, but if they could have squeezed in 'Pure And Easy' it would have been even greater.

The band thought highly of the song though, continuing to play it live in the UK and America in 1971 at least up until the release of the album which did not contain it. It was eventually released in the form of Pete's home recording on his album *Who Came First* in 1972.

8. 'FAITH IN SOMETHING BIGGER'

Written by Pete Townshend
Produced by Kit Lambert
Recorded at CBS Studios, London, January 1968

Another song recorded early in 1968, but unlike 'Little Billy' and 'Glow Girl', here the band don't go for power-pop, but something much milder and more akin to The Beach Boys. At the time, Pete would mention the song to the press, joking that The Who would be preaching along the lines of 'You've got to have faith in something bigger!', going on to say that hearing Roger sing it, no one would believe they were serious.

In the liner notes of *Odds And Sods*, Pete acted embarrassed over the song's subject matter of God, and in the expanded notes from the 1990s reissue called the guitar solo the worst he'd heard, remarking that the rest of the band were good lads for putting up with 'this sort of nonsense'. Although Pete might be overly harsh here, it's true that 'Faith In Something Bigger' is an oddity for The

Who and not really one of the better ones. Despite reportedly being Irish Jack's (long-time Who fan, friend of the band and part-inspiration for the character of Jimmy in *Quadrophenia*) favourite Who song, it does feel like yet another 1968 misstep, one that, unlike 'Dogs' and 'Magic Bus', they decided not to release.

The song is nice enough and features some lovely harmonies, but just feels too sweet and lightweight for a band that were getting tougher and more aggressive every day. Perhaps they could have got away with this in 1965 or 1966, but in 1968, this feels like a backwards step, even though, as usual, Keith does his best to make a tame song sound wild and raucous. Definitely an odd inclusion on the album when there were several better songs in the archives, it shows that even in picking songs for a compilation of overlooked gems, The Who could still overlook yet more gems.

9. 'I'M THE FACE'

Written by Pete Meaden
Produced by Pete Meaden and Chris Parmeinter
Recorded at Fontana Studios, London, June 1964

Technically not even a Who song as it was the B-side of the band's first single, 'Zoot Suit', but released when they were temporarily called The High Numbers, 'I'm The Face' was written by their then manager, Pete Meadon, although really it is a rip-off of Slim Harpo's 'Got Love If You Want It' with different lyrics. The song was recorded in 1964 and showcases the early maximum R&B Who, even before Shel Talmy got his hands on them. Overall, the band do a fine job of injecting life into this basic twelve-bar blues, complete with harmonica from Roger and piano played by Allen Ellet, which help to fill out the mix. Apparently, The Who's previous manager, Helmut Gordon, was also involved, providing handclaps. In the grand scheme of things, the song is nothing to write home about, but it is nicely produced and an interesting addition to the album, showing just how far the band had come. 'Zoot Suit' backed with 'I'm The Face' was released on 3 July 1964 and did poorly, selling only around 500 copies and failing to chart.

10. 'NAKED EYE'

Written by Pete Townshend
Produced by Pete Townshend
Recorded at Eel Pie Sound, London, March–May 1970

Developed from improvisational jams throughout 1969, 'Naked Eye' would be transformed into a fully-fledged song and become a live favourite with fans.

The embryo of it can be heard during the band's Woodstock performance of 'My Generation' and a more fully formed version at the Isle Of Wight in August 1970. By this time, the band had attempted to record the song at Pete Townshend's Twickenham studio earlier that year, in the same sessions as 'Now I'm A Farmer', 'Postcard' as well as 'I Don't Even Know Myself' and 'Water', which were left unreleased.

The song begins with Townshend's clean guitar arpeggios, accompanied by Entwistle on bass, before Roger joins, as well as electric piano by Townshend. Keith comes in at the end of the verse, shifting the dynamic, before the up-tempo guitar riff enters. In the second verse, Pete takes the lead vocal, singing an octave above Daltrey's low, bluesy delivery.

A middle section changes up the mood again, becoming mellower before slowly building back up again, with Townshend offering a little taste of his usual live lead guitar improvisations. Again, Daltrey takes the lead on the last verse before the outro section, which sees the song once again slow down and gradually build back up, with further soloing from Pete before a slightly abrupt ending. 'Naked Eye' is a great Who track, but I have to admit I don't feel they really managed to completely nail it in the studio, preferring several live versions such as the one at the Young Vic from 1971 (even though Roger does forget the words) and available on several reissues of *Who's Next*. Townshend himself says in the liner notes for *Odds And Sods* that they never released the track, as they hoped to get a really good live version. For me, it is a track that just works far better as a long-drawn-out live jam, and although there is nothing wrong with this recorded version, it does feel a little subdued compared to live renditions, especially with the addition of electric piano. The band would attempt to rerecord the song during the making of *Who's Next*, featuring acoustic guitar, but this version was left unreleased until the 2023 *Who's Next/Life House* Super Deluxe boxset, which also contains an unedited mix of this 1970 version, clocking in at over a minute longer.

Note that like the other tracks from the Eel Pie Sound sessions in 1970, the original *Odds And Sods* back cover puts down the recording date as 1969, while the 1990s CD reissue dates it as 16 August 1973, though this is possibly the date it was mixed.

11. 'LONG LIVE ROCK'

Written by Pete Townshend
Produced by The Who, associate producer Glyn Johns
Recorded at Olympic Studios, London, June 1972

Written for the abandoned *Rock Is Dead – Long Live Rock* project, this 1950s-style rocker would take an interesting journey, winding up on a film soundtrack and semi-mimed to on BBC television, but going without an actual release by The Who until *Odds And Sods*. The track is essentially a Chuck Berry-type song loosely charting the birth of the rock music scene and offering comic vignettes on it, in a way that almost foreshadows Entwistle's 'Success Story' from 1975's *The Who By Numbers*. Beginning with Townshend's guitar, it soon breaks into the verse, with the addition of piano, and features Entwistle playing an understated bass riff that is straight from Townshend's own home demo, showing that he wasn't too precious to sometimes stick to Pete's lines. Townshend takes the lead vocal on the verses, whilst Daltrey assumes command of the microphone for the chorus and middle eight. Though the song is essentially a I–IV–V-type blues in the key of A, Townshend throws in something different at the end of the progression with a quick-changing F, G and D, giving it a further sense of energy and a more modern feel.

The middle eight sees Daltrey letting go vocally, and we get more of a typical Who sound at the end of it, where Townshend arpeggiates a C add ninth chord, before a run down on the root note.

'Long Live Rock' would be half-mimed on *The Old Grey Whistle Test* in 1973, broadcast on 29 January, the instruments being on tape while Townshend and Daltrey sang live vocals. Interestingly, Daltrey sings the middle verse instead of Pete (probably to give him a bigger role), while Townshend makes an error on the last verse, skipping a line and ending up singing one line twice, half-laughing as he realizes his mistake. A less-spotted mistake is Daltrey singing the full chorus line (including the 'I need it every night') the first time around on the penultimate chorus, which should just feature the title being sung five times. Despite this appearance, 'Long Live Rock' was not released as a single until 1979 to coincide with the film *The Kids Are Alright*, which featured the song over the ending credit sequence. In the time between the *Old Grey Whistle Test* spot and the release of *Odds And Sods*, the song would be recorded for the 1973 film *That'll Be The Day*. The cast of this film included a host of music stars such as Keith Moon, Ringo Starr, David Essex and Billy Fury, with Fury himself singing 'Long Live Rock'. The film soundtrack version of the song would feature both Keith Moon and Pete Townshend on drums and guitars respectively, as well as Jack Bruce on bass, Ronnie Wood from The Rolling Stones on additional guitar, Graham Bond on saxophone and John Hawken (from The Strawbs) on piano.

'Long Live Rock' was played often in concert in 1972, with Roger singing lead for the entire song, before being dropped, only to become a regular again in 1979, with Pete back on verse vocals, and it stayed right through to 1982. It has since then been largely ignored, but it still made a few appearances in 2004 and 2014.

Chapter 8

The Who by Numbers (1975)

Produced by Glyn Johns
Released in the UK on 18 October 1975 as Polydor 2490 129
Released in the USA on 25 October 1975 as MCA 2161
Chart position – UK = 7, USA = 8
Recorded at Shepperton Studios in Surrey
Pete Townshend – Guitars, Vocals, Ukulele and Keyboards
Roger Daltrey – Vocals
John Entwistle – Bass, Vocals and Horns
Keith Moon – Drums, Percussion and Vocals
Nicky Hopkins – Piano

In 1975, The Who marked a decade since their first album release with *The Who By Numbers*. Although each of the band's previous six LPs had all been distinct from one another in sound and approach, their seventh release might have been the biggest departure yet, and one that has come to be slightly overlooked. It is true that the album doesn't quite reach the heights that had been achieved on their previous three records, but what is contained on the release is refreshingly understated and interesting nonetheless.

With *A Quick One*, The Who had pioneered the mini opera, while on *The Who Sell Out* the band concocted a concept album of sorts, following that with a full-blown rock opera and double album to boot with 1969's *Tommy*. *Who's Next* introduced synthesizers, while *Quadrophenia* combined synthesizers with another concept spanning two LPs. In contrast, *The Who By Numbers* is just an album. There is no concept joining the songs, and the synthesizers that Townshend had made such a prominent part of the last two albums are jettisoned. This is a stripped-back record containing no underlying theme, although one could argue there is a concept of sorts – this could be called a mid-life crisis album.

For it isn't just musically that *The Who By Numbers* differs from previous albums, but in its subject matter too. For the first time, Townshend takes a very personal approach to his lyrics, writing songs that would reach into some of the darker corners of his psyche. Although Pete had sometimes used autobiographical elements in his songs, these were often more a way of mirroring his audience.

In the past, he had written oddities dealing with unusual characters, he had written about spiritual themes and, on the most recent album, delved into the mod movement and the band's own history, but these new songs saw Townshend laying his soul bare. Thus, *The Who By Numbers* is an album that simultaneously delivers some of the most thoughtful and tender music, coupled with some of the darkest lyrics Townshend would ever write. Pete turned 30 during the making of the album, by no means old age, but rock was still somewhat a young man's game, and this was the man who had envisioned the breakup of the band almost as quickly as it had been formed, famously penning the lyrics, 'I hope I die before I get old'. That had been a decade ago, and Townshend hadn't died like contemporaries Jimi Hendrix, Jim Morrison and Brian Jones, but instead carried on as one of rock's leading statesmen, a role that he had become increasingly uneasy with. The album vented all of Townshend's demons, and one journalist, Roy Carr from the *NME*, even went so far as to call it a 'suicide note'. Yet although there is a grim air to some of the songs, there are also moments of subtle beauty that revealed something more multi-faceted than just mere despair.

For the four members of the band, 1975 was a very busy time. In January, John Entwistle began a run of solo shows in the UK, before taking to the US for more gigs the following month. February also saw Daltrey, fresh from making the film of *Tommy*, reunite with director Ken Russell to begin production on *Lizstomania*, whilst March saw the premier of *Tommy* and the various press events associated with the film. After this busy first quarter to the year, *The Who By Numbers* began production in April at Shepperton Studios, using Ronnie Lane's mobile studio, produced by Glyn Johns once more, Pete perhaps seeking to alleviate tensions by stepping back from the producer role after his near total control with *Quadrophenia*. Shepperton was chosen mainly because Glyn wasn't a fan of Ramport. According to John Entwistle, Pete was not initially into the project when the band got together, and on 4 April, Townshend, Moon and Entwistle went into Shepperton Studios without Roger, who was still filming *Lizstomania*, and began jamming. John would say that the resulting jams inspired and motivated the band, with them finding themselves playing better than they had in years. Recording continued through April and May, and some overdubs were recorded in June, with long-time Who studio member Nicky Hopkins being invited back to add his skills.

Aside from the other activities like filmmaking and solo careers, The Who also commenced legal action as the band sought to break away from their managers and Track Records, having finally grown tired of what was perceived as gross mismanagement. Daltrey had been the first to question the status quo and had hired Bill Curbishley to be his manager instead of Chis Stamp and

Kit Lambert. Soon, the other members of the band were convinced to jump ship as well, a sensible decision for the whole band, although Daltrey in a way would have rather kept Curbishley to himself.

Another point of acrimony emerged in the run-up to the album's release, as Townshend and Daltrey traded criticisms in the press. In April 1975, Pete did an interview with *Sounds* magazine, followed by one with Roy Carr in the *NME* which was later reprinted by *Creem* magazine in America. Pete talked about his deep dissatisfaction with the previous year's shows in France and New York, going on to say he felt The Who had become a golden oldies band, churning out the old hits, and that he felt too old to be onstage. Pete brought up Chuck Berry acting out his past onstage, and his fears that The Who were becoming the Chuck Berry of the 1960s. He also admitted to feeling deeply depressed and like a caricature of himself. These comments on age are clearly reflected by some of the material on *The Who By Numbers*, so it was obviously something that had been playing on his mind and not merely an interview that had caught him on a bad day. Townshend also identified a difference in him and the rest of the group, especially between him and Daltrey, going on to say he had been the only one in the band to feel this way.

Was it surprising that the man who had written about his wish to die before he got old was now complaining of feeling his age? Probably not, and as Townshend went on in his interview with Roy Carr, he pointed out that Daltrey's desire to rock out in a wheelchair was not one that he shared.

Townshend was also unhappy with the crowds at New York's Madison Square Garden the previous year, noting it was all the same faces that had turned up to prove they were original fans, and he took umbrage with chants of 'Jump jump' from them as well as 'Shut up Townshend' and them shouting out song requests. Another slight grievance was the pressure he felt from the other band members for him to write songs, get back in the studio and go back on the road in an endless cycle.

Pete would reveal that the new album had taken much longer to record because of Roger making *Lisztomania* and John being away touring. He was also unhappy that he was giving away the best material to The Who, stating that he was preparing a solo album, but when the band got together he'd probably offer up all the songs he had and let them take their pick. It was clear at this time that the individual members of the band were fracturing more than ever. John had his outlet as a songwriter with his solo albums, Daltrey was enjoying his own solo career as well as his acting roles, while Keith had moved to America and become part of a different social scene.

In the interviews, Pete praised Roger for his ability to turn on his stage presence at each show, but nevertheless, the remarks and general tone of the interviews did not sit well with Daltrey, who would fire back in an interview in the *NME*, once more reprinted by *Creem* later that year. Roger accused Pete of talking himself up his own arse, going on to say that Pete had taken over control in the studio and that his own suggestions would get laughed at. In addition to this, he took offence to any suggestions that the previous year's shows had been poor, blaming any faults at gigs on Pete drinking too much, reminding the interviewer that he himself had not drunk onstage in the last seven years. Certainly, looking at the footage that was filmed by the BBC at Charlton Athletic football ground in 1974, one can tell Townshend is clearly inebriated, although to be fair, the performance is still fairly good overall. Daltrey, however, would describe some gigs as firing on only three cylinders, opining that the band could have waltzed the gigs under normal circumstances. Overall, Roger had been deeply affected by the interview, his enthusiasm for the group having taken a knock.

The Who By Numbers is an underappreciated record by The Who, one that, for many reasons, seems to have fallen through the cracks of rock history. Firstly, how do you top the three-album run of *Tommy*, *Who's Next* and *Quadrophenia*? *Tommy* had been the groundbreaking rock opera that would forever follow The Who like a proverbial shadow, or at times even a weight around the neck. Even in 1975, the release of *The Who By Numbers* was overshadowed by the film release of *Tommy*, the album that just would not die, in spite of the several attempts Townshend had made to effectively bury it so that the group could move on to new pastures. Although *Who's Next* was not in the end a rock opera, it did contain some of Townshend's finest writing and two of their very best and most anthemic songs in 'Won't Get Fooled Again' and 'Baba O'Riley', as well as their ultimate lighters-out ballad, 'Behind Blue Eyes'. *Quadrophenia* may have divided people, but there was no doubt it was the boldest musical statement the group had made thus far. In retrospect, it would have been foolish for Townshend to seek another grandiose idea, even if one had sprung to mind. The group was too fractured at this point, with solo projects, movies and families preventing them from truly coming together in the way that would have been needed to produce another epic rock record. After the Townshend-controlled *Quadrophenia* had caused tensions, another Pete passion project might have caused irreparable strain.

The other issue is that *The Who By Numbers* doesn't have that one classic song that grabbed the public by the ears. 'Squeeze Box' was a hit, reaching number ten when it was released, but it's thought by many fans to be a lightweight novelty song, one that in concert is best used as a chance to grab a pint of beer or relieve oneself. Could 'Slip Kid' have been a hit had it been released as a single? As much as the song is a worthy addition to The Who's collection of rock cuts, probably not. Thus, what really remains on *The Who By Numbers* is a curious collection of mainly milder more reflective compositions, such as 'They Are All In Love', 'Imagine A Man' and 'Blue, Red And Grey'. It's another side of The Who, one very much more understated than previous records but a refreshing palate cleanser after the previous three albums.

Daltrey stated he was really pleased with it in his 1975 interview with *Creem*, feeling it was a varied album like *Who's Next* instead of *Quadrophenia*, which he said had all been in one vein. Barbara Charone in *Sounds* gave the album praise for succeeding where *Quadrophenia* had failed, stating that it lacked the previous album's self-consciousness, and curiously comparing the harmony vocals on 'In A Hand Or A Face' and 'Squeeze Box' to earlier Who singles like 'Happy Jack' and 'Pictures Of Lily'. Dave Marsh would pick up on the hidden theme of the album, even recognizing Entwistle's 'Success Story' as fitting in with the overall picture of ageing rock stars and the downsides to fame and fortune. Though he would offer that it might have been their best album to date, he somewhat bizarrely also seemed to take aim at Daltrey as a singer, describing his vocals as barely on key, emotionally and musically flat, going so far as to say The Who could function as a three-piece without him. In my opinion, Daltrey's vocals had been outstanding so far throughout the band's 1970s output, elevating key material on both *Who's Next* and *Quadrophenia*. On *The Who By Numbers*, he would be presented with tricky questions, as the material became for the most part more mellow and nuanced. There's nothing quite as visceral as the scream on 'Won't Get Fooled Again' or 'Love Reign O'er Me', but Daltrey again manages to find another facet to his voice, singing beautifully on the softer tracks. However, there is still plenty of his famous aggression when needed, and songs like 'Slip Kid', 'How Many Friends' and 'Dreaming From The Waist' test every aspect of his range.

For the cover, John drew the illustration in an hour, but it took about three hours to put the dots in. When he got someone to join them up, he discovered he had left out two inside legs. The original UK and US copies were numbered on the back.

In 1996, the album was reissued on CD, containing live bonus tracks from Swansea in 1976.

TRACK BY TRACK

1. 'SLIP KID'

Written by Pete Townshend
Produced by Glyn Johns
Recorded at Shepperton Studios, Surrey, 30 May 1975

On an album defined by Townshend's sense of unease at growing old, 'Slip Kid' is a track that looks at generational divide, exactly ten years after the band had released 'My Generation'. In a way, like *Quadrophenia*'s 'Punk And The Godfather', we find the young man challenging his elders, and here Townshend sums up the truth that ultimately, as much as the young will point the accusing finger at their forefathers and swear themself to a different path, inevitably they will end up in exactly the same place. Idealism will fade as the soldier at 13 becomes the soldier at 63, unfortunately finding out that there is no easy way to be free.

The song begins with percussion and then, after a count in by Townshend, things spring to life, driven by the piano chords, while the guitar plays climbing octaves. The song reaches the chorus quickly, and its lurching chord sequence gives a sense of movement and is instantly catchy. The piano comes to the fore in the middle section as the song calms down with Roger's impassioned warning to the old man, before Townshend's spiky guitar solo, which is a real delight and most probably played on a Flying V gifted to him by Joe Walsh. Before the final verse, Entwistle plays a lovely bass run which is matched by the piano's cascading notes. As the song ends, Townshend plays jazzy octaves in one side of the mix and more spiky leads in the other.

'Slip Kid' is a great Who track and fine album opener, but an unusual one. Keith is incredibly restrained on the song, sounding entirely unlike himself as he lays down a steady-paced groove with virtually no fills or show-off moments. It would prove to be a popular song with Who fans, however, and would often be requested at concerts. The band did play the song in 1976, but it was dropped after just seven performances. In 2008, at a small London show at The IndigO2, Townshend and Daltrey would play an unrehearsed version featuring just the two of them. As lyrics were forgotten, Daltrey would explain this was the reason they never played it, while Townshend would comment on his current age matching one of the ages mentioned in the lyrics, saying that he knew he'd end up singing it when he was 63. The band would revive the song in full band format on *The Who Hits 50* tour in 2014 and 2015.

2. 'HOWEVER MUCH I BOOZE'

Written by Pete Townshend
Produced by Glyn Johns
Recorded at Shepperton Studios, Surrey, 7 May 1975

Perhaps the darkest and most personal of Townshend's confessional songs, 'However Much I Booze' hides the helpless gloom within the breeziness of its country-tinged music. Indeed, its bouncy nature is not far removed from the good-time hoe-down of 'Squeeze Box', but its lyrical content is so bleak that reportedly Roger Daltrey refused to sing it. Whatever the truth, this was a sound decision as Pete delivers the song with an emotional conviction and dynamic range that would be hard to top by anyone but its own author. Built on double-tracked acoustic guitars, with capo on the seventh fret for a bright, high sound, the arrangement is complimented by an electric part which comes in after the intro led by the brilliant Moon and Entwistle, who come tumbling in, in tandem like drunks falling downstairs. The verses are relaxed as Pete sings of being a 'faker' and a 'paper clown', before he injects more passion into his vocals as he declares, 'There ain't no way out'. The instrumental section becomes filled with country guitars and features some more complicated playing from Moon and Entwistle, before a sudden change in the middle eight as we shift to the melancholy of C major seventh, and for the first time the music matches the darkness of the subject matter. 'However Much I Booze' is a weirdly catchy and musically upbeat song considering its subject matter, and was played in concert in 1975 before being dropped for good.

3. 'SQUEEZE BOX'

Written by Pete Townshend
Produced by Glyn Johns
Recorded at Shepperton Studios, Surrey, 30 May 1975

If there is one track that really divides Who fans, it might just be 'Squeeze Box'. Of all The Who's songs, this seems to be the one people either love and look forward to hearing, or hate and find throwaway and embarrassing. Much has been written about its subject matter, with the feeling that surely it's about something sexual. The lyrics about going in and out, and the squeeze box being something mama wears on her chest, certainly do lend themselves to the sort of hidden dirty joke Townshend had displayed on 'Pictures Of Lily'. However, Townshend has always maintained there is no hidden meaning and it is simply about a woman who plays accordion, explaining that there's something very attractive about a woman who plays an instrument. The inspiration seems to have been the accordion itself, as Pete bought one and learnt how to play it quite quickly, attributing the simplicity of the song to the shortness of time spent with the instrument. Indeed, it's one of the band's most basic songs, effectively using only three chords for its entirety, a rare thing even in the early days of the band. For The Who, it's very lightweight, but is damn catchy and has some brilliantly bright and chiming electric guitars over the infectious acoustic strumming. Pete also adds his banjo skills, playing the solo on banjo rather than guitar for an authentic country vibe, while the rest of the band sound like they're having fun. It was the obvious single and reached number ten in the UK when it was released in 1976, an added success considering the album had already been released. One gets the feeling that its chart success might have been down to a large number of non-Who fans drawn in by its lighter tone, danceable quality and catchy simplicity. 'Squeeze Box' would be played live in concert throughout 1975 and 1976, as well as in 1982, and would also be revived for the band's *The Who Hits 50* tour in 2014.

4. 'DREAMING FROM THE WAIST'

Written by Pete Townshend
Produced by Glyn Johns
Recorded at Shepperton Studios, Surrey, May 1975

Although Roger Daltrey and Pete Townshend are on the surface vastly different people, the former did a wonderful job of interpreting the latter's words and feelings, finding himself into the heart of the songs and building his own connection to them. Some themes and topics were far easier than others, and he was often a more believable mouthpiece for Townshend's own macho side.

This very device had been at the heart of the four personas of Jimmy in *Quadrophenia*, and again here Daltrey finds himself singing a topic he can easily make his own – matters of uncontrollable sexual frustration. In a 1975 interview with Roy Carr, Townshend talked about how he hated getting old and recounted turning up at the BBC and seeing a group of girls waiting for The Bay City Rollers. As Townshend passed by, he was recognized, but not with much fanfare or star-struck adulation. Being asked by the doorman what it was like to no longer get much reaction from the young fans, Townshend admitted it brought a tear to his eye. Although The Who had forever been a geezers' band, there would always be a section of screaming girls, as with any major pop outfit of the 1960s. Those times seemed gone though, and this perhaps figured in the writing of 'Dreaming From The Waist'.

The song starts out with prominent use of acoustic guitar playing a series of chords over an A pedal tone, with Townshend's subtle electric guitar leads, until the band kicks in and the pace picks up. Townshend's biting lead tones are ear-catching, as are Keith's drums and Daltrey's aggressive vocals, but the star of the show is the audacious bass from Entwistle, which is melodically expressive, whizzing around the fretboard with fluidity and finesse. Townshend's saw-toned electric rhythm guitar is simplistic in its approach, with its ringing open A string acting as a kind of drone over the acoustic chords, while the lead in the opposite side of the mix is quite nimble, its delay effect adding to the atmosphere. The song's chorus returns to the intro chords, offering a mellower energy with its dreamy harmony vocals answered by Daltrey using his angelic voice in great contrast to the full-throated bravado of the verses.

'Dreaming From The Waist', which had the working title 'Control Myself', was played regularly in 1975 and 1976, and also at Kilburn in 1977 (which is available on DVD), where Daltrey forgot the words and John unleashed a particularly astonishing bass performance. It was featured in concert up until 1981.

5. 'IMAGINE A MAN'

Written by Pete Townshend
Produced by Glyn Johns
Recorded at Shepperton Studios, Surrey, 29 May 1975

A heavily acoustic-based track, Townshend recorded this in drop B tuning (low to high – B, F#, B, E, G#, C#), giving the beautifully picked chord sequence an interesting voicing and added weight. The song is all about subtlety, with a faint hint of piano coming in halfway through the first verse and the bass adding melodic phrases during the second. Keith doesn't play at all until the chorus, where he accentuates the song's climbing melody with some lovely work on the toms, with the backing harmonies also lifting the song. Daltrey puts in perhaps one of his most underrated vocals; nakedly vulnerable and nuanced, you can feel the performer in him come to the fore. Indeed, the song has a touch of a stage musical song about it in its drama and storytelling.

Lyrically, though, the song seems like abstract poetic imagery at times, the themes of growing old again seeming to run through it. Townshend summed up the song by saying it was about when a man is over the hill, can't pull women, isn't keen on drinking or getting out of the house to play football, and instead stays in to watch television, going on to say he realized the song was about himself. Daltrey's brilliant vocal on the song was an indication of how much he loved it. Indeed, in an interview in *Creem* magazine in 1975, he described it as the best song Townshend had ever written.

Being so far removed from the band's live ferocity, 'Imagine A Man' was never played live by The Who until 2019 for the band's orchestra-accompanied *Moving On* tour, although it had been played by Roger Daltrey in 1994 and Townshend in 2006 at solo shows.

6. 'SUCCESS STORY'

Written by John Entwistle
Produced by Glyn Johns
Recorded at Shepperton Studios, Surrey, 23 May 1975

A typically wry and cheeky song by Entwistle, 'Success Story' is dominated by the eight-string bass he plays, with the guitar taking a backseat altogether. The song opens with a bass riff and is soon joined by the rest of the band, the gritty vocal – complete with harmony – lending itself perfectly to the loud rock vibe. Townshend lends his own vocal to a repeating section, and John uses his more nasal singing style on the middle eight, contrasting with his deep 'fairy manager' voice that answers, declaring, 'You shall play Carnegie Hall'. This middle eight also features a line about smashing guitars and a brilliant drum fill by Moon, leading back to the verse.

In the verse, the lyrics tell the story of a nine-to-five worker watching a rock and roll singer who has given up music to turn to religion, possibly a reference to Little Richard. The second verse relates the struggles of the working musician waiting for the big break and the pressure to make it when as young as possible. In the third verse, the band has made it, but most of the money is going to the taxman and the endless time in the studio recording multiple takes is no longer fun – something that John knew plenty about, having initially hated multiple takes before later becoming a perfectionist with his bass parts, often unnecessarily redoing them. The final verse sees our protagonist returning home early in the morning from a gig with ringing ears, to find the preacher has turned back to being a rock and roll star, a nice way to bring the song full circle. 'Success Story' also features an instrumental section which is effectively a bass solo, where the sound is absolutely monstrous, as John plays yet another bass over the top of the arrangement, producing a sonic assault which ends on a sustained fuzz-toned note that feels as if someone is drilling into your brain. Glorious!

7. 'THEY'RE ALL IN LOVE'

Written by Pete Townshend
Produced by Glyn Johns
Recorded at Shepperton Studios, Surrey, 30 April 1975

A piano-led track courtesy of Nicky Hopkins that also features a strong acoustic guitar presence, 'They're All In Love' was a song that Daltrey at first didn't want to sing, stating that although he knew what the first two verses were about, the last one stumped him until Pete clarified matters. Roger would explain the 'Goodbye all you punks' line as being about Who fans that were still living in nostalgia, while Pete summed up the whole song as being about what the band had become, which was lawyers, money and accountants. Townshend said that this was never what they had been about and felt like crawling off and dying. Of course, this was at a time when The Who were involved in legal proceedings against their former managers, so it's easy to see where Townshend was coming from.

Musically, the song – originally titled 'She Loves Everyone' – displays the softer side of The Who, featuring no electric guitar and containing some beautifully understated drums by Keith, putting paid to the myth that he couldn't sit back on a track. Having decided to sing the song, Daltrey puts in another mature effort, starting off with a mellow touch in the first verse but offering more bite and toughness in its second and third, being backed up nicely with harmonies on the chorus. As with many Who songs, there's a key change worked in, this forming an instrumental section that repeats the chorus sequence, up a tone, with the piano and bass providing a striking point of interest for the listener. The song finishes with a touch of strummed ukulele, which leads into the next song.

8. 'BLUE, RED AND GREY'

Written by Pete Townshend
Produced by Glyn Johns
Recorded at Shepperton Studios, Surrey, May 1975

Pete Townshend's second lead vocal, and one of the undoubted highlights of the album, 'Blue, Red And Grey' is unique in The Who's catalogue, for as well as lacking bass and drums, being the only song they ever recorded to feature ukulele as its main instrument. Although a full band version is rumoured to exist, it's difficult to imagine a more fitting and affecting arrangement than the one presented here. The song is the perfect antidote to the mid-life crisis and disillusionment theme that permeates *The Who By Numbers* – this is a joyous

Townshend, taking the time to reflect, one who finds pleasure even in the cold and rain.

The song enters on a D to D suspended fourth chord refrain before changing to G and A. Pete's high-pitched and tender vocal immediately stands out and is easily one of his most beautiful and moving performances recorded. The chorus sees a heart-tugging change to E minor and B seventh, before the middle eight, where the authentic wartime brass enters, played by Entwistle, who, contributing no bass to this track, still manages to make an indelible mark that immediately lifts the song. The brass arrangement, which was recorded at Ramport, is an outstanding piece of work in its own right, showing Entwistle's musical genius beyond just being a bassist.

In the song, Pete refers to Ronnie Wood when he talks about the people on the hill, as Ronnie at this time lived on Richmond Hill at a property called The Wick. This house featured a studio where many recordings were made, and ended up being bought in 1996 by Townshend, who lived there until its sale in 2021. According to Townshend, he was called lazy for his habit of late rising.

'Blue, Red And Grey' has become a bit of a favourite for many fans of the band, even as one of the songs most untypical of them, once again proving that for a loud angry rock group, they could produce a song of tender beauty to rival anyone. This incredibly old-fashioned song was a point of embarrassment for Townshend, and he was against it appearing on the album. However, he was convinced by Glyn Johns, who, upon hearing it, was adamant it should be included. Townshend recalled he was in a depressed state and couldn't believe Johns wanted to include a cheery ukulele song. In a 2006 interview, he commented that Roger had selected the song for him to sing, and that he (Townshend) hated singing it, seeing it as cheesily optimistic. Townshend would come to play the track occasionally at solo performances in the 2000s, while Daltrey would also take to performing the song at his solo shows, doing so often from 2009 onwards.

9. 'HOW MANY FRIENDS'

Written by Pete Townshend
Produced by Glyn Johns
Recorded at Shepperton Studios, Surrey, 28 May 1975

'How Many Friends' is a fairly laid-back song but one that still packs quite a punch, both musically and lyrically. Apparently, the song reduced Keith to tears when he heard it, as the sense of loneliness hit home. The arrangement wastes no time in making an impression, with Keith's relaxed beat allowing John's melodic upper register bass work, the piano and Pete's delay-saturated country guitar lines to shine through. Daltrey again mixes a softer, soul-tinged vocal with his more typical rock style to great effect. The song comes to life in the chorus as John's bass drops in register to provide extra power in an effective dynamic shift, matched by Keith's harder-hitting approach. Pete's lead playing also becomes more intense and frantic before the whole thing calms down at the end of the chorus. The middle eight raises the drama even more and is a perfect musical contrast to the chorus, which, despite its bleak lyrics, is more triumphant in feel.

The general sense of paranoia that pervades the song is painfully honest, with the lyric about talking shit behind each other's back being particularly apt considering Townshend and Daltrey's war of words in the press throughout 1975.

'How Many Friends' was never played by The Who in concert, but Roger Daltrey would add the song to his live shows in 2017.

10. 'IN A HAND OR A FACE'

Written by Pete Townshend
Produced by Glyn Johns
Recorded at Shepperton Studios, Surrey, 27 May 1975

In one way, 'In A Hand Or A Face' is a great Who rocker, but in another it's possibly the most underdeveloped song on *The Who By Numbers*. Built around a biting, simplistic, but catchy riff that had been repurposed from 'Waspman' – the B-side of the 1972 single 'Relay' – the song is nice enough, but doesn't really go anywhere. After the riff, Entwistle and Moon come in, in typical explosive fashion, while Daltrey delivers his vocal, half-laughing on the first line, singing the song with a cool, cynical edge that gets to the heart of the lyrics. The line about firing the pistol at the wrong end of the race has been said to allude to suicide, while the verse about a stranger going through the dustbin has a grim poignancy. It's the chorus where the song slightly falls short of Townshend's usual brilliance, as we get the same 'I am going round and round' phrase repeated, whilst the chords move up over a pedal tone, feeling a little lacking in a real hook or moment of inspiration. At the end of the second chorus, we get a short section of Keith going wild on the drums whilst Entwistle demonstrates his rapid-fire bass skills, leading to Pete's pick-scrape and a trademark Who key change. This is followed by a new 'Round and round' refrain, consisting of the verse chords, which is actually far catchier than the chorus.

'In A Hand Or A Face', which was originally titled 'Round And Round', is not the best track on the album, but is lifted by some biting lead work from Townshend, delightful bass and drums from John and Keith, as well as a sneering vocal from Roger.

Chapter 9

Who Are You (1978)

Produced by Glyn Johns and Jon Astley
Released in the UK on 18 August 1978 as Polydor 2490 147 (WHOD 504)
Released in the USA on 25 August 1978 as MCA 3050
Chart position – UK = 6, USA = 2
Recorded at Ramport Studios, RAK, Olympic Studios and Goring Studios in London, between September 1977 and April 1978
Pete Townshend – Guitars, Vocals, Piano and Synthesizer
Roger Daltrey – Vocals
John Entwistle – Bass, Vocals and Synthesizer
Keith Moon – Drums and Percussion
Andy Fairweather Low – Backing Vocals
Rod Argent – Piano and Synthesizer
Ted Astley – String Arrangements

Following the release of 1975's *The Who By Numbers*, the group embarked on a large amount of live shows, stretching from that year into the next. For many people, this was The Who at their very best as a live band, and it was to be their last proper shows with Keith Moon. In the course of these gigs, they set a new record for the loudest-ever concert when they took to football stadiums for a series of UK shows in 1976, dubbed the *Who Put The Boot In* tour, playing at Swansea and Glasgow as well as famously cranking the decibels to Guinness World Record levels at South London's Charlton Athletic football ground.

By contrast, 1977 would be a year of relative quiet for the band; while Townshend and Daltrey would both release solo albums (in Pete's case it was more of a duo album, a collaboration with ex-Small Faces and Faces member Ronnie Lane), no Who shows were planned. Townshend had stressed in a band meeting early in the year that he did not want to go back on the road, having grown especially tired with the static set lists they had been playing, with little material from their two most recent albums. According to Pete, it was to his surprise when the famously road-keen Roger backed him up. However, in the press, Daltrey expressed his desire to begin touring once more. Either Townshend had misinterpreted his bandmate's words or Daltrey had sided with

Townshend out of understanding and friendship rather than his own reluctance to tour. Whatever the case, 1977 would be a year away from concert stages, the only Who gig to take place being a special concert at the Gaumont Theatre in Kilburn, London, in December, the sole purpose of which was to capture performances for an upcoming film about the band by Jeff Stein. That film, *The Kids Are Alright*, included archive performances and interviews from the band's career, but the lack of quality footage for certain songs (namely, 'Baba O'Riley' and 'Won't Get Fooled Again') presented a problem, for which the solution was the specially arranged gig in Kilburn. A brief announcement made on radio on the morning of the show was the only promotion, and around 800 people turned up.

In the end, this concert was never used for the finished film, as the performance was thought to be substandard, though it eventually was released on DVD in 2008. During the show, the band were rusty, but particularly concerning was the condition of Keith Moon, who had spiralled out of control, gained weight and noticeably deteriorated in drumming finesse in the year since the last tour. Distanced from the band now and still residing in LA, Keith would often phone Townshend late at night to tell him he loved him and say goodnight. Perhaps the signs were already there that Keith was badly lost in more ways than one, though Keith would move back to the UK in September just before sessions for *Who Are You* started.

According to people surrounding these sessions, which began at Ramport, Pete, John and Keith were drinking very heavily during this time and would often spend much of the day talking about old times rather than doing much work. Glyn Johns, who was once again in the producer's chair, became frustrated with the slow progress on the album, having other commitments coming up, namely producing for Joan Armatrading. Keith was hugely erratic during recording, at times being on the money but on other occasions unable to hold it together, his alcohol use being an issue, but also the weight gain causing sluggishness and a lack of stamina.

More problems occurred away from the studio when Townshend became frustrated trying to stop an argument between his parents, so much so that he ended up putting his hand through a window in desperation. The resulting injury took time to heal, which curtailed recording for the time being. Added to that, John 'Rabbit' Bundrick, who had been brought in to provide keyboards, fell out of a taxi (or jumped out of it whilst it was moving to avoid paying the fare, depending on which version of the story you go by) and broke his wrist. Townshend's hearing was also worsening, and the control room at Ramport was very loud, leading him to have special headphones made to listen back to mixes at a lower volume.

Townshend and Daltrey hardly saw each other during sessions, the former preferring to record in the daytime and return home to his family, whilst the latter recorded in the evenings when his voice had warmed up. Townshend apparently told his brother-in-law and studio engineer, Jon Astley, to make sure Roger sang the melodies, suggesting that Pete was wary of Roger altering them. Comparing many demos over their career to the completed song, one has to say Daltrey was usually very faithful, but any small changes made were mostly for the better, although this may be down to the bias of familiarity with the released version.

Eventually, the band upped tools and moved recording to the newly opened RAK Studios, set up by Mickie Most. At one point, Glyn Johns brought in Dave Marquee to play second bass, the idea being that the band could play live, with John doing his usual lead bass style, Marquee simply holding down the bottom end. However, it didn't really work and the idea was scrapped, although Rod Argent, who was also brought in, did contribute keyboards and synth to the final album. Adding to the problems, an incident occurred during a playback of 'Sister Disco' when Glyn and Roger came to blows in the studio after disagreeing over a rough mix. Though the two patched things up, Johns' time on the record was nearing the end as they were now running over schedule and he had to start work on the album with Joan Armatrading, so Astley took over production for the rest of the recording.

Of course, 1977 would also prove to be the year that punk really took off. Back in 1975, Townshend had made his dissatisfaction clear in both the material written for *The Who By Numbers*, and in the press, expressing that he felt too old to be onstage and that he was deeply upset that The Who were, in his opinion, becoming a golden oldies band. Perhaps Pete could sense the coming of the punk movement, and in 1976 it began to emerge with bands like The Damned and the Sex Pistols. Of course, The Who might be seen as pretty much the first punk band, their anger, raw energy and visceral 'up-yours' to the establishment and older generations having been the template for many of the bands that would pick up the mantle of youth rebellion as part of punk. Townshend found himself in Soho one night, drowning his problems with copious amounts of alcohol, only to end up berating two members of the Sex Pistols, a band that were fans of The Who and would even cover 'Substitute'. This encounter and what followed that night would form the inspiration for the title track 'Who Are You'.

Overdubbing would continue into April and May 1978, these mainly being the drum tracks of Keith, who by this point had been given an ultimatum by Pete that he needed to sort himself out or leave the band. He had taken this on board by improving his playing sufficiently to lay down nearly all his drum parts in a couple of weeks.

May was also the month where, on the 27th, the band convened at Shepperton Studios to re-film three tracks for Jeff Stein's *The Kids Are Alright* film. The band wore the same outfits from Kilburn the previous year, so that if needed, some shots could be inserted from that show, all except Keith, who noticeably changed clothes. The three songs to be performed were 'Baba O'Riley', 'Won't Get Fooled Again' (both included in the film) and 'My Wife', but the band ended up playing a longer set to a specially invited audience made of up of some of the new punk and new wave bands, including members of the Sex Pistols, The Pretenders and Generation X. Although Entwistle's playing again scaled new heights, and Townshend was at his animated best, Moon struggled to hold things together, gamely powering through the songs but a shadow of his former self, and apparently overdubs were made in the studio to get the drum parts to a more satisfactory level. This gig would be the last concert Moon would perform with The Who, as he was found dead on 7 September after overdosing on prescription medication.

After the Shepperton gig, the members of the audience were assembled and lined up on the lawn, each behind a member of The Who, for a shot intended to be the cover for *Who Are You*. Ultimately this was not used, and a photo session was arranged the following day, where equipment was set up, Keith ironically sitting on a chair reading 'not to be taken away'. He was only sitting down, to hide his large stomach. The idea for The Who's album covers was usually taken in turns by band members, and this time it was due to be Keith's idea, but apparently he never really came up with anything.

Johns and Astley would mix the album, first at Olympic, but unhappy with the sound, it was given a second attempt at CTS, which did the trick. During the remixing, Roger returned to the studio to record a clean version of a line from 'Who Are You', replacing the word 'fuck' with the word 'hell', thus giving the single a chance on the radio.

One track titled 'Choirboy' was tried but left off the final record. This would turn into the song 'Empty Glass', which would end up as the title track for Pete's solo album, though a version of the song recorded for *Who Are You* was released as a bonus track on the 1996 reissue.

As an album, *Who Are You* might have been only three years since its predecessor, but it seemed vastly different, the back-to-basics style of *The Who By Numbers* perhaps inflating this contrast more than if the band had simply gone from *Quadrophenia* to *Who Are You*. For while *The Who By Numbers* threw away the synthesizers, this album piled them back on, and in a less rock-like way than ever before, moving towards the electronic feel of the 1980s.

Pete would tell *NME* that a lot of the songs on the album had been inspired by his *Lifehouse* story, which he had hoped to resurrect instead of making an album that year. Certainly, 'Music Must Change' has a link to it, while even 'Who Are You' and 'Sister Disco' would be included in his *Lifehouse Chronicles* boxset released in 2000. '905' was also said to be a track John had offered for inclusion towards a resurrected *Lifehouse* project.

Who Are You is in a way the last hurrah for the old Who, and of course with Keith's death shortly after the release, no Who album was ever going to be the same again. But this is the first Who record to fall short of the high standards they had set, with only a handful of tracks really hitting the mark in the way the band had previously managed. That's not to say it's a bad album; there are definite highlights, but also some unfocussed tracks that were beginning to lead away from what the band did best, as Townshend's writing began to change. An upside of this, which would continue on the next two Who albums, would be the elevation as a writer of John Entwistle, whose contributions would keep the band connected to their rockier roots and balance some of Townshend's more experimental and 1980s pop-influenced songs. On *Who Are You*, John gets an unusual three songs (his most since *The Who Sell Out*), and while 'Had Enough' is fairly throwaway, his other two contributions, 'Trick Of The Light' and the futuristic '905', are definite highlights. Curiously, Townshend doesn't sing lead vocals on any song, the first album since *A Quick One* where this was the case.

The album fared well with the public, reaching number six in the UK and a joint record high for the band in America of number two.

TRACK BY TRACK

1. 'NEW SONG'

Written by Pete Townshend
Produced by Glyn Johns/Jon Astley
Recorded at Ramport Studios, London, 24 and 27 October 1977

A brisk and upbeat album opener, 'New Song' immediately announces that The Who have a new sound, though in a way it's not too far removed from the steady stride of *Quadrophenia*'s 'Bell Boy' with its tempo and prominent synth. However, this is a more modern Who, reaching for the sonic textures of the approaching 1980s. The slight 'Bell Boy' feel is ironic (or perhaps intentional), considering what the song is about, with Townshend admitting to now writing the same songs with different lines and being wary of plagiarism. Of course, as diverse a writer as Pete was, he had often relied on using the same type of riffs to build his songs, something which he was now coming clean with on the opening song of The Who's new album. This is Townshend laying bare every writer's main problem – how do you keep doing it year after year? How do you remain fresh and avoid repeating yourself without totally alienating your core audience? The song's lyrics also poke fun at Pete's receding hair line, a leftover from the midlife crisis themes of the previous album.

Townshend's guitar sound is modern and processed, a million miles away from his country Gretsch tones that had been a mainstay of his 1970s studio sound, but overall the track is dominated by several synth parts. The song also features a rather funky section which pretty much forms a chorus, featuring Entwistle introducing some influences from the then-popular disco, with climbing and falling octaves. 'New Song', which also features added backing vocals from Andy Fairweather Low (ex-Amen Corner) and Billy Nicholls, is a decent album opener, which edges away from rock and towards pop but still manages to find a tolerable balance. Not by any means one of The Who's best songs, it is still an album highlight for many fans.

2. 'HAD ENOUGH'

Written by John Entwistle
Produced by Glyn Johns/Jon Astley
Recorded at Olympic and Ramport Studios, London, September and December 1977

Not to be confused with the similarly titled 'I've Had Enough' from *Quadrophenia*, 'Had Enough' is the first of three Entwistle tracks on the record, and also the weakest. By this point, John had realized he stood more chance of getting his songs onto Who albums if he wrote them with Roger in mind and allowed him to sing them. This approach seemed to work, although Roger would admit over the years to not being particularly fond of John's songs. 'Had Enough' opens with heavy synth work that bears quite a resemblance to Van Halen's 'Jump', which would be released more than five years later, and soon breaks into an ominous and steady pace. The chorus features multiple layered harmonies for a rather soft contrast to the toughness of the verse melody, while lyrically, the song dispenses with John's usual black humour in favour of something more standard, with Daltrey singing doom and gloom feelings for the future of the world and life in general. Daltrey sings the words with conviction, but there's nothing that quite authentically hits home. It thus comes off as a bit of a 'written by numbers' track, something that you could easily imagine in a 1980s film soundtrack but not one that really captures the imagination.

Interestingly, the song includes a string arrangement composed by Pete's father-in-law, Ted Astley, and recorded at Ramport Studios, which does add a unique flavour to an otherwise standard song. Billy and Michael Nicholls also add their vocals to the surprizingly mellow and sweet sections featuring layered harmonies, while the synthesizer is played by Rod Argent.

3. '905'

Written by John Entwistle
Produced by Glyn Johns/Jon Astley
Recorded at RAK and Ramport Studios, London, March 1978

For the first time, a Who album sequences two John Entwistle songs back-to-back, and while 'Had Enough' is nothing to write home about, '905' is one of the best songs on the album, as well as being one of Entwistle's finest contributions to the Who's discography. Furthermore, after the first two songs, The Who at last sound like the group we're used to. Keith's drum groove is steady and minimalist, but his fills have his usual character and energy, complete with screaming, most noticeably just before the middle eight. Townshend provides acoustic rhythm guitar, and his saturated lead is understated but almost certainly his familiar Gretsch setup. The track starts with a gurgling synth part programmed by Entwistle on one of the first multiphonic Polymoogs, at John's home studio in Ealing. Unlike the opening two songs, this synth sound is dirtier and more raw, sounding much closer to a song like 'Relay' than 1980s electronic sounds. This synth forms an underlying base for the track but is never overwhelming, so feels much closer to the early 1970s Who than much of the rest of the album. After the intro, the acoustic guitar and John's vocal enter, being joined halfway through the verse by bass and drums. In the second verse, for some reason the 1996 reissue of this song cuts off the first word, the 'In' of 'In suspended animation', perhaps something to do with damage to the multi-tracks.

Entwistle intended '905' for a proposed rock opera about cloning which he eventually dropped, feeling it was perhaps too similar to the book *Brave New World*. Apparently, the song had been written in the early Seventies, perhaps as early as 1971, and according to Pete, John had offered it up as a potential inclusion in the *Lifehouse* project which Townshend hadn't fully given up on. It's quite strange that John would have kept a song of this quality for so many years, but thankfully he did because it's just what *Who Are You* needs.

4. 'SISTER DISCO'

Written by Pete Townshend
Produced by Glyn Johns/Jon Astley
Recorded at Ramport Studios and Goring Studios, London, October 1977

Another synth-heavy song, 'Sister Disco' manages to retain enough of the old Who power-chord energy to keep it from slipping into pop fodder. Its main sections are fairly standard, but the two different middle eight parts offer more musically clever diversions which lift the song above the usual rock fare. The song starts with the familiar A, G and D chord patterns, with the synth playing a weaving line over the top, before adopting a more complex pattern when the whole band comes in. It's the prominence of the synth in the mix that really sets this apart from the Who of the early 1970s, and it overpowers the song a touch, especially compared to a live in the studio rehearsal version in 1979 with future Who drummer Kenney Jones from the Small Faces/Faces, featured on the *30 Years Of Maximum R&B* video, where the song sounds much tougher. Something that is thankfully high in the mix is John's bass, especially at the end of each section of chorus, where his quickfire playing, making using of open strings and fretted notes, makes the song burst with life. The first middle eight moves into the baroque with Townshend taking lead vocals, and John playing melodic bass, including a diminished scale run to bring out the underlying chord that leads back to the beginning of the sequence. A short musical interlude that employs Townshend's pedal tone technique, similar to the intro of 'Dreaming From The Waist', follows, and then a second middle eight, this time sung by Daltrey. Here, we move to a clever chord sequence starting in C minor and featuring prominent use of suspended chords. The synth is hugely reminiscent of the composer Henry Purcell, who was a huge influence on Townshend with the use of suspensions in his work. In fact, the synth arrangement bears similarity with some of Wendy Carlos' recordings, notably the arrangement of 'Music For The Funeral Of Queen Mary', which was featured in the 1971 film *A Clockwork Orange*. This chord sequence moves from C minor to G suspended fourth and then G. The G then becomes minor, and the sequence repeats a fourth down, and then again a fourth below that, before finally moving to a diminished chord and ending up on E suspended fourth to E. Before the verse comes back in, we have a typical Townshend power chord riff, much like 'Won't Get Fooled Again', slightly hidden by the complex synth line. After the final chorus, we're left with Pete's solo acoustic guitar, playing bluesy chords and embellishments, which is a nice coda on which to end the track.

'Sister Disco' may divide fans, some feeling it's too lightweight or poppy to stand up beside their best work. While it is true that it doesn't really reach the heights of their upper echelon of material, it is a well-written and arranged song that would have perhaps benefited from slightly less busy and loudly mixed synthesizers.

The lyrics have a throwback to *Tommy* with the 'Black plastic, deaf, dumb and blind' line, but also musically we get a lot of Who trademarks in the power chords, baroque suspensions and use of pedal tones.

The song would be played live in concert regularly with Kenney Jones, and even make it back into the set in the late 2000s, despite Pete once describing it, in an interview as part of the *30 Years Of Maximum R&B* video, as the song he most hated playing live. This he attributed to the end section, which in concert would see him and Daltrey singing extra lines in harmony. During this, Roger would stand by Pete, and to paraphrase Townshend, give him a soppy grin to indicate some sort of Everly Brothers-type relationship they didn't in fact have. This act, in which Townshend felt he was expected to collude, would wind him up and prompt his scorn, his exact words on his feelings towards Roger being best left out of print!

5. 'MUSIC MUST CHANGE'

Written by Pete Townshend
Produced by Glyn Johns/Jon Astley
Recorded at Goring Studios, London, with overdubs at Ramport Studios, London, April 1978

Much of 'Music Must Change' is in fact Townshend's demo, with overdubs by Roger and John. The song features no actual drums because of Keith's difficulty dealing with the 6/8 time signature. Though he had played in 6/8 before, such as on 'Love Reign O'er Me', his failing health during this point was perhaps a crucial factor in his inability to nail the song's feel. Keith famously would comment something along the lines of, 'I know this is shit ... but I'm still the best Keith Moon-type drummer in the world!' Of course, who could argue with that? But in the absence of Moon's drumming, Pete took a novel approach, not recording drums himself (which he would have been highly capable of) but making a rhythm track out of noises, mainly the sound of his footsteps and squeaky shoes, as well as a milk bottle being rolled across the ground. Pete also plays some lovely clean jazzy guitar figures throughout, though on the 1996 remix there are some differences in the parts used. The differences seem to occur just after the middle eight, starting at around the 3.23 mark, where a neat little fill from Townshend is completely different on the remix. The liner notes on the remix mention the different guitar takes used but don't explain why, so the best guess would be either a damaged or missing multi-track or simply a preference for the take used. With no drums, the track has plenty of room to breathe, and we get brass from John as well as synth and organ to fill out the arrangement. The song has a wonderfully dramatic tension, almost music theatre in its dynamics, but it does feel a bit odd without any drums. However, the song would be played live in 1979 with Kenney Jones being allowed to put his own stamp on it. According to Daltrey, the song was also being rehearsed in 2002 for the band's American tour, but following the death of Entwistle on the eve of the first gig, it was dropped. Daltrey stated he would never play it again, alluding to it being unlucky, having also been recorded shortly before Keith Moon's untimely death. Thematically, 'Music Must Change' goes quite nicely with 'New Song', showing Townshend once again questioning his place as an artist and wondering whether rock was at a crossroads or the end of the track.

6. 'TRICK OF THE LIGHT'

Written by John Entwistle
Produced by Glyn Johns/Jon Astley
Recorded at RAK Studios, London, 12 and 13 March 1978

Despite the synth-led pop rock of 'Had Enough', John could still be relied upon to produce something loud and aggressive to let you know that underneath any changing styles or efforts to move with the present music trends, The Who were still very much The Who. 'Trick Of The Light' is probably the heaviest track on *Who Are You*, largely thanks to its eight-string bass riff which runs through the track like an iron girder. The intro pummels this riff into the brain, as the eight-string bass is used as an overdubbed lead instrument while Entwistle plays far more conventional bass underneath. As on 'Had Enough', John gives the lead vocal to Daltrey, a job he handles with his usual gusto and power. The song also brings out the best in Keith, who in spite of his difficulties and lack of form early in the album sessions, doesn't display any deficiency in his ability or expression.

Lyrically, the song is typical of John, and its dark, wry subject matter of a man making love to and possibly dating a prostitute, and worrying about his own sexual performance, is a sharp take on male masculinity and ego. Fairly early on we get a solo section, played by Entwistle's eight-string bass. The solo is ironically much simpler than his regular basslines on many songs, but he knows exactly what will catch the ear. Though the guitar is not the leading instrument on the song, Townshend does offer up nice embellishments especially towards the end, where his country-style fills pop out of the speakers.

'Trick Of The Light' was performed live at a handful of shows in 1979, with the unusual arrangement of John on eight-string bass and Pete playing one of John's Alembic model six-string basses instead of guitar. These performances would see Daltrey taking lead vocals as he had on the record, but in 1989, when the song was performed extensively on tour, 'Trick Of The Light' would feature Entwistle on lead instead.

7. 'GUITAR AND PEN'

Written by Pete Townshend
Produced by Glyn Johns/Jon Astley
Recorded at Ramport Studios and RAK Studios, London, March 1978

Townshend once more deals with the ups and downs of the artist in this track tackling the frustrations of, but also desire and value in, writing. The lyrics urge us to never disregard creation, as maddening as it can be, mentioning playing songs to unappreciative mothers (possibly a reference to Townshend's own mother, for whom he wrote *The Who Sell Out*'s 'Sunrise', hoping to impress her), writer's block and unclean rhymes amongst other hurdles one must clear. Musically, it's quite an odd thing, the intro full of eerily shimmering synth and another example of Pete's clean electric, jazzy guitar. The verse starts off with Daltrey's pure vocals, bass, synth, piano and clean guitar before the dynamic shifts as the drums come in along with distorted rhythm guitar. Overall, the track comes across as fun and a little frivolous even, though the lyrics are more meaningful than the music suggests. Again, there is a touch of music theatre to it, Daltrey enjoying himself and going so far as to adopt a funny voice as the mum in the lyric who demands 'more of a tune'. Both Pete and Rod Argent play keyboards on this track.

8. 'LOVE IS COMING DOWN'

Written by Pete Townshend
Produced by Glyn Johns/Jon Astley
Recorded at Ramport Studios, London, 18 October 1977

Another song that displays a touch of music theatre is the melodramatic 'Love Is Coming Down', which immediately sets up a melancholy mood with its major seventh piano chord opening and Daltrey's chilling vocal. John's bass and the string part arranged by Ted Astley sweeten the music, evoking a 1970s romance film, while Keith's light and shade is perfect for the emotional sweep presented through its duration. A beautifully written and recorded song, 'Love Is Coming Down' must be one of the strangest and most un-Who-like songs the band ever recorded, yet it seems to showcase the strengths of the individual members, with powerful bass, drums and vocal performances. Only Pete is really missing as a guitarist, but possibly plays piano.

9. 'WHO ARE YOU'

Written by Pete Townshend
Produced by Glyn Johns/Jon Astley
Recorded at Ramport Studios, London, October 1977

The story behind the writing of 'Who Are You' has passed into legend, but to sum it up the inspiration was a particularly testing day for Townshend. In 1977, Townshend had found that an account containing a large amount of royalty money owed to him had been set up in his name. Businessman Allen Klein offered to get involved and resolve the matter, which led to an eleven-hour meeting involving Townshend, where he felt totally lost within the facts, figures and legal-speak. The result was Pete walking out with a hefty cheque, but he'd been forced to make a deal with Klein, something that irritated him greatly. He and Chris Stamp headed to Soho to the Speakeasy Club to watch Jon Otway, and once there Pete began drinking heavily. After becoming extremely drunk, he spotted Steve Jones and Paul Cook of the Sex Pistols and approached them, mistaking Cook for Johnny Rotten, and began ranting about the state of rock and roll and his place in it. According to Jones, he was going around shouting, 'Who are you?' and being negative about The Who's place in the music industry, prompting a worried Cook to ask, 'you're not breaking up are you? We really like the Who.' Townshend, not in the mood to be talked down, at one point became physically threatening to a photographer who tried to snap him and the two Pistols together. He was awoken in the early hours of the following morning by a policeman who found him lying in a Soho doorway, telling Townshend that he recognized him, and he would be allowed to go home if he was able to get up and walk away. Though the events of that night inform some of the lyrics of the song, the music for 'Who Are You' in fact started earlier, a very basic version appearing in a jam during Keith's last ever full show to a paying crowd at Toronto's Maple Leaf Gardens in October 1976, although it bears only a passing resemblance to the finished article.

The song begins with Pete's synthesized guitar, displaying a very much more rock-like sound than the opening 'Guitar And Pen', and his fuzzy lead lines. The song breaks into the chorus with Keith's tight hi-hat work, a typical Townshend guitar riff and layered harmony vocals, helped out by Andy Fairweather Low. A notable part of the track is the shift between standard time in the chorus and half-time in the verse, Daltrey's voice coming in on the first verse in startling fashion. In the second verse, piano adds to the arrangement, while Keith ups the ante on his pounding fills, still managing to find enough of his old drumming prowess to raise the song's energy levels, and of course his screaming is detectable at times. The breakdown after the second chorus features a tasty acoustic guitar solo from Pete, the strings sounding metallic and new, before the synth signals a classic Who power chord riff. This section is brief, leading back to another soft interlude filled with mellow backing vocals, an interesting piano line and Keith's orchestral tom playing. Another pounding riff then comes in and takes us back to the intro/chorus section to begin again.

'Who Are You' is in many ways the last great Who rock song. Though the next two albums would contain some worthy tracks, and even their last two albums have great moments, 'Who Are You' is a Who classic, played at almost every concert since its recording, the last of their huge rock anthems. This would be further cemented when it became the theme of the TV show *CSI: Crime Scene Investigators* in 2000, introducing it to a whole new generation of fans, the first of an eventual four Who songs to feature in the opening credits of series in the *CSI* franchise.

It was released as a single in July 1978, reaching number eighteen in the UK and fourteen in the US.

A version of this from Kilburn in 1977 is the only filmed live version with Keith Moon, and is available on DVD.

Chapter 10

Face Dances (1981)

Produced by Bill Szymczyk
Released in the UK on 6 March 1981 as Polydor 2302 106 (WHOD 5073)
Released in the USA on 6 March 1981 as Warner Bros WN HS 3516
Chart position – UK = 2, USA = 4
Recorded at Odyssey Studios in London, July–December 1980
Pete Townshend – Guitars, Vocals and Keyboards
Roger Daltrey – Vocals
John Entwistle – Bass and Vocals
Kenney Jones – Drums
John 'Rabbit' Bundrick – Keyboards

Following Keith Moon's death in 1978, Pete Townshend did a very odd thing. For some time, the Who's leader, guitarist and chief songwriter had been growing unhappy with the band. He felt the weight of expectation from the rest of the group to maintain the endless album/touring cycle and longed instead to work on solo albums in the way Daltrey and Entwistle had been doing throughout the 1970s. In 1977, he had put out a joint album with ex-Small Faces and Faces member Ronnie Lane, one that had allowed him to work free of the shackles of everything that came with a Who record. Touring, though, seemed the biggest bugbear, and in this respect, Townshend was done and had vetoed the idea of going on the road for the whole of 1977 and 1978. So it was incredibly surprising that in the wake of Moon's death, he became keen to tour as soon as possible. After all, here was the perfect reason to put the band to bed and focus on his solo career, but by his own reckoning, affected by grief, he decided the band must get another drummer and return to the stage as soon as possible. The drummer in question was Kenney Jones, formerly of the Small Faces and Faces, and while much has been said about his suitability for The Who – or rather his lack of it – particularity from Roger Daltrey himself, it's safe to say that Pete wasn't really looking to continue the group in the same vein as before. The Who were always an unconventional band, but by 1978, Pete seemed to have become tired with their dynamic. Entwistle and Moon were arguably the best rhythm section in rock, but they also sometimes left little room for Pete to do much more than keep rhythm. Of course, the notion that Pete was almost solely a rhythm guitarist is far from the mark, and the Who's live jamming featured much lead work from him, but the band was a train that threatened to derail at any moment, which was part of their excitement. However, one feels Townshend was almost longing for something a bit more conventional, something that didn't require the amount of sheer concentration to keep the whole thing together. Thus, given the chance to hire a new drummer, it's not surprising he didn't opt for anyone who was going to attempt to replicate what Keith did – this was a chance to reinvent the band both live and in the studio. Considering Pete's unhappiness with The Who in recent years, having stated they were pretending to be what they used to be, and that the set lists had become stale and repetitive, it actually makes a lot of sense that the shakeup in the band, albeit by the most tragic of circumstances, had reinvigorated Pete and his desire for their future. Kenney was a friend, an excellent drummer and one who was more conventional than Moon, whilst still possessing expression, and thus was in Pete's mind the perfect choice. Kenney was even made a full member of the band with a one-quarter equal share, something that Daltrey was not in favour of but was outvoted on. However, despite any misgivings, Roger would go on to state to the press that they were still The Who, and in typical diplomatic fashion threaten to break the legs of any journalist that suggested otherwise.

The band returned to the stage in 1979, playing the most daring sets they had in years. The shows were long, with a hugely overhauled set that included rarely played songs. This was a huge departure from their last tour, where by and large the same song choices had been presented on most nights. They played several key shows, including one at the Rainbow Theatre, another at Hammersmith which raised money for the people of Kampuchea and a massive show at London's Wembley Stadium, supported by AC/DC, The Stranglers and Nils Lofgren. Even by Roger's admission, Kenney played brilliantly on these shows, and they were generally well received. During these gigs, Townshend would embark on more and more improvisations, often vocally ad-libbing and coming up with riffs which would lead to writing new songs. However, tragedy struck in Cincinnati, where eleven fans were killed in a crush before the show. Meanwhile, 1979 would also see the release of both the *Quadrophenia* movie and *The Kids Are Alright*, which would serve as an epitaph for the sadly departed Keith Moon, in a way the film perfectly ending that chapter of the band's career.

Pete began recording his solo album *Empty Glass* in November 1979. It was clear that his songwriting was changing, becoming more influenced by current music, but Daltrey would later feel that Townshend had saved most of his best tracks for his solo career, and that several songs on *Empty Glass* would have been perfect for The Who. Back in 1975, Pete had complained that he always ended up offering all his material to the band, with them selecting his best work. Now, four years later, it seemed he was finally making sure he didn't leave himself in this situation again. *Empty Glass* would be a strong solo album, but it still left a Who album to record. Indeed, Pete found himself in the situation of having to fulfil album contracts for both The Who and as a solo artist, putting him under strain to write enough material. In all, he was contracted to release three solo albums in five years, as well as another four Who albums over the next seven years. Seven albums in seven years was a fairly mammoth task, even for the prolific Townshend.

When it came to record the new Who album, Townshend's material would be vastly different to previous releases, and *Face Dances* was in some ways a completely different band. In the wake of Keith's death, Townshend had slipped back into drug use and become estranged from his wife, Karen. He spent much of the time away from home, living instead in an apartment in the King's Road, Chelsea. His social life changed, now frequently hanging out in nightclubs and making new friends, both in London and America. Out of this new nightlife came some of the inspiration in the songs, revealing a slightly seedy underbelly to the cities.

The band would record with a new producer, Bill Szymczyk, at Odyssey Studios in London between July and December 1980. Bill, who had much success producing Joe Walsh and The Eagles, worked methodically, going through three takes of each song and splicing together the best parts. He would describe the album as the hardest he ever made, blaming drug and alcohol issues within the band, as well as inner band acrimony, compounded by the fact it was the only record he would produce outside of the States. One point of contention was the fact that Szymczyk wanted Entwistle to sound like a bassist, and he and John would disagree over the bass sound, with Bill telling John that the band already had a guitarist, missing one of the key and most unique aspects of The Who. Like the band's previous album, Townshend would not sing lead vocals on any track, despite taking the mic on a couple of album outtakes, these being 'Somebody Saved Me', which he would later release as a solo track, and 'I Like Nightmares'. These songs, along with the discarded 'It's In You' and 'Dance It Away', would have been fine additions to the album. They have since been released as bonus tracks on either the 1997 remix or the 2021 two-LP Record Store Day release.

For the album cover, the band turned to Peter Blake, who chose fifteen other artists to join him in each painting 6 inch by 6 inch portraits of the band members. These paintings would be sent back to him and assembled into the final artwork. The artists painting the four members of the band were, all from left to right: Pete – Bill Jacklin, Tom Phillips, Colin Self of Norwich and Richard Hamilton; Roger – Mike Andrews, Allen Jones, David Inshaw and David Hockney; John – Clive Barker, R.B. Kitaj, Howard Hodgkin and Patrick Caulfield; and Kenney – Peter Blake, Joe Tilson, Patrick Procktor and David Tindle.

In the aftermath of the release, Roger blamed Kenney for a lack of fire in the album, saying he loved all the songs and imagined they would have been improved with a better drummer. According to Pete, Kenney blamed the songs, suggesting that Pete had used his best material on *Empty Glass*. For his part, John was unhappy with Bill's production, while Townshend himself blamed the songs not being right for the band and the fact that they were not a tight unit. As for Roger's frustrations with Kenney's drumming, on some of the songs it's hard to even imagine how Keith could have played them if he had still been alive. Meanwhile, many people, including myself, would argue that Pete did in fact release a lot of his better songs on his solo album. The reasoning for the latter might have been simply that he needed his very best material to make a genuine stab at being a successful solo artist, whereas with The Who, the name, their sheer ability as a band, plus the writing contributions of John Entwistle would help share the weight of expectation. Other comments from Townshend suggest that a lot of the songs on *Empty Glass* had actually been offered up and rejected. In the case of 'Empty Glass' itself, indeed the song had been recorded with The Who for *Who Are You*, but for reasons unknown, never made the final cut.

Trouser Press editor Ira Robbins, usually a Who fan, described *Face Dances* as pleasant and meaningless, while *Rolling Stone* said the album neither triumphed nor failed, but questioned whether The Who still had a reason to exist. Nevertheless, the album charted well, reaching number two in the UK and number four in America.

TRACK BY TRACK

1. 'YOU BETTER YOU BET'

Written by Pete Townshend
Produced by Bill Szymczyk
Recorded at Odyssey Studios, London, November 1980

Written for Jackie Vickers (the daughter of Mike Vickers of Manfred Mann), with whom Pete had developed a brief romance, 'You Better You Bet' was the Who's last hit single and another song that divides opinion amongst a Who crowd; some find the song an absolute highlight and others view it as overly poppy, an example of exactly the sort of music that signalled the demise of the band. Musically, it's a bright and breezy song, undeniably catchy and light in approach. It's also a lot more complex than one might imagine, hiding some interesting chord changes within its pop parameters. Opening with a slightly ominous piano chord and a popping synth sound, it's soon joined by twelve-string guitar, more synth and harmony vocals singing the chorus line. The band kicks in, with Daltrey clearly enjoying himself and the backing vocals nicely supporting him. It's a standard I–IV–V in C until the pre-chorus, which throws in an unexpected G minor and a series of nice inversions. The first verse also manages to mention the group's own *Who's Next* album as well as the band T. Rex, a nice nod which doesn't feel too forced. As poppy as it may be, the chorus is hard to resist, the call-and-response vocals and the shift back to standard time after the half-time of the pre-chorus working well. The chorus slows back into half-time in its latter portion, and the middle eight keeps this feel, pushing the song a semi-tone up from G to G sharp, for a slightly unsettling feel. After this we get another section that changes the dynamics yet again, and a clean, chorus-laden guitar solo that feels reminiscent of a band like The Pretenders. Towards the end of the song, we have a drop-out that leaves just synth and vocals, priming us for the leap back into a full band chorus and then a trademark Who key change up a tone to D.

Though it may be corny to some and doesn't rock in the way The Who's best songs do, it feels churlish to criticize what is a well-written, catchy and energetic song. Added to that, this wasn't a cynical attempt to secure a hit, but an effort by Pete to write a genuinely good love song, and while it's certainly not in my list of songs to hear live, it's hard to argue with its success as a general audience crowd-pleaser. Because of these reasons, 'You Better You Bet' is one of those songs that may make you groan at first but might have you tapping your toes and nodding your head minutes later. The song was released as a single ahead of the album on 27 February 1981, reaching number nine in the charts, even prompting a return to *Top Of The Pops*, eight years after their performance of '5.15' had earned them a BBC ban.

2. 'DON'T LET GO THE COAT'

Written by Pete Townshend
Produced by Bill Szymczyk
Recorded at Odyssey Studios, London, 1980

One of the most poppy tracks on *Face Dances*, 'Don't Let Go The Coat' is inspired by a saying of Meher Baba – 'Hold fast to the hem of my robe'.

Townshend explained that the song talks about things that change but also the importance of hanging onto the things that are important, such as love, affection, spirituality or whatever one is into. The song is simple and catchy enough but feels lacking in anything exciting or really moving, although it does contain a lovely acoustic guitar solo, helping to break up the slightly clinical feel of the song and injecting a more organic touch. Daltrey remains in low register until the very end, where he rises higher in range, but the track is rather mellow with its clean guitars played with the use of a chorus effect, shimmering keyboards and smooth backing vocals.

'Don't Let Go The Coat' was a perhaps surprise addition to the live set on their 1981 shows, but didn't last beyond the year.

In 2021, a special two-LP version of *Face Dances* was released for Record Store Day, containing a previously unreleased version of this song with Pete on lead vocals.

3. 'CACHE CACHE'

Written by Pete Townshend
Produced by Bill Szymczyk
Recorded at Odyssey Studios, London, 1980

Townshend explained that while in Switzerland, he decided he was going to give up music forever and grabbed his wallet, passport and bottle of brandy and went to Berne, famous for its brown bears and caves up in the hills. Pete then spent more than half the day walking around, sleeping under trees and, in his words, living like a tramp. Highly drunk, he decided to visit the bears and found himself in a bear pit, although according to Townshend, there were no bears there that time of the year, even though it still stank to high heaven. Townshend wrote the song to be a statement about throwing caution to the wind and acting upon mad impulse, coming up with a whole host of other reckless situations.

The song starts with a semi-punky three-chord riff, which turns into the verse, Daltrey doing his best to sing the unusual lyrics with his customary toughness, over the top of the blokey 'Ooooh Ooh Ooh' backing vocals. Entwistle seems to have a good time with the cool ascending bass runs at the end of each verse that lead to a contrasting melodic chorus, where the song loses its punky nature and becomes more of a pop ballad. The middle eight injects more adrenaline into the song, with Entwistle again providing speedy bass runs, the band overall sounding a bit closer to their usual fire and passion. Before the final verse, the song again picks up a bit, with Pete playing a guitar solo of sorts with a sound that is typical of late 1970s new wave/punk bands – clean but lively. 'Cache Cache' is a bit of a jumble of a song, feeling not quite fully formed and slightly confused, the type of track that may well have worked better as a solo Townshend effort.

4. 'THE QUIET ONE'

Written by John Entwistle
Produced by Bill Szymczyk
Recorded at Odyssey Studios, London, 1980

As Townshend's writing was increasingly steering the band away from the hard-edged rock they had become well known for, you could rely on John Entwistle to prevent them from straying too far, and 'The Quiet One' certainly packs more of a punch than most songs on the album. Showcasing Kenney Jones' energetic ability, quite different from Keith Moon's, but strong and dynamic nonetheless, the song began life as a jam between Entwistle and Jones. John was seeking to write something that could replace 'Boris The Spider' and 'My Wife' in concert, having become bored with singing both, and this would do the job nicely. It is a somewhat autobiographical song, as John was in effect the quiet one in the band – not musically, of course, as he was a loud and unmissable presence on record and on the stage, but as a person, John was notoriously taciturn.

The song begins with a bang with Kenney's pounding drums and ride cymbal work, plus Pete's accented chord stabs. John's scratchy and trebly, double-tracked vocals cut through the mix nicely, while the whole track also brings out the best in Pete, who seems to relish the chance to let rip on distorted guitars, playing nice lead lines and some nifty rhythm work. The song is essentially a rocker rooted in E, but the change in the chorus, up a semitone to F, lifts the songs into more melodic territory and brightens the mood.

Live, the song would fulfil its intended purpose and allow John to semi-retire 'Boris The Spider' and 'My Wife', playing 'The Quiet One' as his vocal showpiece throughout 1981 and 1982, occasionally also playing 'Boris…'.

5. 'DID YOU STEAL MY MONEY'

Written by Pete Townshend
Produced by Bill Szymczyk
Recorded at Odyssey Studios, London, 1980

This song stems from an incident on the band's US tour in 1980, where Pete was given an envelope with $50,000 from merchandise stalls at venues, but had it stolen by a model he met. Pete would be elusive about exactly what had happened for many years, stating that the story didn't make anyone look good, before revealing the truth in his autobiography *Who I Am* in 2012.

'Did You Steal My Money' has a slow groove and a two-part backing vocal throughout the verse, hard-panned left and right, which actually becomes a little distracting, especially on headphones, where it overpowers the lead vocal a little, and then leaves abruptly in the chorus. Roger's voice is plaintive rather than having his usual rock roughness, showing more of a tender side from him, while Pete provides the harmonized middle eight. 'Did You Steal My Money' also alludes to Townshend's drug and alcohol addiction in its lyrics, perhaps some of his most revealing yet, mentioning 'cold turkeying' on a sofa. Although in no way the sort of rocker The Who were known for, 'Did You Steal My Money' sets up a nice groove and manages to stay away from sounding too poppy or slipping into a 1980s cliché sound, and thus ends up less dated than some other tracks on the album.

6. 'HOW CAN YOU DO IT ALONE'

Written by Pete Townshend
Produced by Bill Szymczyk
Recorded at Odyssey Studios, London, 1980.

'How Can You Do It Alone' stemmed from a real-life incident where Townshend encountered a flasher in London. Walking up Holland Park Road one night, Townshend stopped a random man in a trench coat and asked him for a light for his cigarette. The stranger reached into his coat to get one, but to Townshend's surprise, he saw that the man was naked underneath. Realizing that he was probably a flasher who had just come off the train, Pete noted the shame in his face but said nothing, only afterwards wondering to himself, how could that bloke do it? How did he get his kicks from something Townshend described as more alone than masturbation?

Opening with a dark melodramatic chord run down, 'How Do You Do It Alone' quickly turns into a cool bouncy rhythm, the keyboards adding to its cheeky swagger and Entwistle playing some slick, metallic-sounding bass embellishments. The chorus changes to the anguished drama of the intro as light is suddenly shed on the dark inner horror. It's a startling and effective musical change, with Daltrey's voice rising in register and changing in tone.

Throughout the song, Daltrey sings with a wry smile in his voice, and although Townshend noted in his demos compilation album *Scoop 3* that he liked what Roger did with it, he also commented it might have needed his own acidic tone to fully work.

Several times in 1979, the band played a song in concert noted as having the same name, although musically totally different and sung by Pete, a version performed in Chicago featuring as a bonus track on the 1990s reissue. In early 1981 at St Austell in Cornwall, the band would play the song in a version that was again different from the album, with Pete singing much of the lyrics from the first verse and Roger joining to sing some of the chorus, but musically still closer to the 1979 take, and again mainly a free-form jam. Daltrey eventually would sing the second verse with the melody of the recorded version before the rest of the band steered the song into the studio version, indicating that Townshend was probably just jamming and borrowing some of the words, with the rest of the band trying to keep up.

7. 'DAILY RECORDS'

Written by Pete Townshend
Produced by Bill Szymczyk
Recorded at Odyssey Studios, London, 1980

'Daily Records' is a very upbeat-sounding song, another that one feels probably would have worked better as a Pete Townshend track. The lyrics, however, appear to find Townshend once again struggling with his place in life, noting that with the changing styles, he doesn't know how to wear his hair anymore, this sentiment reading like Jimmy from *Quadrophenia* facing the same dilemmas of fitting in with a scene, now in approaching middle age. Other issues are that his newfound sex and drugs lifestyle weren't doing anything for his home life, and a particular consideration was being a good father to his two daughters. During all of this, Townshend resolutely wished to simply make records. As the lyrics attest, though, he finds the problem is in his job as a performer, calling the trouble a stage, in this case the concert stage.

The music is full of jangly guitars in the verse and becomes slightly more driving and hard-edged in the pre-chorus and chorus. Once again, Townshend provides harmonized vocals as a counterpoint to Roger's more full-throated singing, and he also plays a quite joyful twelve-string guitar solo which gives the song another shot of life. Towards the end we get duelling guitars panned left and right, which add more colour to a fairly sweet and pretty Who song.

8. 'YOU'

Written by John Entwistle
Produced by Bill Szymczyk
Recorded at Odyssey Studios, London, 1980

Entwistle again brings a hard-rocking feel to the album, with this track sung by Daltrey. After the quick-fire power chord riff opening, which is almost classic Townshend, we get into the main groove that runs through the verse, containing some nice double stop bends from Pete's overdriven, delay-laden guitar. John's ominous low end bass riffing during the verse almost has a 'Peter Gunn Theme' feel to it, whilst Roger adds the necessary grit and cold disdain to the vocals. In the pre-chorus, the song raises the energy as John's bass starts to glide around in a more fluid fashion, before the actual chorus, which changes from the minor of the verse to major for a sweeter and more melodic feel. Through the course of the song, Pete displays some of his more familiar crunchy guitar work, which undoubtedly John was pleased with, even though Townshend himself would blame the recording of John's songs for further hearing problems.

Lyrically, there isn't much here of John's normal clever black humour, and though the song is welcome just for its rock edge and the quite enjoyable bass-led groove, it is still a fairly throwaway track which would have been unlikely to be included on any classic Who album.

9. 'ANOTHER TRICKY DAY'

Written by Pete Townshend
Produced by Bill Szymczyk
Recorded at Odyssey Studios, London, 1980

Probably the most Who-sounding and overall best track on the entire album, 'Another Tricky Day' has the trademark 'yaggerdang' guitar flourishes from Townshend, whilst also managing to not sound like a complete rehash of 1970s Who. Each member finds themselves doing what they do best, and they knit together so well that you feel optimistic about this new line-up. Bopping along with a great rhythm, the song starts with a striking electric guitar power chord, underneath which we get the acoustic playing a classic A, G, D guitar riff, transposed up three semitones with a capo to C, B flat and F. John's bass nicely highlights the change to B flat with a slide to it in an upper octave, while subtle synth and piano pad out the mix. Roger and Pete sing the melodic verse in harmony, and as we get to the pre-chorus they switch to a 'call and answer' part. The chorus switches keys, moving up a fourth, with Entwistle's bass becoming busier, whilst Townshend's guitar chord part also becomes more involved. For the middle eight, the band strips things back, Entwistle's clanging bass playing single notes and the mood becoming more dour as Townshend's chords become darker.

'Another Tricky Day' addresses the troubles that Pete and probably everyone goes through at times, chalking it up to a tricky day, but offering some sort of hope in its defiant upbeat rock, and this is where The Who were often at their best, dealing with universal dilemmas and problems but with an uplifting musical sense rather than a downbeat one.

'Another Tricky Day' was played live in 1981, before being revived by the band in 2002 and 2004. It would again be brought back to the band's set in 2022.

Chapter 11

It's Hard (1982)

Produced by Glyn Johns
Released in the UK on 4 September 1982 as Polydor WHOD 5066
Released in the USA on 4 September 1982 as Warner Bros WB 23731
Chart position – UK = 11, USA = 8
Recorded at Turn Up-Down Studios, Surrey, June 1982
Pete Townshend – Guitars, Vocals, Keyboards and Synthesizer
Roger Daltrey – Vocals
John Entwistle – Bass, Vocals, Brass and Synthesizer
Kenney Jones – Drums
Andy Fairweather Low – Rhythm Guitar on track 2
Tim Gorman – Synthesizers on tracks 5, 8 & 9, Electric Piano on track 6, and Organ on track 5

After the release of *Face Dances*, Townshend continued to further spiral into alcohol and drug abuse, one night overdosing on heroin in the presence of Thin Lizzy singer and bassist Phil Lynott and having to be resuscitated. Townshend became addicted to smoking the drug as well as getting hooked on Ativan, but was touched when his wife asked him to return to staying at the family home despite this. Given strength and resolve, Townshend decided to turn his life around and in early 1982 he came off heroin with the N.E.T. system pioneered by Meg Patterson.

After recording and releasing his solo album *All The Best Cowboys Have Chinese Eyes*, Pete's attention turned back to The Who, who had been rehearsing without him, with Andy Fairweather Low filling in on guitar. Whether the band were just keen to play together whilst Pete was otherwise occupied, or they felt unhappy with the material on *Face Dances* and decided to be more proactive in songwriting, is up for discussion.

In June 1982, they began working at Turn Up-Down Studios, Glyn Johns' home studio in Surrey. According to Townshend, he only had two songs to bring to the table at the time and felt like the band would have made a record with or without him. Pete would also talk in the press about seeing the end of The Who coming after this album, but intriguingly stating that he felt they were working on the album because they enjoyed each other's company, although perhaps this was meant more in a musical sense. Nevertheless, there was a definite feeling that this might be the last Who album, so there should be a huge effort to produce something worthy of such a swan song. Glyn Johns was back to produce, and this time, with relatively few songs in the pipeline, Townshend turned to the band before writing more, asking them what they wanted him to write about. As Townshend would state, he'd been writing songs for the best part of twenty years and had much experience at writing to a brief. So instead of the batch of demos he usually turned up with, he opened the floor to suggestions. Though it emerged that the band had very little common ground, they did all care about the state of the world and humanity in general, and while it might have been only a small thread to grasp hold of, it did give the album a greater sense of unity and purpose than its predecessor. Pete remembered playing the band four tracks that he had been working on, which were met with silence. John 'Rabbit' Bundrick, who had been invited to participate, tried to offer some encouragement, but Townshend was left a little hurt and disgruntled. In an interview with *Musician* in 1982, Pete would describe the new songs as the most aggressive ones they'd ever come up with, remarking that it was a dangerous record. Entwistle certainly does brings an aggressive edge to the material, apparently causing more hearing damage for Townshend, who was forced to play louder than he wished. In the inner sleeve, John also thanked Roger and Pete for help on subject matter and lyrics, showing that he too was receptive to the rest of the band's input.

The cover, again shot by Graham Hughes, which features a child playing an arcade machine, has often been seen as a reference *Tommy*, but Townshend had also become addicted to playing Space Invaders in the early 1980s and this might have more to do with this fact.

It's Hard reached number eleven in the UK and number eight in the USA. Although not a commercial success, *Rolling Stone* gave it a good review, stating it was their most vital and coherent album since *Who's Next*, giving particular praise to the admittedly great 'I've Known No War'. Gary Bushell, writing in *Sounds*, was less appreciative, calling it watered-down Who and comparing it (in typical cockney geezer fashion) to a fat old footballer who still kicked a ball around.

Daltrey would perhaps be most scathing of the album, insisting it should never have been released. Indeed, upon hearing the finished article, he had arguments with Pete over it, telling him it was below par, or words to that effect. Townshend himself would later say that part of the issue was the fact he had just come out of rehab to find the band rehearsing without him, and they were unaware of the problems he was facing at the time.

For all the criticism *It's Hard* is singled out for, the main faults are ones that were already present on *Face Dances*. The songs aren't quite the usual quality, and the arrangement and production is often too clean, lifeless and lacking in the customary guitar-driven edge. But overall, as a collection of songs, *It's Hard* is a more consistent and well-written album than its predecessor, and one which has its moments of magic.

Following the release of the album, the band embarked on a farewell tour, which was meant more as an end to large-scale touring rather than a complete end to the band. However, in 1983, Pete Townshend would officially quit, breaking the band up.

In 1997, the album was reissued in a remixed form on CD, containing several live bonus tracks, while some of the original tracks were also presented in slightly different forms, including longer takes and alternative guitar parts. In 2022, for Record Store Day, a special two-LP version was released, with bonus tracks including 'Eminence Front' with Roger on co-lead vocals and 'One Life's Enough' with lead vocals by Pete.

TRACK BY TRACK

1. 'ATHENA'

Written by Pete Townshend
Produced by Glyn Johns
Recorded at Turn Up-Down Studios, Surrey, 1982

In 1980, Pete became infatuated with actress Theresa Russell, who was at the time the girlfriend of Nicolas Roeg, the director of such films as *Performance* and *The Man Who Fell To Earth*. Roeg had also directed Russell in the film *Bad Timing*, starring Art Garfunkel, a film which featured 'Who Are You' in its soundtrack. Roeg had a history of working with musicians, and Townshend was interested in collaborating to perhaps get *Lifehouse* made in some form. Pete would travel to America while Roeg was away in Paris, inviting Russell to accompany him to see Pink Floyd performing The Wall, but was shattered when he was ultimately turned down by Russell, and proceeded to write 'Athena', which was initially titled 'Theresa'.

Despite it being written from a place of lovesick misery, 'Athena' is musically uplifting, riding along on its infectious bouncing rhythm. Though Daltrey does a good job vocally, Pete's original demo has a manic and unhinged quality that Roger doesn't quite nail and is probably a case where Pete's half-crazed delivery works a little better for the song.

The track starts out with a typical Townshend open A power chord before picking up pace with its fast strummed G to D chord change. The verse is catchy and upbeat, with the addition of brass used sparingly adding to the joyful feel. Though the song is fairly straightforward, the middle eight sung by Townshend, with prominent use of brass, moves to D major seventh and adds a reflective moment to the track before it picks up again. One of the catchier songs on *It's Hard*, 'Athena' has been maligned by some due to its rather breezy nature, but in my personal opinion, its rhythm and energy are hard to resist and it remains something of a pop gem.

2. 'IT'S YOUR TURN'

Written by John Entwistle
Produced by Glyn Johns
Recorded at Turn Up-Down Studios, Surrey, 1982

Like 'Had Enough' from the *Who Are You* album, 'It's Your Turn' is another Entwistle track which opens with synthesizer, sounding a tad like the Van Halen hit 'Jump', although the latter wouldn't be released for another year. The song is another of John's rockers, with Daltrey delivering some especially gravelly vocals at times. Entwistle appears to be challenging the next generation to take up the rock and roll mantle, while at the same time reminding them that he was 'A face in a magazine' when they were but children. Lines about middle age perhaps tap into John's own feelings on getting old, a subject that Townshend had been tackling on the band's last three albums, but here it seems less genuine and there are times when the lyrics are either tongue-in-cheek or slightly ridiculous. Kenney Jones does a nice job of giving the song firepower when it needs it, while John tends to hang back on the bass, making this much more of a straight-up 1980s rocker without much of his usual fretboard fireworks. Townshend also keeps it largely simple, but his guitar parts still do enough to overpower the synth. Andy Fairweather Low plays rhythm guitar.

3. 'COOK'S COUNTY'

Written by Pete Townshend
Produced by Glyn Johns
Recorded at Turn Up-Down Studios, Surrey, 1982

This track is a song about Cook County Hospital in Chicago, which was a free facility on the brink of closure due to financial difficulties and had been refused a government grant to remain open. The hospital was in a rough area and tended to deal with drug addicts, poor people, black communities and those in need, and Townshend was moved by its plight and those served by it.

The track has a nice interplay in the verse between Pete's guitar part in the left-hand channel and the synth part in the right, while later it changes gear for a section with multiple vocals by Pete, the pulse beginning to quicken. Later, this section finds even more grit as the guitars get louder and more violent, with Pete tapping into some of his usual aggression. Though not one of The Who's best tracks, and certainly not the best-written song on *It's Hard*, the arrangement does at times sound tough and at least a fair approximation to The Who's rock credentials, showing that they hadn't let the synthesizers totally subdue them.

4. 'IT'S HARD'

Written by Pete Townshend
Produced by Glyn Johns
Recorded at Turn Up-Down Studios, Surrey, 1982

The album's title track started off as a song called 'Popular' which Pete delivered to the band, along with three others, but they did not appear keen on it. Changing the song slightly, he managed to sell it to them. The track is a curious one, opening with a dark and dramatic chord sequence beginning in D minor before its classical changes sweep through C minor and resolve on D major. Here, it unexpectedly turns into a mellow and perhaps overly pleasant I–IV–V in G for the verse, this pattern changing key to D for its chorus, with the synthesizer sounding particularly cheerful in contrast to the lyrics. The opening section repeating manages to kill the sweetness for a short while before we head back to the verse, while later on in the song we get a solo section where the I–IV–V plays out in the key of E, Pete using the trick of multiple key changes to keep a simple chord sequence fresh, something that he had used as far back as 'My Generation' in 1965. As a title track, 'It's Hard' comes across as nice enough, but apart from its darker intro section, it is a song that is lightweight and mostly forgettable. Despite this, it would make it to the stage, where it was played in 1982.

The 1997 remix of the song replaces the end of the opening lead guitar intro with a different take.

5. 'DANGEROUS'

Written by John Entwistle
Produced by Glyn Johns
Recorded at Turn Up-Down Studios, Surrey, 1982

'Dangerous' is a much more commercial and pop-orientated song than Entwistle's other two contributions to *It's Hard*, but it's well written and far catchier than the makeweight 'It's Your Turn'. The track makes great use of changing the pace and features a nice sense of melody. Starting with a melodic intro featuring synthesizers and some extremely high-register bass, Entwistle soon drops down low to prepare for the verse, a section which starts in half-time before picking up in its second half, Entwistle switching from a simple ominous bassline to even simpler root notes for the verse. The static feel of the verse with its one-note bass then gives way to the chorus' sense of movement in its chord changes, the melody rising in anthemic fashion.

'Dangerous' is more typical of The Who's 1980s sound, featuring much less guitar than most Entwistle-penned tracks, and although it sometimes feels like John was almost singlehandedly keeping the band from straying too far from their status as rock giants, this one fully gives in to commercial music trends. However, it does this well, and is upbeat enough to be enjoyable without slipping into saccharine pop. So often a writer of unusual and darkly comic songs, here Entwistle shows he's just as capable of not only knocking out a commercial pop tune but doing it better than most. Entwistle plays synthesizer along with Tim Gorman, who also contributes organ.

The 1997 remix of this song is a longer unedited take, which features an extra return to the intro part after the first chorus and is roughly twenty seconds longer.

6. 'EMINENCE FRONT'

Written by Pete Townshend
Produced by Glyn Johns
Recorded at Turn Up-Down Studios, Surrey, 1982

After a two-album absence, Pete finally takes a lead vocal on a Who track again, the dark and edgy 'Eminence Front'. The lyrics again have a hint of the vapid world Townshend had glimpsed and even become part of, and here we find him calling out the facade of big money, speedboats, parties and the superficiality of fashion.

The song starts with a synthetic beat, shortly joined by dancing synthesizer notes. Soon, the drums kick in with their simple relentless groove, the echo-loaded snare going off like a shotgun in the night. The guitar riff is a simple two-note phrase which lasts a whole sixteen bars before being joined by the lead guitar. Townshend's opening lead guitar break is clean and jazzy, bouncing around the fretboard and towards the end hitting a particular sweet minor third to second interval which catches the ear. After waiting since 1975 to sing lead vocals on a Who album track, Townshend certainly makes up for lost time, having been made even more confident by his work as a solo artist. The song's verse works on a haunting two-chord sequence, the bass at its most minimalist, with Entwisle hitting a single note on each chord, lasting two bars each. In the chorus, though the chords remain the same as the verse, Entwistle contrasts his basic two-note work, with a more elaborate line that snakes its way through the mix. The chorus also sees the addition of backing vocals, where in the original mix there is a small but noticeable mistake in the first chorus, with Pete's vocal coming in late and thus not syncing with Roger's backing vocal, though this was corrected in later remixes. The original mix also hard-pans Townshend's vocal, whereas remixes place it in the centre.

After the first chorus we do get a brief riff that breaks up the two-chord pattern, before another vocal variation over the same F minor to D flat change, finally moving up to C, to create a period of tension that resolves back into the usual chord pattern.

'Eminence Front' would go on to become a regular live inclusion that would last to the present day, becoming Pete's most often played vocal showpiece in concert and featuring Roger Daltrey playing electric guitar. Although not really a diehard Who favourite, it would seem to have a cult popularity with many people with a more casual interest in the band and those who are not as much a fan of the band's typical style. The song would even find something of a new audience after featuring in the video game *Grand Theft Auto – San Andreas.*

A version of the song was recorded with Roger Daltrey on lead vocals which would remain in the archives until 2022, when a 40-year anniversary vinyl release for Record Store Day appeared, featuring a mix that alternated between Roger and Pete singing lead.

Tim Gorman plays electric piano on the track.

7. 'I'VE KNOWN NO WAR'

Written by Pete Townshend
Produced by Glyn Johns
Recorded at Turn Up-Down Studios, Surrey, 1982

Townshend stated that this song started off with just the word 'War' and developed from there. One of The Who's most underrated songs and one of the best tracks of the Kenney Jones era, 'I've Known No War' is another example of the band managing to sound modern whilst still hinting at the power and defiance of their glory days. A fairly slow-paced rocker, we find Pete writing some specifically autobiographical lyrics as he tackles the position of being born less than two weeks after the surrender of Germany in the Second World War and having grown up without the evils of global-scale military conflict. After the rudimentary synth fades in, Kenney Jones' echo-loaded drums enter. Daltrey's vocals sound as hard-edged and intense as ever as he rages over a sparse backing, which is joined by guitar on some classic Townshend power chord stabs. With the full band playing, the song marches on with an airy but organic rock vibe that is very catchy, while the lyrics explore a very deep subject. Townshend (through Daltrey) talks of children bored with the stories of war, but who wouldn't be alive had it not been for the sacrifices of the older generations, though he is essentially laying this criticism at his own feet since, as the words state, he has never known war, nor will he ever be likely to. Going further, the song states, even if he did see war in his time, he'd likely be gone in a nuclear flash rather than have to suffer front-line battle.

After two verses and choruses, the song has an interesting period with its relentless drum pattern joined by a simple piano figure and then some uplifting orchestration, as if lifted from a vintage old-time movie, before the song roars back in with Townshend's chiming guitar chords and Daltrey's rock howl.

At a time when The Who were struggling to really find a place as a rock band in the 1980s, both musically and with what they actually wanted to say, 'I've Known No War' is a remarkably successful song, brimming with clever lyrics on an interesting theme and displaying the band moving in a musical direction that combines modern flavours with what The Who did best. This seems to be the dangerous Who that Townshend had spoken of, and if the band could have produced more songs of this quality and style, *It's Hard* would have perhaps been seen as a return to form.

8. 'ONE LIFE'S ENOUGH'

Written by Pete Townshend
Produced by Glyn Johns
Recorded at Turn Up-Down Studios, Surrey, 1982

Written for Pete's wife, Karen, 'One Life's Enough' has to be another one of The Who's most unusual songs, almost like a theatre number, opening with synth and odd expressionistic piano chords. Daltrey does a fine job of tackling its soft and reflective vocals, and the arrangement is so sparse that the vocal is left exposed throughout. The lyrics are also minimal, alluding to making love, and the whole song only clocks in at a little under two-and-a-half minutes. The middle section of the track features drums as the song becomes more romantic, before it ends with further dark and expressionistic piano.

Townshend plays piano, while Tim Gorman and Townshend also play synth.

In 2022, *It's Hard* was released as a two-LP version for Record Store Day and contained a version of this song, with Pete on lead vocals, which in my opinion works slightly better.

9. 'ONE AT A TIME'

Produced by Glyn Johns
Written by John Entwistle
Recorded at Turn Up-Down Studios, Surrey, 1982

Although on the surface a fairly throwaway song from Entwistle, 'One At A Time' is hugely enjoyable and energetic, filling the same sort of role as 'The Quiet One' did on *Face Dances*. Here, the feel is slightly more of a straight 1950s-influenced rock and roller, with Kenney Jones propelling the song along on the back of a lovely tumbling drum part.

The song starts with a nice brass arrangement from John before a crash-and-tumble drum roll that resolves into the main groove. After some slightly ominous-sounding bass and guitar, the song breaks into its feel-good, fast-paced verse. Everyone sounds like they're having a great time on the track, Townshend playing some delightful, wiry rock and roll guitar phrases and Entwistle delivering a rough and ready vocal as he serves up a typically black-humoured tale. Here we have a man with a cheating partner, who instead of being upset is actively trying to offload her onto the other man, as he himself already has someone better lined up. The protagonist in question even suggests the other man phones up, promising he'll let his partner answer the phone, and insisting, 'If you want her, you can keep her'. A middle section featuring synthesizers played by Entwistle and Tim Gorman is a slight change in mood and briefly removes the song from its more traditional style, but it's a deviation that work well.

'One At A Time' is for me a highlight on *It's Hard*, one in which the band sounds like they are simply having a blast jamming with each other.

10. 'WHY DID I FALL FOR THAT'

Written by Pete Townshend
Produced by Glyn Johns
Recorded at Turn Up-Down Studios, Surrey, 1982

With its title, one might assume this song is about a relationship, but it was in fact written about the apathy during the Cold War, with people getting on with their lives and ignoring what was unfolding. 'Why Did I Fall For That' is a melodic track that works fairly well as a pop-rock song of its time, with its mix of catchy melody, old-fashioned music hooks and some nice lyrics. Opening in a slightly 1950s Doo-wop feel, with deep warm bass set against the chiming electric guitars, Daltrey sings in a lower register until we get to the chorus, where he can open his range and is backed by some nice harmonies. After the second chorus, we have a crafty key change down a semi-tone to D for an instrumental section replicating the verse, and then halfway through the chorus chords we modulate back to the original key for the final verse.

Overall, it is a track which is commercial and a bit lightweight on the surface but contains deeper meaning in its lyrics as well as a few musical touches that elevate it and make it an enjoyable Kenney Jones-era Who song.

11. 'A MAN IS A MAN'

Written by Pete Townshend
Produced by Glyn Johns
Recorded at Turn Up-Down Studios, Surrey, 1982

Townshend deals here with the issues facing the male of the species and what really makes a man a man – and this time it definitely isn't tattoos! Dispensing with macho notions of being a John Wayne-type, the lyrics speak of opening one's heart and offering an ahead-of-its-time take on toxic male stereotypes.

Beginning with some clean and chorus-rich guitars, the song soon settles into a piano-led ballad in a similar vein to 'How Many Friends' from *The Who By Numbers*. Daltrey is in a way the perfect singer to tackle this, a figure of duality with his toughness and macho side but also possessing a hidden sensitivity, which was apparent in both his image and singing. Roger had already expressed the pain, sadness and need for love inside the tough guy, as evidenced in a song like 'Behind Blue Eyes', and here again he does a wonderful job of bringing Townshend's words to life in a very authentic-sounding way.

Musically, the song is a fairly simple chord progression, but it has a melancholy feel that pulls in the listener and features a rousing chorus with Townshend adding harmony vocals. The only real curve ball is the middle eight, which key-changes to E and features a small section where the song speeds up into a kind of punky rock and roll pastiche.

As a ballad, 'A Man Is A Man' is heartfelt and poignant enough to be a worthy inclusion on *It's Hard.*

12. 'CRY IF YOU WANT'

Written by Pete Townshend
Produced by Glyn Johns
Recorded at Turn Up-Down Studios, Surrey, 1982

Often seen as one of the best tracks from the latter-period Who, 'Cry If You Want' certainly offers more old-style Who bite than most. Guitar-wise it's a classic Townshend piece, with his trademark open A chord riffage. The song starts with a persistent martial-style drum beat from Jones and the rumbling bass of Entwistle. After the first verse, Pete comes in heavier, thrashing away at the guitar with more vitriol than we've come to expect from this incarnation of the band, providing a taste of the still-present musical rage that made them so exciting. By contrast, the chorus is mellower, allowing a brief respite before the assault starts again. Daltrey relishes the moment, spitting out rapid-fire words like venom and calling out the follies of idealism, naivety and bitterness. A middle section sung by Townshend is interestingly melodic and reflective before the song bludgeons the listener over the head once more, Daltrey coming thundering back in, full of rage.

Towards the end of the song, we get some violently distorted guitar from Townshend, sounding like it's been pushed into the red on a mixing desk, such is the savageness of its fuzzy tone.

'Cry If You Want' would be played live in 1982 and then revived in its usual form for a few shows in 2006. Later in 2006, the band would rework the song into the end of 'My Generation', changing the music significantly, but with Roger singing the words from the song. In 2014, the band would play the song in its usual form at several shows, before returning to it as a 'My Generation' jam add-on in 2016.

Chapter 12

Endless Wire (2006)

Produced by Pete Townshend
Roger's vocals produced by Bob Pridden and Billy Nicholls
Released in the UK on 30 October 2006 as Polydor 1709519
Released in the USA on 30 October 2006 as Universal B0007967-10
Chart position – UK = 9, USA = 7
Recorded at Pete Townshend's home studio and Eel Pie Oceanic, Twickenham, London, between autumn 2002 and summer 2006
Roger Daltrey – Vocals.
Pino Palladino – Bass on tracks 10, 11, 14, 16, 17, 18 & 21
Zak Starkey – Drums on track 5
John 'Rabbit' Bundrick – Keyboards on tracks 10, 11 & 18
Simon Townshend – Backing vocals on tracks 10, 11, 14, 20 & 21
Peter Huntington – Drums on tracks 8, 10, 11, 14, 16, 17, 18, 20 & 21
Billy Nicholls – Backing vocals on tracks 10, 11, 14, 20 & 21
Lawrence Ball – Electronic music on tracks 1 & 15
Rachel Fuller – Orchestration supervisor on track 13, Keyboards on track 8
Gail Morley – Violin on track 13
Brian Wright – Violin on track 13
Ellen Blair – Viola on track 13
Vicky Matthews – Cello on track 13
Stuart Ross – Bass on track 8
Joylon Dixon – Acoustic guitars on track 8
Pete Townshend – Everything else, including Guitars, Vocals, Bass, Piano, Keyboards, Mandolin, Banjo, Violin, Drum Programming, Drums, Orchestration.

In 1999, the Who went through something of a resurgence. In October, they played as part of the iBASH 99 concert bill for the company Pixelon, which was launching a new technology designed to advance internet video streaming. This event was set to be streamed by an estimated billion viewers, but in fact the technology did not exist, with people trying to use Pixelon's technology unable to watch the show. The event went down in history as a scam.

One good thing to come out of this fiasco was the return of The Who. Although it is true they never really left for very long – first re-forming for

Live Aid in 1985, just two years after their split, followed by a huge tour in 1989 playing *Tommy* and other songs, and then *Quadrophenia* shows in 1996 and 1997 – this was very different. The Who's tours in 1989 and 1996–1997 had been elaborate affairs, far removed from the glory days of the band as a lean and mean four-piece, when they had even turned down the option of adding Nicky Hopkins on keyboards for fear of the way it would interfere with the group dynamics of their onstage jamming. The 1989 shows in particular featured a vast array of musicians, including brass sections, percussionists, keyboards and the almost unthinkable addition of a second guitarist. Worse still, Townshend would spend most of the time playing acoustic, allowing the second guitarist, Steve 'Boltz' Bolton, to handle most of the electric lead work. Bolton was a fine guitarist, but his style was vastly different from Townshend's, and although Pete was an excellent acoustic player – with many of The Who's studio cuts featuring his acoustic work – in a live setting it would rob the audience of much of his customary fire and improvisation. This would continue with the *Quadrophenia* shows, where again much of the set saw Townshend playing acoustic guitar, allowing at first Geoff Whitehorn and then his own brother, Simon Townshend, to handle the lead work. Simon Townshend perfectly dealt with his role, providing the right feel for the songs, but the touring band was still a world apart from The Who of the Sixties and Seventies.

In 1999, however, the fans showing up to see The Who were about to witness something of a rebirth, as they went back to basics as a tight and aggressive five-piece, consisting of Townshend, Daltrey, Entwistle, drummer Zak Starkey (son of Ringo Starr) and John 'Rabbit' Bundrick on keys. The difference was huge. The 1999 gig was just the starting point, as the band returned with renewed vigour to their old stomping ground for two homecoming Christmas shows at the Shepherd's Bush Empire in West London. The following year, a full-blown UK and American tour got underway, culminating at the Royal Albert Hall with a gig for Teenage Cancer Trust, the charity with which Roger had become involved. This concert saw The Who perform with an array of special guests including Paul Weller, Eddie Vedder of Pearl Jam, Noel Gallagher from Oasis, Bryan Adams and Kelly Jones of the Stereophonics.

For the first time in decades, it felt like The Who were an ongoing band rather than one temporarily coming out of retirement to do one last tour. There were more dates in the UK in 2002, including two shows at the Royal Albert Hall, again for Teenage Cancer Trust, as well as a handful of warm-up shows in Portsmouth and Watford. In June of that year, the band were about to start another American tour when tragedy struck. On the eve of the first date, John Entwistle passed away from a heart attack, possibly brought on by cocaine use. With Entwistle gone, this might have been the end for the band, and one does wonder if the tour hadn't already been booked, would they have found the impetus to pick up their guitars and play? However, with a contract in place and crews relying on money, the group soldiered on, recruiting renowned session bassist Pino Palladino.

Finally, in 2004, two new Who tracks appeared, the first being 'Real Good Looking Boy', a song about the twin subjects of growing up and the boyhood idolization of Elvis. The second was 'Old Red Wine', written about Entwistle and having been developed from a live jam on the band's last tour. But these two new songs were not part of a new original album, and instead were released as a single and as part of a compilation, *Then And Now*, in a classic move all bands now seem to do in order to shift an album which contains mostly tracks the fans already own elsewhere.

However, in 2006 it emerged that finally, after more than two decades, The Who were about to record a new full album, and this new record would even contain a rock opera of sorts. Was this really happening? After all these years, was Pete Townshend about to launch a rock opera again? In a way, this was the perfect time. Rock operas can be wearing, for both the band and the listener, and after putting out two such epic records in *Tommy* and *Quadrophenia* within four years of each other, the band had effectively exhausted the medium in the 1970s, especially considering the attempted *Lifehouse* in-between the two. As the 1970s wound towards their end, the advent of punk left some feeling that the notion of concept albums was an archaic remnant of rock – pretentious, ponderous and best left in the past. But in 2006, enough time had elapsed, during which *Tommy* and *Quadrophenia* had been celebrated in many forms, from films to stage shows and theatre productions. The Who were now a legendary band, so who could argue with one last triumphant and bold return to what made them famous? On paper it was a potentially good idea, but in classic Who style, the ability to fully pull it off would elude them. The rock opera would end up being half a rock opera, not a true mini-opera in the sense of 'A Quick One' or 'Rael', but more a song suite, longer than the aforementioned mini-operas but still only part of an album. The rest of the record is made up of standalone songs of varying styles and quality, but the overall effect is disjointed and confused. Because of the compromise, parts of the mini-opera 'Wire And Glass' sound a tad rushed, as though they had to be squeezed into a time slot. Some of the tracks sound like properly fleshed out songs in their own right which would benefit from being longer, while others are just short pieces. Put simply, it's neither one thing nor the other. The rest of the songs are a mixed bunch, but at times the album feels more like a Pete Townshend solo record with Daltrey as a guest vocalist, with the former taking lead vocals on six of its tracks.

Having not released a record since his solo concept album *Psychoderelict* in 1994, a big question remained as to what sort of songs Pete would come up with in 2006. Townshend would speak to *Relix* magazine of wanting to make a simple record, one that didn't sound like stadium rock or pseudo-metal, choosing to produce it himself rather than let a producer bully them into reinventing themselves in a way in which they (the producer) saw fit. The record would have significant religious themes in many of its songs, but would also deal with other unique topics, such as terrorism and the comforting effect of TV upon our lives.

The *Wire And Glass* mini-opera itself is based on a novella of Pete's called *The Boy That Heard Music*, which had links back to Pete's last solo album and even *Lifehouse*. Pete recalled sending the novella to Roger, asking if he felt it could form a basis for new Who music, to be told by his long-time bandmate that it was 'the same shit', presumably referring to the complexity of Townshend's concepts.

In an interview with *Mojo* magazine in January 2006, Pete revealed that he had delivered twenty-six songs for consideration for the new album, with Daltrey being unsure if he could even sing some, such as 'In The Ether', which would end up being sung by Pete. He also mentioned a track called 'Cinderella' about the actress Leslie Ash, as well as songs titled 'There's No Doubt' and 'He Said, She Said', none of which were released. Townshend described sending tracks to Daltrey, expecting him to hate 'Tea and Theatre', 'A Man In A Purple Dress' and 'Two Thousand Years', though feeling he might have liked the hoe-down element of the latter.

Daltrey would state that he'd written six songs himself, but none were suitable for The Who, admitting he was not the writer Pete was. In an interview with *Rolling Stone* in 2006, Townshend explained that in 2000, both Daltrey and Entwistle had talked of new songs they'd written for a Who album. He went on to say that when he asked Roger if he could hear them, he hadn't actually written any, and that when he asked Entwistle, the bassist said he had hundreds but wasn't willing to play them to Roger, feeling they would instantly be shot down.

Working titles for the album were *Who2* and *Glass And Wire*, and the working title of the mini-opera was *The Glass Household*. The final title of the album is said to have come from a misunderstanding Roger had about Pete's *Lifehouse* story, when he apparently remarked that there wasn't enough wire in the world to connect everyone up to the experience suits and grid in the plot.

For the album's personnel, although touring bassist Pino Palladino played for much of the record, regular drummer (since 1996) Zak Starkey was unavailable for much of it and only appeared on one track.

Preceded by an EP featuring six songs from the *Wire And Glass* mini-opera on 17 July, *Endless Wire* was released on 30 October 2006, reaching number nine in the UK and number seven in America. Reception was mainly positive, with veteran journalist and friend of the band, as well as writer of *Before I Get Old*, Dave Marsh saying *Endless Wire* was the closest album to classic Who since *The Who By Numbers*, declaring it truly a Who album rather than a glorified Townshend solo record.

As time has gone on, I've come to appreciate the album more, and there isn't much on it that falls flat. Indeed, there are some fantastic songs and moments of magic, but it still feels a little bit of a compromise between too many different ideas and styles to fully achieve its potential.

The band would play much of the material live, including a performance of the mini-opera at The Electric Proms series of concerts at Camden's The Roundhouse in October 2006, a performance that was broadcast on BBC TV.

TRACK BY TRACK

1. 'FRAGMENTS'

Written by Pete Townshend and Lawrence Ball
Produced by Pete Townshend

The cynical might suggest the opening track on *Endless Wire* displays The Who ripping themselves off a tad, while the more generous might instead view it as a clever nod to the band's past. Either way, one can't ignore the similarity of the opening synth part to perhaps the greatest ever Who album opener, 'Baba O'Riley', from 1971s *Who's Next*. *Endless Wire* would contain themes and links back to that album, so perhaps it's no surprise that Townshend might have consciously evoked a little of its spirit, but if the intro is like 'Baba O'Riley', the rest does not follow suit. However, the crashing guitar chords that enter also recall to mind the 1981 track 'Another Tricky Day', even appearing in the same key.

The song is slightly unconventional in structure, not really having a standard verse and chorus format, and featuring Daltrey switching between upper and lower register on what would best qualify as verses, sounding much more comfortable in his lower range, the higher end obviously not quite as easy as in his younger days, but one still can't fault the commitment he puts in. Complimenting Daltrey's vocals are Townshend's carefully arranged, rich harmonies, which form the familiar contrast to Roger in classic Who style. Towards the end of the song, we get a shift to the minor as the song briefly becomes darker before its end.

Overall, 'Fragments' is quite a simple song which uses changing dynamics to keep the listener's interest. The track credits Lawrence Ball, who worked with Townshend on *Lifehouse Method*, a website that would partly realize Pete's idea from the 1970s about creating unique electronic music based on individual users. Lawrence used software designed by his colleague Dave Snowden to input data about Meha Baba and convert it to the electronic music we hear throughout the song.

2. 'A MAN IN A PURPLE DRESS'

Written by Pete Townshend
Produced by Pete Townshend

Written after seeing Mel Gibson's *The Passion Of The Christ*, 'A Man In A Purple Dress' is a Bob Dylan-esque folk song featuring just the two surviving original members of The Who, Townshend and Daltrey. Here, the subject is religion, but rather than an attack on God, the accusatory finger is pointed at religious leaders whose pompous misuse of power is an affront to both God and man. The lyrics ridicule, reducing the fancy robes to 'a dress', and lay bare the hypocrisy and vanity that can emerge in organized religion. The song sounds like something which might have been released on *The Who By Numbers*, beautifully stripped back with Townshend's elegant acoustic playing (tuned to open G) and Daltrey's heartfelt vocals producing a standout moment on the album. 'A Man In A Purple Dress' would be played live in concert in 2006 and 2007 before being dropped from sets.

3. 'MIKE POST THEME'

Written by Pete Townshend
Produced by Pete Townshend

Mike Post is an American composer, known for writing several TV show theme tunes, including *NYPD Blue*, *Hill Street Blues*, *The A-Team*, *Quantum Leap* and *The Rockford Files*. This ode to his work is a novel subject for a song and tackles the way TV shows can become a part of our lives, offering us comfort and a sense of familiarity. These moments are where we can escape our everyday lives and be calmed for a while, as well as live vicariously through the characters, and feel in touch with emotions we once expressed more freely in our youth. What makes the subject more interesting is the fact The Who had in recent years found their songs becoming TV themes, with *CSI: Crime Scene Investigation* beginning in 2000, using 'Who Are You' as the theme song, followed by *CSI Miami* in 2002 ('Won't Get Fooled Again') and *CSI New York* in 2004 ('Baba O'Riley'). Whether this had any influence on 'Mike Post Theme' is uncertain, but the TV connection gives an added sense of meaning to the track.

Starting with Daltrey's roaring vocals and furiously strummed acoustic guitar, the song certainly makes an impactful entrance, after which we get a cool, laid-back verse, Townshend's nicely picked acoustic being complimented by Roger's smooth vocal. This light and shade between the mild verse and more powerful chorus is played for all it's worth, but the real highlight of the song is the tender middle eight which is both lyrically and musically touching and displays Townshend's still present knack for coming up with the perfect change of pace in a track that seemed straightforward. 'Mike Post Theme' is a nice enough song with an original idea, but perhaps does overstay its welcome a little, though at the end we get a nice instrumental section before a reprise of the middle eight, complete with some mandolin work from Townshend, which is a lovely way to finish. This song also features Townshend playing drums.

'Mike Post Theme' would be played in concert throughout 2006 and 2007, even popping up twice in 2008.

4. 'IN THE ETHER'

Written by Pete Townshend
Produced by Pete Townshend

If there is any song on *Endless Wire* that really comes as a shock and feels out of place on a Who record, it's 'In The Ether'. That's not to say it's a bad track, but it does come across as a tad bizarre and certainly not one for casual fans. According to Townshend, when he delivered the demo to Roger, the Who frontman questioned how he was going to sing it and suggested that Townshend take the vocal instead, perhaps playing it on just guitar instead of piano as well. Pete would go with the first suggestion but not the second, so what we get is essentially a Townshend solo track with him singing over his acoustic guitar and piano on a song that's part jazz and part music theatre. The music is actually very beautiful and emotional, but it's the singing that really divides people, as Townshend ignores his usual vocal style for a rough deep growl that has been described as sounding like Tom Waits. In a way it's a shame, because if you can get past the unusual singing style, the song is a well-written ballad with effective chord changes that show yet another side of Townshend's writing. Unsurprisingly, the song was never performed live by The Who, but Townshend would play it solo a handful of times as early as 2005.

Although the track is not strictly part of the *Wire And Glass* mini-opera, it is based on *The Boy Who Heard Music* and its words feature in the novella.

5. 'BLACK WIDOW'S EYES'

Written by Pete Townshend
Produced by Pete Townshend

Probably the most emotionally charged and controversial song on the album, 'Black Widow's Eyes' deals with terrorism, but instead of presenting the perpetrator of human death as merely a villain, Townshend goes for something deeper and more unusual. Inspired by an account of a suicide bombing survivor, who moments before the explosion remembered the female bomber having beautiful eyes, Pete constructs a haunting tale in the form of a commercial modern rock song. The track is propelled by Townshend's insistent acoustic fingerpicking, while his electric guitar provides the sparser power chords he is known for. The verses switch between straight and half-time, Daltrey matching the change by switching octaves, while the chorus by contrast is mellow and haunting, but again the real striking moment is a sort of middle eight or second chorus sung by Townshend in multi-layered harmonies, with his guitar chords played over a pedal-tone.

Zak Starkey makes his only appearance on the album on this track but does a brilliant job of periodically adding Keith Moon-like drum fills, as well as setting a laid-back pace when required.

'Black Widow's Eyes' was referred to as possibly being called 'Stockholm Syndrome' during an interview with *Music Week* in May 2005. According to Townshend, when he delivered the song to Daltrey, the singer immediately connected it to the Beslan massacre of 2004. The song was an obvious choice for live shows, being played throughout 2006 and 2007.

6. 'TWO THOUSAND YEARS'

Written by Pete Townshend
Produced by Pete Townshend

Another folk song, the mandolin-led 'Two Thousand Years' also finds its subject matter in religion, as it speculates that Judas, rather than betraying Jesus, might have in fact acted as part of his plan, but 2000 years on, Christians still wait for answers. This simple and pretty song rests on its hypnotic rhythms, which are driven by Townshend's mandolin strumming and aided by handclaps, whilst Daltrey and Townshend offer harmony vocals and we get orchestration too. Even though a minor song in The Who's catalogue, it's enjoyable enough to justify its short running time. The Who (consisting of just Pete, Roger and Simon Townshend) would perform the song in a guest spot at the Royal Albert

Hall's annual concerts for Teenage Cancer Trust in 2008, playing a mini-set, with Simon on mandolin.

7. 'GOD SPEAKS OF MARTY ROBBINS'

Written by Pete Townshend
Produced by Pete Townshend

Effectively another Pete Townshend solo track, 'God Speaks Of Marty Robbins' would easily fit on Pete's 1972 solo album, *Who Came First*. Indeed, the obviously aged vocal is the only thing that really indicates it's a 2000s recording, though if anything this age adds depth and warmth to the performance. The track is far from the traditional Who sound, but is one of the highlights on the album and a beautiful piece of music, Pete displaying his acoustic guitar mastery, playing once again in non-standard tuning (apparently D, A, D, A, D, E) and also contributing a tender and affecting vocal. It's only towards the end of the track that he adds a second guitar part, which gives the song another layer without getting in the way of the intimate feel.

The song is named after country performer Marty Robbins and is based on the idea that God created the world to hear music by humans like Marty.

The song had been previously released in demo form on the Pete Townshend compilation album *Scoop 3* in 2001, where it was titled 'Marty Robbins' and featured no vocals, although essentially being instrumentally the same song.

Some of the lyrics also feature in *The Boy Who Heard Music* novella.

8. 'IT'S NOT ENOUGH'

Written by Pete Townshend and Rachel Fuller
Produced by Pete Townshend

Perhaps the most commercial track on *Endless Wire*, 'It's Not Enough' is a dark rocker with an up-tempo beat and a rich arrangement, co-written by Townshend's then partner and current wife Rachel Fuller. A classically trained musician and composer, Fuller had worked on a backing track for a modern pop song, but the track, titled 'Magic Flute', was left unfinished. Townshend then took the piece and added his own words and style to it, transforming it into a more aggressive track in the process. The words find inspiration from Jean Luc Goddard's 1963 film *Le Mepris*, which starred Brigitte Bardot. In the film, Bardot asks her husband several times if he likes different parts of her body, to which he replies 'yes' each time, but Bardot insists, 'It's not enough'. From this line, Townshend creates a lyric dealing with relationships and the toxic dynamic where one partner can never do enough to please the other. The darkness in the lyrics (which even explicitly name-checks Bardot, Goddard and the film *Le Mepris*) is something universal and timeless and is mirrored by the music, which is tempestuous and urgent. Daltrey delivers the required rough aggression and Townshend too brings out his anger, delivered through his distorted and delay-heavy electric guitar, lending the song a 1980s Eric Clapton vibe. Pete also adds some subtle acoustic guitar picking and the customary harmony backing vocals. The song makes use of a dynamic shift between the loud and aggressive chorus and a more calm and chilling verse, Roger in particular doing a fantastic job of riding the emotional changes.

Sadly, the emotionally charged and energetic 'It's Not Enough' would never be played live by the band or either Pete or Roger solo, perhaps being a bit too complex arrangement-wise to have been carried off as well as on record.

9. 'YOU STAND BY ME'

Written by Pete Townshend
Produced by Pete Townshend

Another solo Townshend folk song, 'You Stand By Me' is also one of the shortest Who songs, clocking in at just over 1.30, but despite the brevity of the track it's a nice addition to the album.

Its message is straightforward and pure, speaking of his partner Rachel Fuller's unwavering support, but also perhaps a little bit of the unlikely but long-lasting partnership with Roger Daltrey. Musically, it feels like a Paul Simon song and features pretty fingerpicking (again in non-standard tuning) and an especially lovely middle eight. As with 'God Speaks Of Marty Robins', Pete gives us a tender and authentic vocal, expressing his own words perfectly and giving us perhaps the most naked look at the artist of any song on the record.

Chapter 13

'Wire and Glass'

This mini-opera is based on Pete's novella *The Boy Who Heard Music* and follows the story very closely. The plot features the largely autobiographical character Ray High, who was central to Pete's 1993 solo concept album *Psychoderelict*.

In this story, we find Ray in the year 2035, incarcerated in a mental facility, where from his cell his consciousness can enter another realm called The Ether, from which he can view both past and present. Here, he focuses on three individuals who met as children and grew up in Ray's old neighbourhood. These are Gabriel, a boy of Christian faith who hears music; Josh, from a Jewish family, who hears voices; and Leila, a Muslim girl, who can fly. Together, they create a band called The Glass Household and find Ray's old notes about his Gridlife concept (based on Townshend's own *Lifehouse* ideas) through Leila's father, who co-owned a studio with Ray.

The band become an international success and Leila marries Gabriel, but although he finds himself unable to give her a child, he does impregnate another girl, causing both his marriage to fail and the breakup of the band. Leila and Josh begin a relationship and become involved in dark sexual games at fetish clubs, whilst Gabriel becomes an addict of several vices and is disgraced by various stories that are revealed to the press.

Leila eventually decides to use modern technology to finally bring the Gridlife concept to fruition, allowing audiences to created music based on themselves which will then play out in a giant concert in New York. Gabriel at first refuses to re-form The Glass Household or allow one of his songs to be used, but is convinced to do so by a now broke Josh, who needs the money from the concert. Gabriel travels to New York for the concert but is shot dead by Josh, who is now suffering from mental illness and has stopped taking his medication. A giant staircase opens, with a host of demons and angels awaiting above, and Gabriel ascends, passing through the Mirror Door, winding up at a pub called The Black Hole.

Back in 2035, Josh resides in the next cell to Ray, where he is often visited by the voice of Gabriel. He is also visited by Leila, who takes tea with him, both now in old age.

10. 'SOUND ROUND'

Written by Pete Townshend
Produced by Pete Townshend

The first song from the 'Wire And Glass' mini-opera opens with a Keith Moon-esque drum roll and wastes no time in getting to the point, with a great vocal from Daltrey and some classic chiming chords from Townshend. On the chorus, the upper register bass work does enough to recall some of the melodic nature of Entwistle, whilst not trying to really emulate him. The lyrics talking of campervans help to evoke a bit of a *Lifehouse* connection, while the music definitely has a Who feel to it, and if anything it's a shame it's condensed down to under a minute thirty, as one feels it could really work as a full-length song.

In the song, the character of Ray High, a rock star based on Townshend and the central character of Townshend's solo rock opera, *Pyschoderelict*, is driving in his campervan in his past, and this seems to be Ray looking back at his life from his cell in 2035. According to the *Who's Next/Life House* Super Deluxe boxset released in 2023, 'Sound Round' was possibly a leftover song from around 1971 that doesn't seem to have been even demoed, or at least a song with the same title had been noted at the time.

11. 'PICK UP THE PEACE'

Written by Pete Townshend
Produced by Pete Townshend

'Pick Up The Peace' also does a fairly good job of distilling some classic Who sounds into the modern format of the band. In this part of the story, Ray High waits in another realm called The Ether, where he watches three children discovering his work, an idea that is basically Townshend's own *Lifehouse*, changed here to Gridlife. Musically, the song starts off with ringing power chords and explosive drums, and develops into a steady-paced verse, while its chorus has a swagger and slightly funky edge that recalls something like 'Smash The Mirror' from 1969's *Tommy*. Although brief, the song still manages to squeeze in a nice middle eight, and again is a track that feels a bit too truncated and something that would have certainly worked as a longer song.

12. 'UNHOLY TRINITY'

Written by Pete Townshend
Produced by Pete Townshend

'Unholy Trinity' sets up the main characters, three kids from different religious backgrounds who become friends and will form a group called The Glass Household. The three are Gabriel, who is from a Christian background, Josh, who is Jewish, and Leila, from a Muslim background. Despite their different religions and lives, they note they have 'identical smiles'. Musically, the song is based around a banjo and is sparse in arrangement. Not a standout track, it's a nice enough song and one which advances the plot in the necessary way.

13. 'TRILBY'S PIANO'

Written by Pete Townshend
Produced by Pete Townshend

Another example of Townshend writing in more musical theatre style, and a track that many fans were less than fond of, 'Trilby's Piano' is nevertheless by no means a bad song. Opening with eerie, expressionistic piano, the song is partly autobiographical and based on Pete's Aunt Trilby. As a child, Townshend would play her piano, and even though not skilled at that time, he was encouraged by his aunt, who told him he was a real musician. Of course, this encouragement to a child who is interested in music can be vital, even if the child might only be playing random disconnected notes.

In the story, Townshend adapts this and makes Trilby Gabriel's aunt, and this song, which is about the love Trilby has for Josh's Uncle Hymie, is performed by the youngsters at Leila's father's studio, in front of their families as part of a play they put on.

The piano and Pete's vocals are backed by a beautiful orchestral arrangement composed by Pete and supervised by Rachel Fuller, and although the song is baulked at by many rock fans, lovers of classic film and stage musicals might just find this at least a tad enchanting. 'Trilby's Piano', along with 'Fragments Of Fragments', are the only two songs from *Wire And Glass* that were never played live.

14. 'ENDLESS WIRE'

Written by Pete Townshend
Produced by Pete Townshend

The title track of the album, hidden within the mini-opera, is one of the highlights of both 'Wire And Glass' and the entire *Endless Wire* album. A very simple but catchy track, and another sung by Townshend, the song exists in two versions on the CD release of the record, the standard, fairly short version and an extended one which features as a bonus track and is the preferred version. The song tells of the teenagers finding the writings of Ray High, referred to here as 'The Ether Man'. After finding his writings, they begin to find a purpose and decide to try to resurrect his ideas of using the network of wires to spread music to everyone.

Musically, the song is a laid-back country-influenced track, with Townshend playing acoustic guitar as well as banjo. An example of a very basic but catchy song, 'Endless Wire' is an extremely likeable ballad with a singable chorus.

15. 'FRAGMENTS OF FRAGMENTS'

Written by Pete Townshend and Lawrence Ball
Produced by Pete Townshend

Joining the mini-opera with the rest of the album, this is just a reprise of 'Fragments' with a slightly different arrangement, essentially a remix, with Townshend this time providing lead vocals which are altered with various effects. If anything, this track feels a tad superfluous, especially as better tracks have been trimmed to very short lengths.

16. 'WE GOT A HIT'

Written by Pete Townshend
Produced by Pete Townshend

'We Got A Hit' sees the teenagers in the story finding success with their song, which turns them into stars. The song opens with a nice drum fill and we're straight into the verse, Daltrey sounding great, and he is joined in the second half by some nice backing vocals which recall more of the 1960s-era Who, especially something like 'Rael'. The song is arranged nicely, with crisp jangling electric guitars, acoustic guitar and mandolin providing a typically strong and infectious Townshend rhythm. The chorus makes use of a call-and-response vocal between Townshend (singing in harmony with himself) and Daltrey, as the drums briefly stop, before rushing back in, showing Pete's still-evident knack for writing a hook.

This song also exists in an extended version which features a middle eight that includes a nod towards the next track, 'They Made My Dream Come True'.

17. 'THEY MADE MY DREAM COME TRUE'

Written by Pete Townshend
Produced by Pete Townshend

This Townshend-sung track is written from the point of view of Ray High as he sits in his cell, able to see the teenagers' success in their band The Glass Household as they manage to bring his ideas to life. In this song, whose slow Americana vibe conjures up images of dusty highways, Townshend again alludes to his own past with the opening line about people dying when he performed, referencing the disaster in Cincinnati in 1979 where eleven fans were killed in a crowd crush.

The song has a great atmosphere, with Townshend's acoustic picking complimented nicely by the sparse, twangy electric and some nice bass work from Pino Palladino. It's a nice track which possibly would have been good as a full-length song if it had another section to extend it. As it is, though, the length works for it, and the track does its job of leading the story towards its finale.

18. 'MIRROR DOOR'

Written by Pete Townshend
Produced by Pete Townshend

And so we get to the standout track of 'Wire And Glass', and what may very well be the best track on the entire album. 'Mirror Door' sees the culmination of The Glass Household's success, but Ray High has foreseen that a great tragedy will take place at a concert by the band. Tragically, Josh, who suffers from paranoid schizophrenia, stops taking his medication and ends up shooting Gabriel. It's here that a stairway opens, and it is revealed that several dead artists and actors are above, as well as angels and demons, and Gabriel ascends to join them.

The track begins with the cheers of a concert crowd before breaking into the intro, a run through of the chorus chords, before a typical Townshend G to D chord change snaps us into the verse. This is based on another set of tough power chords, over which Daltrey half-growls. The song changes to the minor for a brief pre-chorus, and then we get more power chords in the actual chorus as Daltrey uses his higher register. The end of the chorus has a great climbing chord sequence which introduces a sense of ascending the staircase to the Mirror Door and adds a lighter and more melodic touch.

The song represents some of the best songwriting on the album and allows the band to perform dynamically, Roger displaying his range of pitch and intensity, while Pete pulls out his usual rhythmic chord playing tricks, including suspensions, power chords and pedal tones There's also some subtle but great organ work by John Bundrick, and the drums and bass do just enough to give a little of the classic Who magic. If there's one criticism it is that the bass could actually be higher, as there's some lovely playing going on underneath everything, but nowhere near as loud as it would have been if it was Entwistle.

At the end of the song, Townshend plays partial chords over a D pedal tone (a trick that instantly has shades of older Who songs such as 'Sparks' or 'Another Tricky Day'), over which Roger drops in range to read out a list of departed stars. In this list, though, Townshend made a mistake, as he included Doris Day, who was still very much alive and didn't pass until 2019.

'Mirror Door' succeeds in being a modern Who track that distils the essence of the band without two irreplaceable members. Much of that is down to Pete's writing, using all his tricks but staying the right side of the line that stands between a well-composed track with subtle nods to the past and simply repeating oneself.

19. 'TEA AND THEATRE'

Written by Pete Townshend
Produced by Pete Townshend

The low-key and sentimental closer of 'Wire And Glass', 'Tea And Theatre' wraps up the story with Leila visiting Josh, who is now in a sanatorium cell next to Ray, to drink tea together.

The basic, stripped-back arrangement leaves Townshend's acoustic guitar (again in open G tuning) and Daltrey's naked vocal as stars of the show, but adds a simple drum machine and later bass guitar. Live, the song would feature just Pete and Roger in an even more intimate version. The song alternates between a dry vocal and one loaded with reverb, which adds a more atmospheric touch to it, and is a heartfelt end to the mini-opera, if a little sentimental. Live, the band would often play this song, not as part of the mini-opera itself but as an encore number after the usual big hits. This two-man version, with just Pete and Roger, would wind the night down and leave it on a note of calm reflection rather than high adrenaline and energy. The only song from *Endless*

Wire to survive in concert as a regular inclusion, the band would perform the track from 2006–2009 and again in 2012 and 2013, as well as 2019 and most recently 2023, where it returned as a show-closer after having been earlier in the set for some years.

Chapter 14

Who (2019)

Produced by Pete Townshend and Dave Sardy
Roger's vocals produced by Dave Eringa
Associate Producer and Assistant to Pete Townshend – Myles Clarke
Released in the UK on 6 December 2019 on Polydor
Released in the USA on 6 December 2019 on Polydor
Chart position – UK = 3, USA = 2.
Recorded between February and August 2019 at Metropolis Studios in London, British Grove Studios in London, Sunset Sound in Los Angeles and Hillside Manor in Los Angeles. All basic tracks recorded at Eel Pie Upper Woody Studios. Orchestra recorded at Newman Scoring Stage, Fox Studio Lot, Los Angeles
Roger Daltrey – Vocals
Pete Townshend – Guitars, Vocals, Harmonicas, Synthesizer, Percussion, Hurdy-Gurdy, Violin, Cello and Orchestration
Pino Palladino – Bass on tracks 1, 2, 4, 5, 6, 7, 8, 11 & 12
Zak Starkey – Drums on tracks 1, 2, 4 & 7
Simon Townshend – Backing Vocals on tracks 1, 3 & 5, Piano on track 9, and Percussion.
Joey Waronka – Drums on tracks 5, 8, 11 & 12
Carla Azar – Drums on tracks 3 & 10
Matt Chamberlain – Drums on track 6
Benmont Tench – Organ on tracks 1, 2 & 10, Mellotron on track 1
Gus Seyffert – Bass on tracks 3, 9 & 10
Rachel Fuller – Orchestration on track 6
Dave Sardy – Percussion, Mellotron

In January 2019, it was announced that The Who were recording a new album, thirteen years after their previous studio effort. The news was somewhat unexpected, as the band had shown no real signs of continuing as a recording group after 2006's *Endless Wire*, that album having largely been seen as a swansong for the group. The band had released a new song in 2014, called 'Be Lucky', which was possibly the worst thing they had ever recorded. Like 'Old Red Wine' and 'Real Good Looking Boy', its release was obviously a tactic to sell copies of the new compilation album, *The Who Hits 50*, but unlike those songs, which were genuine songwriting efforts, 'Be Lucky' felt more like a contractual obligation, written in haste, using a popular Roger Daltrey phrase delivered to the crowd at the end of each gig. The throwaway nature of 'Be Lucky' didn't seem to do much for any hopes of new material, but Townshend became adamant that if the band were to tour again, they needed a new album. Townshend's demand was not born of any desire to have a hit or make money, but instead a matter of artistic pride. Townshend spoke of wishing to stay away from romance or nostalgia on the new material, though the album contains elements of both these, but crucially, in just the right dose.

Townshend worked on demos from June to September 2018 and submitted fifteen songs to Roger, but was a little put out that his bandmate didn't get back to him for several months. Daltrey stated that he'd have to work to make them Who tracks, saying he felt like the songs were singing *at* him, and though they were great, they felt to him more like they belonged on a Pete Townshend solo album. Consequently, he wasn't sure if he could get inside them and make them something the public would accept as The Who.

The sessions began at British Grove Studios in February 2019, with producer Dave Sardy and engineer Jim Monti. At the time, Roger was away on a rock cruise and wouldn't return to the UK until March. In the meantime, Townshend did preliminary work on songs with his brother, Simon, who would contribute one of his own tracks to the record. Pete also worked on rhythms with Zak Starkey, who this time would play a much greater role on record, after playing on just one track from the band's previous album. In addition to this, Pete's wife, Rachel Fuller, would contribute orchestration. When Roger entered the recording process, he elected to have his vocals produced by Dave Eringa, with long-time soundman Bob Pridden helping to engineer.

Townshend would keep video diaries during production of the album, producing a series of blogs for The Who's website that showed clips of the progress, many of these demonstrating the songs being developed with Pete's guide vocals in place and him using a variety of instruments. For the record, he would play not only guitars and synthesizer but even cello, violin and hurdy-gurdy. Guitar-wise, Pete used several models, including his 1952 Telecaster, a stage-used Stratocaster and a Gibson J200 acoustic. A hollow-bodied Gretsch was also spotted in the studio, though not his famous 6120. For the recordings, which later moved to Metropolis Studios, Sardy would often record live drums and bass to Townshend's demos.

The resulting album is a surprisingly good listen, with a strong line-up of songs that do for the most part sound like The Who of old, but with enough new wrinkles to avoid pastiche. The topics cover a wide range of issues, from the Grenfell Tower fire to death, reincarnation and music itself, and the album isn't ever short of ideas. Daltrey's voice is a revelation, sounding back to somewhere near his best, better than a 75-year-old man has any right to sound. After showing signs of age on the previous album, it is remarkable that Roger manages to sound younger and more vital than he did thirteen years previously, but this could be partly down to throat surgery he'd undergone in the interim.

Pete's writing is solid overall, and at times inspired, showing that the knack of crafting a catchy and clever rock song was still as present as ever. Of course, there are some interesting curveballs thrown in too. Aside from this, the rest of the assembled musicians do a great job in giving things a 'Who' feel.

The cover art was created by Peter Blake, who had also worked with the band for their album *Face Dances*. Similarly to that record, which featured the overall image made up of smaller boxes, the cover of *Who* comprises twenty-five squares. Three of these display the letters of the album's title, while the rest contain various images, mostly associated with the band's history. These include baked beans, a poster of Pete Townshend smashing a guitar, a roundel (commonly identified as a mod target), a picture of the cassette edition of *Face Dances* and a scooter.

Who was released on 6 December 2019, reaching number three in the UK charts and number two in America. Reception was very positive from both fans and critics. *The Times* would say it was their best album since *The Who By Numbers*, while *Uncut* would go one better, declaring it their best since *Quadrophenia* and awarding it 9/10.

A CD version featuring bonus tracks was also released. These songs were three Townshend-sung tracks – 'This Gun Will Misfire', 'Danny And My Ponies' and an old 1960s demo called 'Got Nothing To Prove'. The first two tracks are fantastic and would have made fine additions to the album, though the third stands out like a sore thumb, being a home recording from the 1960s. On a Japanese release, another old Townshend demo called 'Sand' was also added.

TRACK BY TRACK

1. 'ALL THIS MUSIC MUST FADE'

Written by Pete Townshend.
Produced by Pete Townshend and Dave Sardy. Roger's vocals produced by Dave Eringa

Possibly The Who's strongest album opener since 'Slip Kid', 'All This Music Must Fade' finds Townshend returning to the familiar subject of music itself, and forty-one years after he proposed that 'The Music Must Change', here we find Pete addressing the state of music in the late 2010s and coming to the conclusion that repetition and borrowing is all part of the game.

The song starts with faded-in organ and Townshend's refrain of 'What's yours is yours and what's mine is mine' before the band comes in, Daltrey singing better than in decades as he declares 'I don't care, I know you're gonna hate this song'. This line seems aimed at critics, maybe also some fans but possibly even Daltrey himself, who had proved a tough singer to please, particularly on the later Who albums, when Townshend's writing changed significantly. However, this is the sort of track you feel Daltrey would have been dying to sing and feels instantly right as a Who song. As the track gets into its pre-chorus, it shifts groove and we get the admission that the song is nothing new or diverse, but it doesn't matter, as the fantastic chorus races in with chiming guitars and a nice set of backing vocals. The second verse adds violin, while the second chorus suddenly sees Townshend roaring out an answer vocal with such vigour it takes the listener aback slightly. A brief interlude, which is a repeat of the intro lines, is followed by the third verse, which is a nice call back to the band's 1965 song 'The Kids Are Alright', featuring a similar lyric to that song's opening line, Daltrey singing this time that he doesn't mind other guys ripping off his songs, another example of the band revisiting their past from a new angle. The song closes with a repeat of the 'What's yours is yours' section, with Townshend carrying this on by himself before declaring, 'Who gives a fuck?' as he sums up his communal attitude towards music in the bluntest of fashions.

'All This Music Must Fade' is a gloriously fresh track that is catchy, powerful and shows that the band had a real reason to make new music. It recalls the spirit of The Who in a way that feels right for its time but without selling out to modern fads or trends. However, according to Daltrey, Pete originally had written a rap into the song, which he wanted him to perform, but Roger refused.

Sadly, despite being one of The Who's best tracks in decades, it has to date never been performed live. The song was the second to be released from the album, in October 2019, ahead of the album's December release.

2. 'BALL AND CHAIN'

Written by Pete Townshend
Produced by Pete Townshend and Dave Sardy. Roger's vocals produced by Dave Eringa

This song was previously released as a Townshend solo track on the compilation album *Truancy* in 2015, under the title 'Guantanamo'. The song deals with Guantanamo Bay and the harsh treatment at the detention camp there, a place described here as a 'pretty piece of Cuba, designed to cause men pain'.

The track begins with some electric guitar string noise before a simple but hypnotic piano part starts to play, a more organic version of a typical synth riff, almost a cross between 'Baba O'Riley' and 'Love Reign O'er Me'. Other noises enter the soundscape, setting up a slightly psychedelic feel, before we get some crisp acoustic guitar adding a more bluesy tone. When the track kicks in, we get earthy blues with Daltrey's deep vocal working a treat, while the other instrumentation keeps things slightly airy. Being essentially a blues track, there isn't really a verse and chorus, but at the end of the progression the song hangs back, allowing the piano and acoustic guitar to take over. However, it's just the calm before the storm, the second verse roaring in with Daltrey's vocals sounding even more savage and Townshend playing more biting electric guitar, tapping into the ever-present fretboard firepower at his fingertips.

Though a pretty basic track, the performances and arrangement elevate it to a fairly enjoyable one. Townshend plays some gloriously aggressive electric guitar here, while Daltrey performs with levels of grit and muscle that make him sound tougher than ever. Add to this the slick bass playing from Pino Palladino and pounding drums from Zak Starkey, as well as added instrumentation including the orchestration, and you have something that's far greater than the sum of its parts.

The song was debuted live at Wembley Stadium in July 2019, but was referred to as 'Still Waiting For The Big Cigars'. 'Ball And Chain' was released in September 2019 as the first single, ahead of the album release date in December.

As a side note, Townshend played guitar on an Elton John song of the same name in 1982.

3. 'I DON'T WANNA GET WISE'

Written by Pete Townshend
Produced by Pete Townshend and Dave Sardy. Roger's vocals produced by Dave Eringa

A song which seems to deal with the past and the flaws and imperfections of youth, 'I Don't Want To Get Wise' sounds partly autobiographical but relatable to just about anyone. Daltrey would alter some of Townshend's lyrics, replacing many instances of the word 'I' with 'We', making the song sound less directly about himself and more about both him and Townshend.

Structure-wise, the song is a little unusual, not really having a defined verse and chorus but featuring a series of contrasting sections, offering enough hooks and melodies to make for an enjoyable song.

'I Don't Wanna Get Wise' was released as the third single from the album in November 2019.

4. 'DETOUR'

Written by Pete Townshend
Produced by Pete Townshend and Dave Sardy. Roger's vocals produced by Dave Eringa

Even the title of this is a bit of a nod to the band's past when they were called The Detours, and the music itself has a retro feel to it. The song starts with pounding toms and is soon joined by backing vocals and low, rumbling bass as it sets out its R&B groove. Townshend unleashes grittier guitar as Daltrey puts in another outstanding performance, singing as well as ever and recalling his 'My Generation' days, but if anything sounding even more authentic in his bluesy delivery. The song drives on with its vibrant rhythm, employing handclaps and a host of interesting percussion instruments including a tamarind seed pod shaker, but a contrasting section sees the song veer towards acid jazz, Daltrey now crooning more than roaring. It's an odd change, but one that just about works and leaves the song as more than just a pastiche of the band's past. An actual middle eight takes the song into more melodic territory, with Daltrey using his voice in a purer way, before we get back to the chunky rhythm and blues that form the main part of the song.

'Detour' comes across as the band's 2019 version of 'Magic Bus', a basic song brought to life by the rhythms and instrumentation. Townshend would explain in a blog entry that the song was about men finding new ways, paths and routes to find an honest, decent way to reach women, elaborating that we need to swerve to avoid the old ways.

Townshend also plays bass harmonica for the first time since 'Join Together' in 1972.

5. 'BEADS ON ONE STRING'

Written by Pete Townshend and Josh Hunsacker
Produced by Pete Townshend and Dave Sardy. Roger's vocals produced by Dave Eringa

Apparently one of the most popular songs from the album with fans of the band, 'Beads On One String' is a slow pop-rock ballad that advocates human unity and decries wars, especially conflicts waged under the banner of religion, noting that whoever your God is, we shame him when we kill in his name. Co-written by Josh Hunsacker, who provided the music backing, with Pete writing the vocal melody and lyrics, the song gets its name from a quote from Meher

Baba, who on a 1932 trip to London said he had come to draw the people of all religions together like beads on one string.

The song starts with heavy use of synthesizer, which in my opinion is far too clean, sounding just too much like Euro-pop. The song is a catchy one no doubt, and Daltrey sings it well, while Townshend takes lead vocals in the chorus, which thankfully introduces more guitars and the track begins to sound more like a rock song.

Townshend would remix the track in October 2020, though this still keeps much of the electro-pop feel.

To date, The Who have played the song just once in concert, at the Royal Albert Hall in March 2022 at an acoustic-based concert.

6. 'HERO GROUND ZERO'

Written by Pete Townshend
Produced by Pete Townshend and Dave Sardy. Roger's vocals produced by Dave Eringa

Like 'Ball And Chain', 'Hero Ground Zero' would be debuted at Wembley Stadium in 2019, takinng full advantage of the live orchestra present at the concert. On record, the orchestral arrangement is a major part of the song, a welcome addition to an otherwise straight melodic rock track. It has to be said that the opening chords do sound an awful lot like 'Another Tricky Day', a song intro which had already been repurposed for the track 'Fragments' from the band's previous album, *Endless Wire*, with all three songs even being in the same key. The similarities with this song and 'Fragments' are deepened by the opening violin pattern, which like the opening synth from 'Fragments', has a slight 'Baba O'Riley' quality to it. We already know Townshend tends to reuse ideas and almost copy himself at times, but more often than not he pulls it off, and in this case he definitely does.

As the band kicks in, the song races along at a nice pace, the orchestration adding a sense of urgency. The verse settles back into a more relaxed pace and gives plenty of room to Townshend's acoustic guitar, while the chorus sees the return of the trademark Townshend power chords, bolstered by uplifting strings which add a grand expansive beauty to the song throughout. An already rousing track, there's another trick up the sleeve in a great middle eight, leading to an instrumental section with pounding drums and Pete slashing away on electric guitar, which sounds a little reminiscent of his classic Gretsch tones.

'Hero Ground Zero' is a nice addition to The Who's catalogue and one of the most exhilarating later additions, full of great guitars, lush orchestration, commanding drums and a star vocal performance from Daltrey.

7. 'STREET SONG'

Written by Pete Townshend
Produced by Pete Townshend and Dave Sardy. Roger's vocals produced by Dave Eringa

'Street Song' was written by Townshend after the events of the Grenfell Tower fire, in which seventy-two people lost their lives and others were injured as a block of flats in London went up in flames. During this tragedy, trapped people called loved ones as they faced their own mortality, and this informs the opening lyrics and repeated chorus refrain. The song starts with some light percussive cymbal work and then a synth, before the chords arrive along with Daltrey's emotive voice. Soon, the drums come in with heavy tom hits, aiding the anthemic feel, as Pete's harmony vocals take over the refrain. The verse moves to half-time and is more laid back, Daltrey singing over the sparse backing, with the synths adding a busy psychedelia to the arrangement. When the chorus comes in, the track picks up pace and turns into a U2-esque stadium rocker, Roger's impassioned vocals rising from the streets like a cry for humanity. Towards the end of the song we get another refrain from Townshend, explicitly referencing Grenfell, while Daltrey wails over the top. A song with few sections and for the main part only three chords, it really relies on the dynamics, and towards the end we have another chorus with some stops, and tom fills firing like a barrage of cannons, before a very odd ending which almost sounds like the band hitting a wrong note and grinding to a halt. Sadly, for a song perfect for stadium rock crowds, 'Street Song' has never to date been played live.

8. 'I'LL BE BACK'

Written by Pete Townshend
Produced by Pete Townshend and Dave Sardy

After singing the unusual and un-Who-like 'In The Ether' on the band's previous studio album, here Townshend once again makes an interesting choice of what is his only lead vocal on *Who*. Steering clear of rock or even country, Townshend makes a foray into 1970s soul for this romantic track that deals with mortality and the possibility of the eternal existence of the soul. In 'I'll Be Back', Townshend comes to terms with the fact that at his age, he may not have much time left, but reflects on the love he has shared with his partner and is calm in the belief that his consciousness will carry on and the two will find each other again. This track, in alluding to reincarnation, is thus a love song that isn't bound by the physical, and not even contained by just one life, almost an interesting follow up to 'One Life's Enough' from *It's Hard.*

Musically, the song is slow-paced, with lush orchestration and a warm soft-focus feel that's so far removed from anything else by the band that for many it will be a bizarre inclusion. However, it's hard to fault the song for what it is. Starting with a Stevie Wonder-type harmonica played by Townshend, it instantly develops into a nice chord progression and is adorned by Pete's smooth vocals, being complimented later by delicate harmonies. A moment that will divide even those who have been thus far won over occurs midway through, when Townshend performs a kind of rap, a stream of autobiographical lines relating to his youth, delivered in a rough London accent and processed through effects. It's something of an odd passage, but somehow it's not too jarring and soon after we get a quite frankly ridiculously good harmonica solo from Townshend, showing his multi-instrumental prowess. After all this, Pete still squeezes in a charming and beautiful middle eight, again mining some tasty jazz chord changes.

I must admit, for a while 'I'll Be Back' was my least favourite track on *Who*, but after multiple listens, it's become one of my favourite Townshend-penned ballads. That's something not many would agree with, but if this had been released by a 1970s soul artist, it just might have been a classic.

9. 'BREAK THE NEWS'

Written by Simon Townshend
Produced by Pete Townshend and Dave Sardy. Roger's vocals produced by Dave Eringa

After nearly two decades as a member of The Who's touring band, Pete's brother, Simon Townshend, marks his first writing credit on a Who album with this up-tempo and lively yet slightly dark acoustic-led track.

Simon had been asked by Bill Curbishly to co-write with Roger, as he felt a new Who album might happen and they may need a few songs, seeing as Pete didn't have many at the time. Simon sent a few songs to Roger, but never expected either him or Pete to want to include 'Break The News', as it was only planned for his own solo album.

Simon said that the opening lines came to him one day in the studio and were about the fact that people are afraid to break bad news, later speculating he might have had a medical test around that time. The rest of the song then came to him quickly, and he soon got to work recording it.

Based in E minor, the song starts with a picked acoustic part outlining the chorus chords, before the chorus itself starts, its stomping rhythm being accentuated by handclaps. The arrangement simmers down for the verse, which shifts to the relative major of G and is a fairly standard chord progression until the A minor to A minor/G and the haunting and ear-catching change to C add nine add sharp eleven, with its dark F sharp note. The song is undeniably catchy, utilizing the contrast between the gentle fingerpicked verses and the punchy choruses with a tidy arrangement that includes piano and backing vocals by Simon. According to Simon, The Who took the song's original half-time feel and sped it up, Dave Sardy encouraging the stomp-like feel.

'Break The News' is a worthy addition to *Who* and would be performed at four special acoustic shows at Kingston upon Thames' Pryzm nightclub in February 2020, as well as an acoustic-based show at the Royal Albert Hall in March 2022 and several Roger Daltrey solo shows.

10. 'ROCKING IN RAGE'

Written by Pete Townshend
Produced by Pete Townshend and Dave Sardy. Roger's vocals produced by Dave Eringa

'Rocking In Rage' is another example of the musical theatre side of Pete Townshend's writing which has sometimes revealed itself on their later albums. Here, it's blended with a hard rocker, making for an interesting song that tackles the modern phenomenon of cancel culture and online abuse from keyboard warriors. The subject matter must surely have struck a chord with the outspoken Daltrey, and his vocal performance certainly suggests so, as he ranges from weary forlornness to agitated fury.

The song starts with a pretty piano part before the verse, which uses a series of dissonant, jarring chords. Over this, Daltrey sets out his stall, feeling the pressure to conform to the accepted viewpoints and fearing retribution or simply being shunned, should he not do so. As the song enters the pre-chorus, the strings add an air of sadness, with Daltrey further describing the feelings of isolation and vilification, while the bass expertly highlights the emotionally wrought chords. Suddenly the song turns, becoming tougher as Townshend enters with an edgy descending guitar riff and Roger switches from mournful pleading to righteous resistance. As the song fully kicks in, Daltrey's campaign of self-expression grows stronger, and the song enters a more typical Who-like section of power chords based in A. It's the only moment where it feels like Pete is slightly writing by numbers, but the power of the track, with some meaty bass and Roger's apt promise that he won't leave the stage, overcomes such criticism.

'Rocking In Rage' is a great track that combines several different styles and tackles a subject many people of different generations will relate to. It is especially fitting for those of Townshend and Daltrey's age group, and Pete is still writing here about his generation, a generation now in their eighth decade and still as defiant as ever.

11. 'SHE ROCKED MY WORLD'

Written by Pete Townshend
Produced by Pete Townshend and Dave Sardy. Roger's vocals produced by Dave Eringa

The Who show they still have one further surprise with the sultry and Latin-influenced album closer, 'She Rocked My World'. One of Daltrey's favourites from the album, the song speaks of a mysterious girl pressed up against a wall, who rocks the world of the narrator. Townshend has the self-awareness as a writer to admit this is a bit of a cliché, but asserts that this time it's true. Townshend described the song as being about a fabulous girl from the past, and the lines talking of himself having a teenage daughter at home seem to indicate that this might be about a one-night stand sometime in the 1980s, which certainly was a time when Townshend was something of the promiscuous rock star about town.

The song, featuring Gordon Giltrap on guitar, simmers away, with Daltrey singing in low register for much of it, growling and teasing, but also rising up an octave in the second verse to heighten the drama and raise the temperature.

'She Rocked My World' provides a cool yet steamy end to *Who*, its arrangement aided by dreamy piano and nice light drumming. The song would be performed at four special acoustic shows at Kingston's Pryzm in February 2020, as well as an acoustic show at the Royal Albert Hall in March 2022.

Conclusion

Of the first wave of British Invasion bands of the 1960s, there are arguably four names that sit at the top of tree. The first is of course, The Beatles, the band who started it all, and remain the biggest guitar act of all time. Joining them in second place, we have their southern bad boy counterparts, The Rolling Stones, and making up places three and four, surely there can be none other than The Who and The Kinks. Although there are others, these are the four biggest British bands that released music in 1964 or before and carried on producing hit records until at least the end of the decade. Of these bands, only The Rolling Stones and The Who remain as actively touring bands today, over sixty years after forming.

As I write this in February 2025, The Beatles have just won a Grammy award, with the song 'Now And Then', released in November 2024, this being in spite of having broken up in 1970 and the deaths of John Lennon in 1980 and George Harrison in 2001. The Rolling Stones have themselves also won a Grammy with their most recent LP, *Hackney Diamonds*, their first album of original material in eighteen years, and one which topped the charts in October 2024. It seems the main players in the first generation of British rock bands are still going strong, but what of The Who? As I write this, they have announced another two shows for Teenage Cancer Trust at The Royal Albert Hall, with more shows in Italy lined up and talks of an American tour. This comes after a period of uncertainty in the past year, where Townshend had stated that although the last gig of their 2023 tour shouldn't have felt like the end, there was a feeling of it being the closing of an era, and that he needed to sit down with Daltrey to discuss the future of the band. In 2024 Daltrey had also commented that he needed to meet with Townshend but would be happy to call the part of his life spent with The Who, as being over. With Daltrey approaching 81 years old in 2025, and Townshend a year behind him, it would not be unexpected for them to hang up their stage clothes, but what of the possibility of another album? Townshend has appeared keen to record more music but on the other hand his long-time band mate seems to be less thrilled about the idea, citing the expense of the last album as a key factor.

So, it seems likely that The Who's studio discography will end with 2019s *Who*, which in my opinion would be a fine send off for the band, but we can always hope for one last hurrah - it wouldn't be the first time the band had surprised the public.

Dante DiCarlo,
February 2025.

Bibliography

Barnes, Richard, *The Who: Maximum R&B* (Eel Pie Publishing, 1982)

Clarke, Steve, *The Who In Their Own Words* (Omnibus Press, 1979)

Daltrey, Roger, *Thanks A Lot Mr Kibblewhite* (Blink Publishing, 2018)

Fletcher, Tony, *Dear Boy: The Life Of Keith Moon* (Omnibus Press, 1998)

Jones, Kenney, *Let The Good Times Roll* (Blink Publishing, 2018)

Neill, Andy & Kent, Matt, *Anyway Anyhow Anywhere: The Complete Chronicle Of The Who 1958–1978* (Virgin Books, 2005)

Rees, Paul, *The Ox: The Last Of The Great Rock Stars* (Constable, 2020)

Townshend, Pete, *Who I Am* (Harper Collins, 2012)

Townshend, Pete & Barnes, Richard, *The Story Of Tommy* (Eel Pie Publishing, 1977)

Unterberger, Richie, *Won't Get Fooled Again: The Who From Lifehouse To Quadrophenia* (Jawbone Press, 2011)

Wilkerson, Mark, *Who Are You: The Life Of Pete Townshend* (Omnibus Press, 2008)

Various articles originally printed in the following publications:

Rolling Stone, *Sounds*, *Beat Instrumental*, *NME*, *Record Collector*, *Record Mirror*, *Eye*, *Mojo*, *Melody Maker*, *Zig Zag*, *Music Now*, *Disc And Music Echo*, *Creem*, *Trouser Press*, *Musician*, *Relix*, *Music Week*, *The Times*, *Uncut*.

The following writers and journalists:

Nik Cohn, Charles Shaar Murray, Penny Valentine, Dave Marsh, Chris Charlesworth.

The following films and television programmes:

Amazing Journey: The Story Of The Who (Paul Crowder, 2007)

Classic Albums – The Who: Who's Next (Bob Smeaton, 1999)

Classic Albums – The Who: The Who Sell Out (Bob Smeaton, 2021)

Quadrophenia: Can You See The Real Me? (Matt O'Casey, 2012)

Sensation: The Story Of Tommy (Martin R. Smith, 2013)

The Kids Are Alright (Jeff Stein, 1979)

The Who: Thirty Years Of Maximum R&B (1994)

Album liner notes, including contributions from the following people:

Pete Townshend, Chris Stamp, Richard Barnes, Matt Kent, Andy Neill, Keith Altham, Matt Resnicoff, John Swenson, Penny Valentine, Pete Drummond, Chris Huston, Arnold Schwartzman OBE, Roy Flynn, Richard Evans, Mark Blake.

The following websites:

Thewho.info

Petetownshend.net

Thewho.com

Justbackdated.blogspot.com

www.thewho.net/whotabs

www.thewholive.net

Index